Competing Conceptions of Academic Governance

Competing Conceptions of Academic Governance

Negotiating the Perfect Storm

Edited by William G. Tierney

The Johns Hopkins University Press
Baltimore and London

The Johns Hopkins University Press
2715 North Charles Street
Baltimore, Maryland 21218-4363
www.press.jhu.edu

Library of Congress Cataloging-in-Publication Data

Competing conceptions of academic governance : negotiating the perfect
storm / edited by William G. Tierney.
    p.   cm.
Includes bibliographical references and index.
  ISBN 0-8018-7920-5 (hardcover : alk. paper)
  1. Universities and colleges—United States—Administration.
2. Education, Higher—United States—Administration.   I. Tierney,
William G.
  LB2341.C7234 2004
  378.1′01—dc22

                                          2003018759

A catalog record for this book is available from the British Library.

George Keller, Consulting Editor

Contents

Why Governance? Why Now?

Mary Burgan

There has been a great deal of talk in the past decade about the governance of institutions of higher education. The conversations started from a number of perceived crises in the early 1990s. University and college presidents came to be seen as overworked and bereft of power; there had been relatively high turnover in the field, with some high-profile casualties. The Association of Governing Boards (AGB) responded with a blue-ribbon task force that issued a report portentously entitled "Renewing the Academic Presidency: Stronger Leaders for Tougher Times" (Baliles 1996). Furthermore, institutions seemed to be growing like Topsy with little rational direction or aim beyond "surviving by adding on." Their struggles were spurred by a number of forces—decline in support from state budgets, growing intervention on many fronts by boards and alumni, increasing demand by "nontraditional" students for expanded offerings, competition with proprietary schools, and competitive impulses from surrounding communities that view local universities as essential for urban renewal at home—and bragging rights abroad. Moreover, whereas boards and administrations appeared intent upon micromanaging higher education, faculty seemed terminally recalcitrant about being managed.

Embedded in this matrix of mid-1990s inspirations, "growth" and "change" have become the mantras. There is no doubt of their relevance to higher education, but growth without direction can be pathological, and change for the sake of change can undermine foundational values in complex social institutions. Questions about who should direct growth and change are therefore logical responses to the current crises in higher education. Such questions have become even more imperative with the introduction into the academy of two major forces for growth and change in the new century—corporatization and globalization. These relatively new forces have intensified issues of governance by inserting nonacademic interests into the heart of education, adding layers of external complexity to institutions, and intensifying the stakes involved in devising new ways of handling them.

An array of programs has been advanced to unravel and regularize the governance of higher education. Among these, I would single out three prime contenders: management, unionization, and shared governance. These general approaches to governance at times may work at cross purposes, but I have hopes that in the future they might recognize common interests and come to compromises that can help to direct our protean activities effectively while maintaining our desire to work collaboratively. There is considerable value in management, unionism, and shared governance, but not if they become so antagonistic that the result of their interactions is conflict rather than cooperation.

Management

The academic studies published by Peter Drucker in the last quarter century—and given additional credence by the rise of the MBA and the mushrooming fame of one or another business strategy—have provided a theoretical foundation to managerial claims for leading colleges and universities. From the board and administrative points of view, the managerial model is compelling in its status and logic. For one thing, it is seen to have generated the economic successes of the last decade, and this appearance has outlasted the dot-com debacle and the fall of Enron—tending to override all that such failures tell us about what happens when governance lapses in business. The continuance of trust in managerial theory and expertise among board members and selected academic administrators is based not only upon a belief in the success of our market-based economy but also on a burgeoning industry in management literature. To some extent, the belief in management has become a secular religion in some academic quarters; management axioms are lifted whole from the *Harvard Business Review* or the business best-seller list of the *New York Times* and deposited in the strategic plans of one institution or another (Birnbaum 2000). The faculty responds with almost automatic opposition when jargon from these sources articulates administrative planning. There is no surer way of arousing faculty satire than using terms like *stakeholder, value added, total quality management,* or *accountability measures* in describing the actors, methods, and aims of university governance.

Nevertheless, faculty members do understand the realities of the economic situation of contemporary institutions of higher education. They have been deeply involved, for example, in the growth of academic research and of interdisciplinary programs, and they have experienced the need to manage the legal and managerial complexities that such growth brings with it. Although there have been a few entrepreneurial professors who can run their own show, most ordinary research faculty assent to the bureaucracy required to meet legal, legislative, and organizational needs in their labs. More reluctant to assent to corporate values, many tenured faculty have participated in the rise of management by sloughing off their own roles in governance. For example, they are more complicit in decisions to outsource teaching and other essential academic tasks to adjunct faculty than they may wish to acknowledge. Some of them are therefore willing to entertain new modes of governing such complexity. But they will be deaf if those modes are not clearly explained, if they don't make sense in the light of the essential missions of teaching and research, and if they are instituted arbitrarily and without consultation. The presumption that management is the answer to all problems also can make faculty downright stubborn when such maxims override notions of the values of traditional teaching and learning. For example, a favorite faculty gripe about management initiatives is the impulse to "reform" for the sake of making a splash on the national scene. This complaint becomes legitimate when reforming administrators have had no experience in the academy either as researchers or teachers. If they do not know about the essentially lonely life of the study or classroom, their big offices and multiple assistants (not to mention their business attire) will undermine their authority with faculty whose culture values the mingy ways of the scholar.

Accentuating this source of cultural division in higher education governance is the changing nature of governing boards. The modern managerial board tends to be less tolerant of delay and dissent now than in the past. It wants quick decisions about reorganization of programs, and it frequently shows frustration about the process of governance when the faculty senate offers opposing views about a favorite project (frequently in the athletics department). Perhaps most controversial of the management practices advocated by boards is the treatment of college and university presidents as CEOs. Faculty believe, for example, that the growing reliance on headhunters to identify their leaders is misguided and expensive, and many faculty (and students and alumni) are scandalized by the board's accession to the norms of corporate CEO pay for academic salaries. They observe the problems that have occurred in high business circles in the past several years, and they conclude—vociferously—that corporate management practices may be totally inappropriate for the academy.

It is no wonder, then, that presidents and boards are, in turn, troubled by faculty governance problems. The accusations that faculty tend to waste time, guard turf, and make departmental compromises that do not benefit the whole are not always misplaced. These flaws in faculty governance could be cured with a little more managerial know-how, artfully exercised by the faculty. But where is this know-how to be found?

Unionization

I hazard to make the novel suggestion that the rise of academic unionizing may be seen as a faculty attempt to gain and employ managerial know-how in support of its own interests. The truth is that academic employees are not educated in managerial expertise and that most faculty do not have the time or incentive to work in governance on campus. Given this occupational lack on the faculty's part, if the administration does not have true skill at mutuality in governance, the institution will suffer. The faculty's recourse in such cases may well be to adapt more rigorous forms of participation that enact specific and definitive arrangements with the administration. Thus the faculty's reaction to mismanagement, authoritarian style, and arbitrary decision making has increasingly led to collective bargaining and thereby to the hope that a contract might become a better instrument to insure the faculty's say in governance. Further, in light of the current growth of undifferentiated academic employees, most of whom do not have the organization or protections of the tenure system, unions envision higher education as a fair field for organizing.

Unionism tends to be a dirty word in managerial discussions of governance in higher education. Most boards and many administrations find the idea of faculty unions a violation of the notions of professionalism and collegiality. Many faculty respond negatively as well, concerned that belonging to a union is counter to belonging to a professional elite. Nevertheless, the impetus to unionization has remained strong, even with the difficulty imposed on efforts to unionize in private colleges and universities by the U.S. Supreme Court's Yeshiva decision of 1980. That decision found that faculty could not organize for collective bargaining because they were "managerial." Through the tradition of shared governance, faculty were supposed to have a major say in the curriculum, in hiring and retaining colleagues, and in setting the standards for grading and graduation. With whom could professional teachers bargain, given the fact that so many of the managerial activities of higher education were theirs alone to exercise decisively?

What more could professors want? After Yeshiva, a number of faculty unions in private higher education were decertified, but meanwhile, in states that have enabling legislation that overrides Yeshiva, almost all faculty in public institutions have chosen to unionize. In addition to the traditional authority they have, they have looked for a better fiscal understanding and stake in the institution as well as hands-on participation in setting institutional priorities.

One reason for the union preference in university governance is that the culture and expertise of union bargaining can give faculty genuine effectiveness and efficiency. There is an expertise in collective bargaining that, at its best, approaches the expertise of managerial know-how. Union dues also fund the staff to aid in leadership, assuring effective continuity. The definiteness in procedures and rules in contracts offer more clarity than less formal modes of institutional participation can do. Finally, nationally affiliated higher education unions may have a powerful voice in the state legislatures; in the current state of public funding for education, there is the allure of "industrial strength" unions, like the United Automobile, Aerospace, and Agricultural Implement Workers of America (UAW), which are imagined to bring extra clout to bargaining for higher education.

Despite the appeal of the collective bargaining approach to academic governance, there has been only sparse study in higher education research of its particular benefits and problems. Since the discussion of unionism in managerial circles tends to be suspicious if not downright negative, ignorance among those who have not worked on union campuses makes it difficult to instigate an objective understanding on the administrative side. On the faculty side as well there can be unrealistic dreams of solidarity, picket lines, and *Norma Rae* triumph. This romance is ignorant of the relevant legislation and the bargaining practices of most unions, for whom a strike is usually considered a sign of failure. The fact is that knowledgeable faculty leaders in "mature" unionized campuses can be far more cooperative with managerial initiatives than those on traditional campuses. They know the realities of budgets, they have studied various modes of negotiation, and their participation in self-management has made some of them less tolerant of faculty obstructionism than their colleagues in less well-defined traditional systems.

Shared Governance

Not all faculty members want a union, and many cannot have one even if they do. Further, even where there are unions, the subjects available for bargaining do not usually include matters that traditional shared governance covers—peer review in hiring and retention of colleagues, curricular revision, control over admissions, standards for courses, and assessment of student learning. That means that for most faculty members, on union or nonunion campuses, participation in running their institutions requires traditional practices to govern matters beyond wages and conditions of work. The standard practices of academic governance were laid out by the American Association of University Professors (AAUP)—working with the American Council on Education (ACE) and the AGB—in the mid-1960s. The result was the classic *Statement on Government in Colleges and Universities* published by the AAUP in 1966 ("Policy Documents," 217–23). The ACE and the AGB fell short of adopting this statement, but did "commend" it to colleges and universities as an approach to cooperation in governance. Since then, the traditional shared governance policies of the AAUP—embodied in the handbooks and faculty senates of colleges and universities around the country, and installed in some of the most important governance processes of most schools—remains as a template for a cooperative system of governance for higher education inside or outside collective bargaining.

It may be useful to sketch the main elements of academic shared governance as codified in the AAUP statement. The 1966 statement delimits the faculty share in governance with great clarity, yet with a caution that all operations of the university bear upon one another. "The faculty has primary responsibility for such fundamental areas as curriculum, subject matter and methods of instruction, research, faculty status, and those aspects of student life which relate to the educational process" ("Policy Documents," 221). The emphasis on professional responsibilities derives from the notion that the faculty alone has the expertise to decide on academic matters—the composition of the faculty, the curriculum, and the student body. This notion of responsibility assumes that academic freedom is fundamental to higher learning and then argues that only the insights of disciplinary knowledge and training can therefore decide about the ways in which that learning is conducted. If scholars are not in primary command of their institutions' academic pursuits, outside influences would surely be tempted to take a hand in censoring knowledge as well as those who profess it. From that concern for institutional control by academic expertise has grown the current system of academic microgovernance, mainly at the departmental level. It is here that the faculty may have substantial power in hiring, reviewing, and retaining colleagues. The system of tenure has also led to particular practices—from search and screen through peer review and annual review procedures—that have built up a unique system of personnel management in higher education; indeed the location of tenure processes in a peer-review system may override management initiatives and union oversight. Generally, it has been agreed that experts must decide upon the quality of other experts in the field, and administrations and unions alike tend to honor that agreement. (When they don't, there is likely to be major institutional uproar.)

Despite current controversy about tenure as guarantor of permanent status for faculty, its structural function in managing a large work force has never been fully appreciated. Further, the tenured faculty's say on curricular development, revision, and initiation of new programs usually has been admitted as appropriate by administrations and boards. At the microlevel of department and school, the faculty's influence on courses and course content has remained almost inviolate. I say *almost* due to the recent entry of proprietary schools into curricular matters—with their emphasis on standardization of courses and on student demand as critical in determining the curriculum.

It is at the macrolevel that traditional shared governance has been most criticized in recent times. The managerial segment of our institutions desires clearer borders between decisions on course offerings and decisions on institutional mission and budget, and thereby more freedom for its own activities in making moves in these areas. At a time when an emphasis on the vocational aspects of higher education seems inevitable, for example, university management can be exasperated with the faculty's insistence on maintenance of liberal arts requirements. The unions tend to side with the faculty here, seeking to protect the jobs of such rarified specialists as French teachers and geographers. The AGB has reflected this uneasiness with shared governance in recent years. In 1999, it issued its own report on shared governance, seeking to include more "stakeholders" in governance processes and according faculty only a subsidiary role as one among many interested parties. This view strongly asserts the managerial prerogative and recommends that unions be denied any role in traditional governance bodies (AGB 2001).

The AGB critique of faculty governance is not the only one. The faculty itself is concerned that the managerial project in governance has been successful because the faculty is too preoccupied with research, overworked with teaching, or engaged in microgovernance to attend to the good of the whole. The regnant faculty leaders tend to be on the verge of retirement, and their replacements are either powerless part-timers or young faculty who are too enmeshed in the contest for tenure to stand for election in the faculty senate. Thus while management worries about too much faculty involvement in governance, the faculty is concerned that shared governance may be withering away.

I believe that most thoughtful observers of higher education would count such withering as a loss. It is clear that governance in our universities demands a system of checks and balances. In the past, the faculty has provided a challenge to administrative initiatives, and rightly so. But an informed faculty will monitor rather than impede administrative progress. The question for shared governance is how to inform the faculty.

The question for college and university governance writ large is how to inform all of its participants—the board, the administration, the students, and the alumni, as well as the faculty—that their participation is critical. This book adds to recent attempts to do just that. It does so with thoughtful criticism from past presidents, higher education scholars, and voices from the business school. It brings in the law school as well, to keep fresh the agreed-upon assumption that academic freedom is paramount in all discussions of academic governance. Management, union, shared governance—these values seem mutually supportive when they are invoked as abstractions. The task of governance in the coming decades is to make them mutual in practice. For it is clear that without such effective mutuality, without the practice of a collaborative model of democracy in our colleges and universities, American higher education could lose that vigorous independence that has made it so powerful a force in freedom and progress both at home and abroad.

REFERENCES

American Association of University Professors (AAUP). 1966. *Statement on government in colleges and universities.* Washington, DC: American Association of University Professors.
Association of Governing Boards (AGB). 2001. *Governing in the public trust: External influences on colleges and universities.* Washington, DC: Association of Governing Boards of Universities and Colleges.
Baliles, G. L. 1996. *Renewing the academic presidency: Stronger leadership for tougher times.* Washington, DC: Association of Governing Boards of Universities and Colleges.
Birnbaum, R. 2000. *Management fads in higher education: Where they come from, what they do, why they fail.* San Francisco, CA: Jossey-Bass.
Norma Rae. 1979. United States: Trimark.

A Perfect Storm: Turbulence in Higher Education

William G. Tierney

Sailors have long known the dangers of sailing in harm's way. The forces of nature constantly threaten or assist the crew. Waves and winds move the vessel in one direction or another. Storms may cause delays, or the sun's rays may be so brutal that the passengers and sailors feel oppressed. Icebergs in the high latitudes are visible dangers above the water, and deadly and silent below. Rocks and shoals have taken their toll.

Of course, the kind of vessel and the water it sails in are best if matched one to the other. An oceangoing ship is likely to be less troubled by stormy seas than a small fishing boat. A boat that functions under its own energy is less concerned with the wind than a sailboat. A raft or canoe may be at home in a river or lake but not in the open ocean.

The ship's captain has frequently been portrayed as a hero or villain, or simply as mad, incompetent, or irrelevant. Captain Bligh was court-martialed even though he was known as a skilled navigator; the sailors rose up against Captains Queeg and Ahab; John Kennedy was a profile in courage on his PT boat, but Gilligan and the skipper were fools; Noah was little more than a passenger once he built the ark, and the old man floated listlessly on the sea. John Paul Jones, however, knew when to fight and when to adapt and overcome.[1]

Some will say that sailors and captains matter, and others that they are irrelevant. The heroism of the sailors in *Two Years before the Mast* is coupled with the treachery of the Barbary Pirates. Billy Budd had his own problems to deal with, but George Tilton, the third mate of the whaling ship *Belvedere*, covered 3,000 miles on foot to rescue his mates who were trapped in ice off Alaska.

Certainly the Polynesians who set out on outriggers for Hawaii showed a fortitude and wisdom that seems amazing today. How did they survive for half a year on such small boats? How did they learn to navigate the time and distance to finally find land? And how did they find their way home again, only to return to Hawaii without either a compass or modern navigational equipment? The times in which one sails, then, matter as well.

The purpose of one's travel is applauded or disparaged depending upon the observer. Christopher Columbus is either a hero or marauder. Pirates are colorful Robin Hoods or thieves. Admiral Nelson saved a nation, but Admiral Kurita contributed to the downfall of Japan in the Battle of Leyte Gulf.

Those who live on the water know that sometimes a perfect storm arises. The wind, the rain, the sea, all combine in a cataclysmic hurricane that is likely to swamp anyone caught in its grip. Some may sense a storm is coming, but no one can predict when all the factors will arise to create a perfect storm. Obviously, those who always stay on shore because a storm may arise will never get where they are going. We are equally impaired if we do not take precautions, not so much to batten down the hatches, but to acknowledge the conditions that may arise.

Colleges and universities are akin to ships at sea: many will say we are adrift. Others will caution that the conditions for a perfect storm are in the air. As with traditional ships, the kind of vessel we sail will make a difference, as will those who crew and take passage in them. We are foolhardy if we stay at home, and we are equally at risk if we do not take account of where we are and where we want to go.

This is a book in which we first discuss the conditions that give rise to academe's perfect storm, and then consider how our governance structures might respond. Our vessels matter. Those who are on the ship—the captain, the crew, and the passengers—do, too. Where we are heading and where we want to go makes a difference in how we deal with the perfect storm.

Neither sailing nor governance is a science. Just as one cannot predict when a perfect storm will arise, one also cannot develop a precise manual for a president, a board, or a faculty about what to do when a storm hits. Accordingly, the authors I have assembled offer competing conceptions of what to do. The point, of course, is not to confuse but to highlight the complexities academe faces. The kind of postsecondary ship we sail, and the nature of who we are as individuals, will likely help us in deciding to make one plan and not another. But without a plan we will be tossed about and unable to get where we want to go. We may even sink. What we really need to do is to echo John Paul Jones who, when asked to surrender after a ferocious battle, replied: "I have not yet begun to fight."

Storms and Perfect Storms

If the problems to be faced were merely the anticipation of a downturn in the funding of higher education, or the expectation of a smaller cadre of entering students, then we might look to the past to figure out how to respond. Indeed, over the past generation, there have been several times when one or another problem has beset academe and an institution's leaders have had to figure out what to do. However, the underlying premise of this book is that the problems academe currently faces are combining to create a unique storm. True, state budgets will continue to fluctuate and public institutions will experience the ups and downs that state revenues afford. Small private institutions will still be particularly influenced by the ability of their constituents to afford the cost of college. Research universities will still chase after federal and philanthropic monies that are either flush or meager based upon the health of the economy. The upkeep and maintenance of buildings will remain a priority, as will the desire to hire tenure track faculty, all things being equal.

But in this new world all things are not equal. As Simon Marginson and David Collis outline in the first two chapters, the environment of higher education has gone through a sea change; or, rather, colleges and universities are going through a sea change, for if we could say that the storm was over and the seas had settled, then it would be clearer how to respond. What makes the current environment so confusing is that, as with a perfect storm, the conditions are unique. Those who are in academe are unable to predict how one action will likely create an alternative reaction. The point, then, is not simply that a budget shortfall exists or a particular school or college is having trouble recruiting students. Rather, there are new underlying premises of *why* shortfalls exist and *why* recruitment and a host of other issues are problems. If we continue to respond in familiar ways when new situations arise, we are likely to face decline. The first two chapters expand on what these changes are and how they have come about. As Marginson and Collis elaborate, the forces that create the changed environment are threefold.

Competition

A competitive atmosphere in some aspects of higher education is not new. The ubiquitous football bowl games on New Year's Day provide athletic competitions. Requests for proposals from the government or a foundation end up with teams of professors competing against others to win a prestigious contract. Indeed, academic competitions have been in existence at least as far back as 1769, when the American Whig Debating Society started at Princeton.

However, the structure of higher education has been in large part a closed market. When words such as *college* or *university* or *campus* have been used over the past half-century, most individuals have conjured up a specific set of institutional types. If one wanted a postsecondary degree, the choices pretty much involved a fixed set of institutions within the universe of higher education. If research needed to be done, then more likely than not, especially after World War II, the assumption was that the research was going to happen at a research university or its affiliate (such as the Jet Propulsion Laboratory of Caltech).

New entrants have created the potential for competition in ways with which traditional colleges and universities are unfamiliar. Organizational change and experimentation is currently greater than at any time since the 1960s. Even in the 1960s, however, those who created new institutions still held to traditional precepts about how to define a college or university. Gerald Grant and David Reisman labeled the experimental colleges of the twentieth century in general, and of the 1960s in particular, as "telic reforms" (1978, p. 17). They thought a telic reform occurred not when an institution's participants merely tinkered with organizational processes but when the institution's underlying goals were different from the dominant ethos of academe. The experiments in the 1960s, argued Grant and Reisman, were in response to the rise of large research universities. Cowell College at the University of California at Santa Cruz is an example of how they viewed telic reforms; the college was geared toward educating individuals for participation in Western civilization rather than merely a job. Hampshire College and Evergreen State College are additional examples of institutions that sought to be different from the norm not simply by their processes but also by their goals. However thought-provoking the work of Grant and Reisman was, the aspect they missed was that the telic reforms of the twentieth century in general worked within the same paradigm as traditional institutions.

Experimental institutions were private or public in the same manner that traditional colleges and universities have been private or public. Funding either derived from the state or through tuition dollars. Each institution had a board of trustees that functioned in a manner similar to those at traditional institutions; the individuals chosen for the board might well have been chosen for a traditional college or university. How one defined faculty in experimental colleges was similar to how anyone defines faculty today. Similarly, students at experimental colleges were individuals of traditional college age who by and large spent the majority of their time as students on a campus.

The manner in which decisions got made did not differ that greatly from how they are made in much of academe. All of the institutions with telic reforms had a board of trustees, an administration, a faculty governing body, and broad student input. The accoutrements of the reform-minded institutions may have been different—grading, majors, interdisciplinarity, and the like—but virtually all of these institutions sought, and gained, accreditation. The raison d'être of any experimental institution was a terminal degree—an associate arts, bachelor's, master's, or doctorate.

The innovative institutions of today are entirely different. For-profit institutions, corporate universities, certificate programs, and nontraditional private institutions are redefining the marketplace in a manner that was unheard of a generation ago. Some institutions are publicly traded. What one means by *faculty* in a university that is entirely online differs dramatically from its meaning at either traditional colleges and universities or those that were supposedly telic reformers in the 20th century. Students may never set foot on a campus of a new institution, or if they do, the campus classroom may be in a shopping mall, where one works, or virtual. The technology of teaching and learning—the Internet, distance learning, the World Wide Web—have the potential to radically interrupt age-old traditions (Christensen 1997).

Boards of trustees act more like corporate boards than academic boards. Some institutions' boards think of the educational plan as a business plan that will enable the company to earn a profit. College presidents at these new institutions frequently think of themselves as CEOs rather than professors who are first among equals, and they often come from the corporate sector rather than the academy. Faculty may have no voice akin to what they would have at traditional institutions, and student voice is equated with that of a consumer who expects particular goods and services. The focus is less on a degree than on the skills learned. A corporate university, for example, is less concerned that students get a degree than that they learn skills that will enable them to do a better job.

A viable argument can be made that the new innovators are little more than small boats entering a sea full of proven, trustworthy vessels. Although some may succeed, many observers will remain unconvinced that these new entrants will impact traditional colleges and universities in any sustainable manner. When traditional colleges and universities award more than 1.2 million bachelor's degrees in a year, how much should one worry about a collectivity of new entrants that award fewer than 25,000?

As Marginson and Collis argue, however, we ignore the new environment that has given rise to the new competitors at our own risk. The point is not so much that these new entrants will swamp all of academe in a matter of years but rather that how these new organizations will shape specific institutions and disciplines needs to be considered. That is, a research university is less likely to be impacted by providers of certificates for on-the-job training than is a community college. Biomedical engineering is less likely to face immediate consequences from the improvement of distance learning than is teacher education. Thus, the concern ought not to be that a mature industry such as higher education is about to go out of business (Drucker 1998). Nevertheless, we are mistaken if we ignore the fact that fundamentally new ways of configuring higher education are taking place. In the words of Grant and Reisman, these institutions have telic reforms. Their goals are distinct, and the processes they take to achieve those goals are oftentimes different from, if not anathema to, traditional colleges and universities. Accordingly, we need to consider how new forms of competition will change the manner in which traditional higher education responds to its environment. Video and DVDs have not put Hollywood out of business, but they have forced the movie industry to think and act in new ways. So too will the higher education industry need to think and act in new ways with the advent of a competitive market.

Indices of Quality

Throughout the twentieth century, how one judged academic quality was similar regardless of where one taught. Regional and professional accreditation was the foundation from which the institution functioned. An institution had to be accredited in the region in which it worked, or it would be looked on as an academic pariah. Professional schools such as business, law, or accounting in all but the top two or three elite institutions also had to gain their own accreditation or students would not be able to transfer their courses or have them count toward their academic degrees.

The academic hierarchy placed research universities at the top of the ladder and community colleges and for-profit institutions at the bottom. Throughout the last century there has been a continual desire to move upward such that a teacher's college could become a state college and then a state university that offered master's degrees, and then joint doctoral degrees, and finally doctoral degrees. The assumption has been that the better the institution, the harder to gain entrance. The more professors who had doctoral degrees, the more respected the faculty. Faculty who were better at doing research were judged the better faculty. If an institution wanted to improve, then it needed to strengthen its requirements for tenure by raising the quality and quantity of the research that individuals produced. By the end of the century premier faculty not only needed to publish more than their confreres of generations past, but they also needed to attract external funding for their research.

Student quality generally followed a similar path. Students with higher SAT scores were more desirable than their low-scoring peers. Students with high GPAs were better than those with lower GPAs. Institutions that had students who earned an award such as a Rhodes Fellowship or were Regents Scholars were better than institutions without such students. Students with a certificate from a premier research university were judged to be better than those who graduated merely from a regional teaching-intensive institution.

To be sure, by the late twentieth century criticism had arisen on many fronts. Some argued that research should not be given prominence in teaching institutions. Others questioned the necessity of tenure. The SAT came under attack—racial and ethnic bias and lack of predictability were among the most prominent criticisms. Individuals pointed out that the majority of student indices of quality said very little about whether students learned anything at the institutions they attended. Others pointed out that the quality and quantity of one's research had little to do with the quality of one's teaching.

The result is that how one judges quality today is more confusing and more important than it has been at any time throughout the history of American higher education. Quality matters. It has been commonplace to acknowledge that colleges and universities are unlike businesses with bottom lines that provide an indication of how well the company's product is selling. If students continued to apply to an institution and if the indirect criteria such as those mentioned above were met, individuals claimed that the institution was doing a good job. Such easy answers no longer suffice. Consumers, the state, funding agencies, and competitors want to know why a particular institution believes it is doing a good job. What is the proof?

The answer to such a question does not simply provide an institution bragging rights. In a competitive world, institutions need to be able to determine how they excel in order to clarify their market position. In a competitive climate the rules are changing. Just as we would not judge Wal-Mart and

Microsoft according to the same criteria simply because they are organizations that seek to make a profit, no longer can one assume that all postsecondary organizations should try to emulate those that are the "best" according to standard criteria. Organizations that do not employ tenure-track faculty will not judge quality by the number of tenure-track faculty they have. Students who have little need of a campus are likely to think that the convenience of where they take their classes has more to do with quality than does an institution that happens to have a large park where students play Frisbee. Some employers will not care where an individual took a particular course of study; what the student learned in the course as judged by a particular exit exam is what counts. Institutions that see their medium as distance learning will question the merit of regional accreditation when their audience is global.

Again, in traditional institutions individuals are able to point out that their institution does not cater to part-time students, does not use distance education extensively, does not have only part-time faculty, so such concerns are irrelevant. As with the issue of competition, however, the point is not to assume that those of us in traditional organizations must adopt wholesale what the new entrants are doing, but to determine among ourselves how we are to judge quality. If previous definitions no longer work, then how ought we to determine the future indices of quality?

Public Goods

Throughout much of the twentieth century public education was seen as a public good in the United States. Although the nation has decentralized education to a largely state responsibility, as a country we have held as a common precept that education is a right extended to all our citizens. Public schools are dependent upon state and federal largesse; in the early twentieth century the same could be said about public higher education. By the turn of the twenty-first century, however, some states supported significantly less than 25 percent of a public state university's budget.

The transformation of the role of the state, and how the public thinks about what ought to be provided to everyone, also has been redefined. In the rampantly capitalist culture of the early twenty-first century the expectation that the state will provide adequate funding for all public postsecondary education has been eliminated. Instead, we have moved to a system that survives on a diversified funding base in which the underlying tenet is that postsecondary education is of greater benefit to the individual than to society; hence, the individual should pay for the costs, and the greater the array of postsecondary options the better it is for the consumer. Education has become a consumer good rather than a democratic good. Postsecondary education's primary role is no longer to prepare the citizenry for participation in the democratic sphere but rather to teach vocational skills that enable individuals to function in a competitive environment. My point here is neither to denigrate the teaching of vocational skills nor to bemoan the current state of events. Instead, I seek to point out the changes that are taking place so that we may consider how traditional colleges and universities might best respond.

Although one may suggest that these two goals are not necessarily in conflict with one another, the fact remains that the underlying assumptions of these goals point toward different beneficiaries and, consequently, different responsibilities. If a postsecondary education is a democratic good, then society shares in the costs; when the consumer is the beneficiary, then the individual presumably should bear the cost. The result is that what we mean by *college* or *university* needs to be reconfigured insofar as previous assumptions rested on financial support from the state. More importantly, the intellectual justification of a postsecondary education based on a particular view of the democratic state is being dropped in favor of a largely privatized, capitalist view of what a postsecondary education entails.

Again, many will suggest that I have drawn too dramatic a picture and that the state continues to play a vital role in the health and well-being of higher education. Community colleges remain largely funded by state coffers, and most of the state universities continue to draw significant fiscal support primarily from the state. Only the research universities have had to dramatically diversify their base of support. None of these changes, however, should be seen as either/or propositions: Either there is increased competition or not; either the same indices of quality remain or entirely new ones are developed; either the state will remain the majority provider for public higher education or it will not.

Instead, in a time of dramatic change, each institution's participants need to take stock of where they are in relation to the significant environmental forces that are occurring. We must not rush off unprepared as if we are academic Chicken Littles proclaiming that the sky is falling and something must be done. Indeed, with the benefit of hindsight the predictions of those who said that a distance-education tidal wave would wash over higher education in the early twenty-first century have proven—so far—not to be true. Yet, few will suggest that the conditions I have sketched here do not exist to some degree. The challenge, then, lies in trying to figure out how to respond creatively to the dynamic forces currently at work.

What makes these forces different from previous problems that academe has faced is that they are interrelated and call for alternative conceptions of what we mean by *higher education.* During the fiscal belt tightening of the 1970s, for example, the challenge was how to cut back, not how to reformulate how we do basic tasks. The discussions about accountability asked that colleges and universities focus on ways to undertake activities in an efficient and effective manner, but the benchmarks for quality remained relatively untouched. Calls for improved business practices such as total quality management were based on the premise that higher education needed to improve on its basic practices.

But what should we do in an era when we need to question what those "basic practices" are? Insofar as the diversity of what is meant by *postsecondary institution* is only going to expand, we must understand that not all sea-worthy vessels will—or should—respond in the same manner to the storms upon us. In chapter 1, Simon Marginson delineates how these issues are impacted and extended when we think of institutions situated not merely in local, regional, or state markets but in cross-national and global contexts. Marginson, then, works from a system level and suggests implications for postsecondary institutions. In chapter 2, David Collis focuses on related societal trends and considers how organizations might respond to such pressures.

Their chapters set the stage for the chapters that focus on internal governance processes and how they might best be arranged to deal with the pressures that are upon us. What ties together these chapters, with their competing ideas about how to respond, is the manner in which the debate is constructed.

Tenor of the Debate and Actors Involved

Debating Change

If a threatening storm is heading our way, then we need to be organized to make decisions that are timely, well informed, and thoughtfully conceived. We also need to maintain a sense of academic integrity and at the same time not remain mired in shopworn ideas. The problem, of course, is that such statements often provoke conflict either because they are said in an overly aggressive manner meant to stimulate reactions or because the assumption is that "timely" decisions that are not "shopworn" is coded language for attacking fundamental precepts of the academy. The underlying assumptions in this book, however, neither seek to generate angry retorts nor to subvert those principles that have made U.S. higher education admired throughout the world.

All of the authors accept that a fundamental premise of traditional colleges and universities is tied to the production and dissemination of knowledge in the classroom, in research, in local communities, and in the larger society. Some institutions are more likely to highlight the teaching function, and others emphasize research. Most institutions are involved in their local or regional communities, but some have a national or global reach. Nevertheless, the assumption is that, unlike profit-making corporations, the output for colleges and universities is not an increase in profits but an increase in knowledge.

Knowledge production is not certain to produce particular results, and no amount of managerial efficiencies can ensure a particular result. The scientist in the laboratory or the teacher in the classroom is involved in an intellectual undertaking to see whether or not a particular hypothesis can be proven and/or material can be conveyed that increases the critical thinking of students. The testing of theories, models, experiments, policies, and the like may fail to produce the desired results, or they may lead one into unexpected areas.

Accordingly, for almost a century there has been a widespread belief in the importance of academic freedom. Academic freedom has provided institutional protections to enable scholars to search for truth wherever it may take them. Thus, to eschew such a basic precept would be to negate a fundamental premise of academic life. However, our contention is that to call for timely decisions or more effective governance structures is not to assert that academic freedom or knowledge production be eliminated as the premises of the institution. Rather, the challenge turns on how to maintain basic precepts of academic life by assuring that the structures we utilize ensure smooth sailing so we reach where we want to go. A static organization is one that can neither maintain the underpinnings of the organization nor chart future directions. To be dead in the water, either on a sailboat or a steamship, is certain cause for destruction.

Unfortunately, one frequently hears clarion calls to "do something" when the organization or system is not adequately prepared. Just as I am claiming that stasis is an inappropriate reaction to change, so too is action by one or another group that has not carefully delineated the purpose and plans of the institution in consort with other key organizational constituencies. Boards, administrators, and faculty more often than not seem at loggerheads when they should be in step with one another.

Creative Engagement

An oddity about academic life in the early twenty-first century is the tension emanating across the decision-making units of institutions. Boards of trustees, administrators, and faculty, principally, are frequently portrayed as if they distrust one another and are opponents rather than colleagues. One might understand such conflict in profit-making firms, where workers try to gain rights related to their jobs and management tries to increase profits. In traditional colleges and universities, however, the expectation ought to be that the various groups work together rather than pull apart. Yet everyone has heard public pronouncements from individual board members who express frustration at the manner in which faculty insert themselves into governance (Carlin 1999). Some senior administrators privately worry about the intrusion of a board member into the affairs of campus life and wring their hands about the lethargic pace of faculty decision making. Faculty on some campuses bemoan what they see as the diminution of their role in governance and the rise of "corporate" tendencies (Ramo 1997).

In a world populated by 4,000 institutions, one is sure to find a maverick trustee, administrator, or professor who is likely to succeed in poisoning the atmosphere on a campus. All too often, we tend to generalize one person's comment as if he or she is speaking for all trustees, or all administrators, or all faculty. However, in a survey (to which I will return in the final chapter) that was sent to 3,500 faculty and academic administrators at 750 institutions, 77 percent of the respondents commented that they believed enough trust existed on campus for decisions to be made (Tierney and Minor 2003). The top five areas in which faculty have a natural voice and authority in decision making were curriculum, general education, admissions, academic standards, and promotion and tenure requirements. Although the processes and structures of decision making may be unclear, based on the data from the survey, I suggest that there is much more agreement on who decides what than anecdotal evidence suggests.

The dual challenge, it seems, is to figure out in the dynamic environment of the twenty-first century how to ensure that enough trust exists so that change can happen and that the various constituencies are clear about what they might do to improve their governance structures so that informed decisions are made. Trustworthiness is an issue I take up in the concluding chapter. However, effective governance structures are matters that pertain to every chapter in the book.

My assumption is that differences of opinion are bound to occur in an intellectual organization. More often than not, there is no one best answer. I disagree with proponents of the collegial model of governance who assumed that all constituents came to consensus on all issues (Millett 1962). Such an assertion was more an academic myth than a historical reality (Tierney, in press). Where one sits in an organization is bound to influence how one sees a particular issue. However, if an organization's actors trust one another and have effective governance structures, then they will be able to weather storms rather than get stuck or perhaps even drown. Instead of cozy consensus, we ought to develop governance structures and processes that enable creative conflict.

An additional mistake that we frequently make is to assume that faculty governance pertains strictly to academic senates. If the senate does not function well, we assume that faculty governance does not function well on campus. However, the survey pointed out that faculty decision making occurs on various levels and in multiple forums. Rather than assume that faculty governance is an either/or proposition, we need to utilize a range of communicative and decisional structures in order to maximize the voice of the faculty.

In chapters 3 and 4, for example, Neil Hamilton and Terrence MacTaggart point out the critical role of state systems of public higher education. By analyzing four states, Hamilton shows how little is known of the faculty role in state governance systems. He picks up on the premises I have just outlined pertaining to knowledge production and academic freedom and considers what needs to be done at the state level to secure a more symbiotic relationship between governing boards and the faculty. Simply appointing more faculty to state boards is not a cure-all to the problem. Instead, Hamilton delineates the manner in which knowledge production occurs and emphasizes the import of having all voices at the system-table. He emphasizes that mission clarity is essential not only for faculty but also for the well-being of the entire system, and that the faculty have a fundamental role in its development and articulation.

A concern for mission clarity pervades the current environment of colleges and universities, as does the need to have governance mechanisms that enable fulsome debate and discussion that reaches closure. A competitive market in which quality is key demands that organizations define what they do and who they see as their students and clients. To make such a decision, the administration, faculty, and board need to be able to communicate effectively.

MacTaggart further underscores the critical need for system boards to identify not only the mission of the system but also the specific roles of the board. At a time when competition is only going to increase, it is critical that a system define what it does and does not do. Similarly, boards need to clarify their roles as the primary agents who deal with the external environment. By way of case studies of different systems, MacTaggart outlines how systems vary from one another and how significant their challenges are. Yet he suggests that environmental pressures create opportunities for state systems to define a public agenda and clarify their roles.

James Duderstadt continues these ideas but uses as the unit of analysis the organization rather than the system. Instead of focusing solely on the role of the board, he considers the individual trustee, administrator, and professor. Duderstadt's concern is the qualities that trustees bring to the board, the power of the president, and the areas where faculty should be involved. He, too, buys into the initial points raised by Marginson and Collis about the increasing complexity of the modern university and suggests that trustees need to become more involved in particular organizational aspects. In doing so, Duderstadt calls for university boards to act in ways that exemplify what they are—public corporations that are accountable to various stakeholders. He argues persuasively that boards need to be less political and more informed about the myriad issues that come before them. Just as business corporations have boards composed of individuals who are chosen for their expertise, so too should academic boards have individuals with particular knowledge pertaining to the governance and management of higher education.

In chapter 6, George Keller offers perhaps the most forceful argument in the book for reconfiguring academic governance structures. He posits that decisions are seldom made in isolation and that a singular decision made by the faculty about the curriculum and courses has inevitable consequences for the fiscal well-being of the organization. Relatedly, if the administration defers maintenance on a building as a fiscal measure, it often overlooks the pedagogical consequences if classrooms are falling apart or a lab is poorly maintained. Thus, rather than suggest that groups be autonomous, Keller highlights the need for a synthetic, collaborative approach. The academic organization is a collective that is going to either thrive or die by the ability of its multiple constituencies to work together.

Robert O'Neil returns the text to a central question of academe: What does academic freedom mean in an organization that faces all these changes, and what are the implications for governance? He refers us back to the initial chapters as well as to Hamilton and MacTaggart's consideration of mission delineation. Insofar as academic freedom has played a central role in the shape of academic life in the twentieth century, I thought it prudent to include this chapter in order to straightforwardly delineate the parameters of academic freedom. One hears misstatements from all sides of the argument. Some claim as a prerogative of academic freedom that they get to teach particular courses at particular times. Others say that academic freedom is no longer germane to the academy. No one is quite sure how to resolve such differences within current governance structures. O'Neil offers a dispassionate analysis of what academic freedom is and then ties his ideas to the book's earlier discussions of knowledge production and effective governance structures.

Again, we find that authors with different viewpoints frequently work from similar suppositions. No one argues that because of the various storms swirling around the institutions the solution is for colleges and universities to drop their key foci. If anything, as Hamilton argues, postsecondary institutions and systems need to be clearer in their basic organizational identities. Rather than simply asserting that presidential authority be increased or that the faculty senate is a primordial structure that must be maintained, the authors consider the indeterminacy and contingencies of governance in academic institutions.

Our solutions are generally more cultural in nature than instrumental. That is, although some of the authors offer suggestions such as to increase the expertise of boards or to place faculty on state boards, the overriding ethos of the book is to engage the reader in culturally nuanced ways to approach the problems that confront us. George Keller, for example, calls for "Kleenex structures" rather than rigid governing bodies so that institutions are able to call upon faculty expertise to deal with special problems. Kleenex structures will work in academic organizations where individuals trust one another but are unlikely to succeed where suspicion and mistrust pervade the organization's culture. Similarly, calls for faculty involvement in budgetary matters are unlikely to meet with a positive reception if governance exists through segmented decision-making bodies.

In the concluding chapter, I offer a cultural framework for considering governance so as to synthesize and highlight what individuals think of when they discuss governance. I focus on the faculty in order to concentrate on one key group so that I might make a summative point. We all arrive at an organization with preformed ideas based on our multiple identities of how organizational life is structured. Too often organizational analysts try to foment one particular version of academic life as if one mental model will suffice. However, by way of interviews and survey data, I suggest that rather than try to dissuade individuals from their own views and to convince them that one true model exists, the goal ought to be to work creatively with multiple mental models of governance from a cultural perspective.

Rather than focusing on structures, participants in the successful twenty-first-century organization will concentrate on culturally held beliefs in order to enhance ways to improve governance and, in doing so, improve institutional performance. My suggestions, then, are ways to improve governance not so much by tinkering with structures or instrumental actions, but by considering ways to create a more cohesive culture in which individuals have bonds of affiliation that enable them to disagree as well as to move creatively toward responding to, adapting to, and interpreting the dynamic conditions that exist in the environment.

The goal of this book, then, is to enable those involved in traditional colleges and universities not merely to weather the coming storm but to ensure we reach our destination in a timely manner and in good shape. We acknowledge the myriad seagoing vessels that populate academe and recognize that not all post-secondary ships are going to make the same ports of call. The manner in which colleges and universities make decisions, the governance structures and processes, however, all need to be effective in bringing forth quality decisions that encourage individuals to pull together rather than apart.

NOTE

1. Sebastian Junger describes a deadly sea disaster in his 1998 book *The Perfect Storm;* Captain William Bligh (1754–1817) was an English navigator and commander of the Bounty; Captain Queeg is the neurotic commander in Herman Wouk's *The Caine Mutiny* (1951); Captain Ahab chases the white whale in Herman Melville's *Moby Dick* (1851); John F. Kennedy's PT-109 was split in two by a Japanese destroyer on August 2, 1943; Gilligan and the Skipper were characters in the television comedy *Gilligan's Island* (1964–1967); the tale of Noah and the flood is described in *Genesis;* Ernest Hemingway's *The Old Man and the Sea* (1952) describes the plight of Santiago, an aging Cuban fisherman; John Paul Jones (1747–1792) was an American naval commander during the Revolutionary War; *Two Years before the Mast* (1840), written by Richard Henry Dana, provides an account of the author's journey from Boston around Cape Horn to California and back; the Barbary pirates were from Morocco, Tunis, and Tripolivigator; Admiral Horatio (Lord) Nelson (1758–1805) commanded a successful battle but was killed by a sniper's bullet at the Battle of Trafalgar; Admiral Takeo Kurita commanded a fleet of Japanese super-battleships in the Battle of Leyte Gulf (October 23–26, 1944), one of the decisive battles in the Pacific during World War II.

REFERENCES

Carlin, J. 1999. Restoring sanity to an academic world gone mad. *The Chronicle of Higher Education*. November 5, p. A76.

Christensen, C. 1997. *The innovator's dilemma: When new technologies cause great firms to fail*. Boston, MA: Harvard University Press.

Drucker, P. F. 1998. The next information revolution. *Forbes ASAP*. August 14.

Grant, G., and D. Reisman. 1978. *The perpetual dream: Reform and experiment in the American college*. Chicago, IL: University of Chicago Press.

Millet, J. D. 1962. *The academic community: An essay on organization*. New York: McGraw-Hill.

Ramo, K. 1997. Reforming shared governance: Do the arguments hold up? *Academe: Bulletin of the AAUP* 83 (5). Washington, DC: American Association of University Professors.

Tierney, W. G. In press. A cultural analysis of shared governance: The challenges ahead. In *Higher education: Handbook of theory and research*, ed. W. G. Tierney. New York: Agathon.

Tierney, W. G., and J. T. Minor. 2003. *Challenges for governance: A national report*. Los Angeles, CA: Center for Higher Education Policy Analysis.

Competing Conceptions of Academic Governance

Going Global

Governance Implications of Cross-Border Traffic in
Higher Education

Simon Marginson

Traditionally we imagine governance in higher education as having two dimensions: internal and external. Internal governance rests on the three estates of faculty, executive leaders, and boards of trustees. Nonfaculty employees do not figure in the traditional view, and students are present only intermittently. External governance involves policy actors, state higher education agencies, and boards located outside colleges and universities. In the United States external governance is largely confined to the state level, though regional accreditation associations and federal agencies also have roles. In most other countries, national government is a major player in governance.

Every methodological move has consequences, both enabling and limiting. No doubt the way that governance is constructed in the mind shapes the way that it is constructed in the world, and vice versa. The question is whether or not this traditional imagining/practice of governance, with its dualism of internal estates and state-level regulation, remains appropriate to the changing circumstances of universities and colleges. This chapter argues that the traditional construction of governance is no longer appropriate for two reasons. The main argument focuses on the second reason.

The first reason is that while the separation between the internal and external dimensions is demarcated in formal rules and lines of authority, in practice the two dimensions overlap at many points. Here governance creates a kind of Cartesian paradox (Dow 1990, 1996): it imposes certainty and simplicity on a problem that is uncertain, organic, and complex. In the real world, executive leaders, managers, and boards of trustees find themselves making judgments that move across both dimensions. Of the three internal estates, only the traditional faculty is purely internal in orientation, and here the traditional conception creates an unfortunate limitation. One of the first moves of the traditional professional culture is to invoke academic autonomy as a defense against the demands of managers *and* calls to social responsibility. More generally, by defining governance in separate internal and external dimensions, we fail to make explicit the manner in which these worlds are intimately and continually related, and to bring an understanding of their relationship into the structures of governance themselves. On one hand, the external context impacts teaching and research, albeit periodically and unevenly. It does so not only through the formal requirements imposed by state agencies but also through the many ways in which the external context shapes internal perspectives and decisions. On the other hand, colleges and universities reciprocally shape the overlapping communities—professional, local, city, state, national—in which they are located. For the most part it is left to executive leaders to manage the relationship between "inside" and "outside" on a day-to-day basis—not so much through formal decisions as by operational strategies, mapping trends, and reading the play. Boards have a primary function in mediating between internal and external governance but do not always explicitly focus on this role.

One might argue for a subtle reconfiguration of internal governance in which external relations are grounded organically inside the university, especially in the work of faculty, and the external dimension is broadened beyond governors' offices, state legislatures, and performance managing agencies to include industry large and small, community and civic organizations, and other educational institutions (Marginson and Considine 2000; Marginson 2002). However, that is not the argument I make here. My concern in this chapter is with the second limitation of the traditional notion of governance. There is now a third dimension—the global—that is impacting the older internal and external dimensions of governance.

Why focus on the global dimension of higher education? Conventionally, there are two motivations. One is aesthetic: a love of international diversity and, perhaps, of things foreign and "other," as ends in themselves. This is too readily dismissed as a distraction from the real issues. The second motivation is comparative: we study international higher education so as to expand our imagination about what is possible for ourselves. We study what is "out there" so as to better fashion what is "in here." At bottom this is a self-centered motivation grounded in a world of nation-states. However, this premise is no longer adequate. The nation-state no longer constitutes a closed horizon. In the last twenty years or so, around the world, global economic, social, cultural, and political influences have become increasingly felt in the day-to-day work of higher education. The global dimension, with its world markets, cross-country consortia, networked systems, and instantaneous communications, is not just something "out there." It is becoming something "in here." We need to understand the global dimension because it has become national and local. Yet this global dimension remains unrecognized in the way we imagine governance, and lacks appropriate regulatory mechanisms. Influential in shaping the terrain on which systems of governance operate, looming larger in the practical agendas of executive leaders and boards, the global dimension of higher education is largely determined outside the mechanisms of formal governance. In this sense, governance runs the risk of losing control of its own destiny.

No higher education institutions are more globally networked than are U.S. institutions. Despite this, U.S. institutions, unlike their counterparts abroad, often see the international dimension as marginal to their "real" activities. This says something about the English-language-based and Americanized nature of globalization itself. Globalization is more about what the United States does to the world than what the world does to the United States. In the United States its transformative effects are muted and retarded so that U.S. educational traditions appear to be more robust than others. Nevertheless, U.S. higher education is globally engaged; it educates an often cosmopolitan student population, and in many disciplines it prepares students to operate in any country. Sooner or later, global engagement must bring with it changes in governance. This chapter discusses the growing salience of global influences in the context of governance and maps early signs of an emerging international regime.

Global engagement broadens faculty practices and adds a new strand to executive strategies. Sooner or later it finds itself part of board agendas. It affects the rules by which institutions recognize foreign qualifications and foreign institutions. There are new issues in how cross-border partnerships and consortia are managed. Whose rules and whose rhythms of decision apply? To what extent do partners take each other's systems of governance into account, and how are heterogeneous systems to be blended? For example, the processes of accreditation and quality assurance, which affect the identity and mission of higher education, were developed originally for local and regional purposes. Now these processes are affected by the need for a workable congruence between North American colleges and universities and those of Western Europe. There is a new obligation to find common protocols and systems that will facilitate mutual recognition; the mobility of people, ideas, and qualifications; and interinstitutional cooperation and exchange. It is not so much a question of which kind of higher education is superior and should be adopted as the dominant model. The fundamental need is for workable cross-country systems.

Local, National, Global

Globalization refers to the spread of cross-national and worldwide phenomena, including their growing influence at local, regional, and national levels. *Globalization* is a broader term than *international* and also a more locally salient term. The term *international* refers to relations between nations as discrete entities, without implying any necessary change in those nations themselves or in the structuring of their relationship. Globalization encourages relationships between nations, on both a bilateral and a multilateral basis, but it does much more. It weakens geographic and political barriers and configures a new world order in which interdependency is fundamentally increased (Held et al. 1999). It is no longer possible for any one nation-state to isolate itself. Notwithstanding the military and cultural fallout from 9/11, this trend to interdependency is irreversible. This is true not only of nation-states but of all agents, institutions, or individual persons. Though globally active institutions and individuals are a privileged minority, this group is expanding rapidly. The logic of rapid expansion is built into the very structure of networks: "When networks diffuse, their growth becomes exponential, as the benefits of being in the network grow exponentially, because of the greater number of connections, and the cost grows in linear pattern. Besides, the penalty for being outside the network increases with the network's growth because of the declining number of opportunities in reaching other elements outside the network" (Castells 2000, p. 71).

The great change, as David Collis discusses in the next chapter, is the evolution of synchronous and near-synchronous electronic communications and data transfer in conjunction with a common system of local identities (for example, web pages), data banks, and standard languages and protocols. This has created a worldwide conversation in every economic and cultural field that draws on a common pool of information, except the most parochial. Worldwide networking and instant data transfer have also facilitated a single system of global finance, the first literal world market, with implications for all economic exchange, public or private, including higher education. National and regional specificities continue, and local zones are partly separable from world financial markets. Ultimately, however, all sites of production are joined, and the mobility of capital and labor is increasing. Facilitated by cheaper travel and electronic intercourse, the cross-border movement of people for business, skilled labor, tourism, and education also has grown. The global element in governance lags behind economic and cultural interdependency, which is an established fact. We remain an international order of nation-states in which global links are more de facto than de jure.

Since the formal origins of higher education in Europe and the Islamic world, it has been subject to international influences. Early on, the characteristic forms of knowledge—theological, medical, scholastic, and, later, scientific—took on a global character. Further, transnational influences have long affected the development of national higher education systems themselves. British models structured universities in the colonial countries. The Bonapartist model that took root in the Latin countries also shaped universities in South America. The German universities affected the United States as well as much of continental Europe and Scandinavia. But these international and transnational patterns were played out behind national barriers. In the global era international influences are more insistent. Research findings are sent everywhere, though the pattern is uneven, with a small number of developed countries (particularly the United States) tending to dominate world research output. Near-instantaneous web publishing is beginning to dominate in many fields, speeding up the old rhythms of scholarly conversation and collaboration. International partnerships and consortia are becoming more important. Cross-border, on-line education is gathering momentum. The U.S. model of higher education, based on mixed public/private funding and provision in autonomous institutions, now directly influences institutions abroad, especially in the developing world and in Eastern Europe. This global policy influence is supported by the global agencies, particularly the IMF/World Bank, with its power to apply targeted funds and attach programmatic conditions to the receipt of its loans by national governments (Mollis 1999/2000).

At the same time, global communications and visibility enable institutions everywhere to be recognized by each other. This creates the potential for a plurality of models and more diverse educational encounters. Whether the potential for diversity in higher education is largely swamped by global standardization, encouraged by the universalization of English as the lingua franca, or held in an uneasy and ever-changing coexistence with standardization, is yet to be determined.

What is clear is that the global, national/state, and local dimensions are combined. We can talk about a *glonacal* framework for understanding higher education, simultaneously *global*, *national*, and *local*. All three dimensions feed into the work of leaders, trustees, and faculty, and affect the missions of colleges and universities (Marginson and Rhoades 2002). The global dimension is the new one, but it is gaining currency. Faculty with international networks take a diverse range of ideas and data into their teaching and research, or they organize international associations of colleagues, or work with global agencies such as the World Bank. Executive leaders see the revenue-raising potential in foreign student education and offshore business, want to become first movers in the on-line education market, and broaden their policies on student diversity and student exchange.

As David Collis discusses in the next chapter, the competition from for-profit providers has created a dynamic new environment. Some boards are dealing with state agencies that want to foster internationalization as a strategy for city and regional development. All are affected by IT networks that bring the national and global dimensions closer to home. It is likely that empirical research would find that the volume and intensity of electronic communications increase each year, as Castells suggests. It is also likely that research would show that the proportion of communications from out-of-state and international addresses is also on the rise. By no means is everyone in higher education working with a broader range of people and ideas than before. For many it remains business as usual, and that means exclusively local business. The point is that the cosmopolitan, globally connected segments of higher education are growing relative to the purely localized segments, particularly, though not only, in the research universities.

How are we to understand the new global order in higher education? Amartya Sen (1999a) identifies two conceptions of global relationships that have tended to dominate our thinking. Neither, he argues, serves as an adequate basis for understanding the global order. The first conception, *grand universalism,* assumes that we can treat the world simply as one unit—that we can apply a single set of rules and values in every country. This cuts across the real diversity that exists, stripping the local element from the global/local dialectic, and negating the continuing potential for nationally determined variations. The second conception is *national particularism.* Each nation is an island of identity, and the global order is comprised of the rules whereby nations relate to each other from behind their borders. National particularism is more sophisticated than bedrock isolationism—the complete refusal of all that is foreign—but at bottom national particularism too is an isolationist conception. It fails to encompass the explosion of cross-border communications and influences, extending beyond relations between separated states to include person-to-person and institution-to-institution activity.

Nowhere is this more apparent than in higher education, which often finds itself dealing outside the frame of states. Higher education is a preeminent site for the formation of what social capital theorists call "bridging" social capital, association between people from different localities, kin, and professional backgrounds (Woodcock 2000). The growing presence of foreign students ensures that these bridges are built between nationals from different countries as well as within them.

To further complicate matters, in higher education the patterning of the different elements—the nation-state, regional or state agencies, the institution, the academic or professional association, and the persons themselves—varies greatly from country to country. The English-language countries traditionally provide higher education in autonomous institutions under the conditions of academic freedom that Robert O'Neil discusses in chapter 7. These institutions are being redefined as quasi-business corporations to varying degrees (Marginson and Considine 2000). The role of national government varies: contra the U.S. experience it is powerful in the UK, New Zealand, and Australia. In Canada provincial and national governments are important. Western European countries are moving away from the old model of state control, in which universities were often run as a department of the state service, but the nation remains a central actor in governance. In the Argentine "reformist" tradition, which affected much of Latin America, the universities had a special role in democratic nation building while the nation-state refrained from direct interference. This model is now being altered under the twin aegises of government steering and corporate reform (Mollis and Marginson 2002). Even without traveling further, say to China or Vietnam, it is apparent that connecting governance across national borders is not a simple process.

Globalization in Higher Education

It is helpful to examine more closely cross-border activities in higher education. Five aspects are briefly considered: the education of foreign students in provider countries; provider institutions operating in foreign countries;

cross-border, on-line learning; institutional partnerships and consortia; and professional association. All forms of international education pose two kinds of problems for governance. First, there are the implications for processes and systems of national and regional/state-level accreditation, quality assurance, and recognition. Cross-border activities need to be factored in, and this usually involves more than one set of national parameters—how are multiple processes of governance reconciled? Second, there are the implications for internal governance, including the roles of faculty and boards. Cross-border education is less immediate to local concerns, less visible to local constituencies, and often subject to commercial pressures that encourage "fast-track" procedures and decisions. This may empower executive leaders but diminish the roles of internal faculty and boards. On the other hand, certain individual faculty that have developed a strong international profile may increase their influence over the trajectory of their institutions.

The Movement of Students to Foreign Countries

For a long time marginal to national systems, cross-national higher education has become a large and rapidly expanding industry. Its growth is driven by the globalization of many occupations such as trade, finance, information technology, and scientific research, and by the growing migration of skilled labor (Tremblay 2002). Education is often the first step in immigration, especially from developing countries and newly industrialized East and Southeast Asia to developed countries such as the United States, the UK, Australia, France, and Germany (Engberg 2001). Of doctoral students from China and India finishing their PhDs in the United States in 2000, more than half had firm plans to stay after completion. Students from Argentina, Iran, and Peru also stay on in high proportions. In many countries, national immigration authorities use fast-track visas to encourage certain categories of foreign students to stay, especially information technology graduates (Tremblay 2002, pp. 42–46). Educational movement between developed countries is more varied and less often immigration linked. There is considerable intra-European movement. However, few nationals leave the United States and Australia for educational purposes, despite the fact that all students spending part of their studies abroad gain in life experience and employability, and their nations augment the collective global competence (Hayward 2001).

For students who do make the move, it is part of a win-win bargain. Foreign students gain status in the country of origin and often enhance their employment opportunities in more than one country. For the provider country, foreign students generate revenues inside and outside education institutions. For example, in the United States foreign students generate $11,000 in additional income in their host region, which is double their marginal cost (Tremblay 2002, p. 63). In 2000 the export of U.S. education and training totaled more than $14 billion and ranked among that country's top five services exports (Adam 2001, p. 36). The worldwide student body is becoming more cosmopolitan, though the degree of cultural diversity varies greatly between nations, subnational regions, institutions, and fields of study. In 1998, 4.8 percent of all students studying in OECD (Organization for Economic Cooperation and Development) countries were foreign students, varying from 30.5 percent in Luxembourg, 16 percent in Switzerland, and 12.6 percent in Australia to 0.6 percent in Japan and 0.1 percent in Korea. In the United States a modest 3.2 percent of all higher education students were foreigners, below the OECD average. Of these more than three in five came from the developing world and the Asian newly industrializing countries (NICs), and almost one doctoral student in every four was a foreign student (OECD 2001; Tremblay 2002, pp. 47, 56). However, the sheer size of the U.S. system, and the global value of U.S. experience and U.S. credentials, ensures that the U.S. foreign student population in higher education is the largest in the world, followed by the United Kingdom and Australia.

The regulation of foreign student education is determined largely by the provider countries, though foreign country governments also can play a role. Student movement and mobility is affected by immigration policies; policies on educational export itself, including government subsidization; procedures for the recognition of foreign students' previous institutions and qualifications; standards and procedures for language testing if required; the cross-national alignment of course structures and course contents; and the quality assurance of provider institutions. Another area of potential importance is consumer protection. Foreign governments may seek to better inform and protect their student nationals when they move to provider countries for educational purposes. Certain provider nations include consumer protection in their protocols, for example, covering the provision of accurate data concerning courses, educational quality, and graduate employment prospects; grievance procedures; refund mechanisms; and contingency provisions for when the provider is unable to complete the course. Not all such regulation is mandatory. Voluntary codes of conduct are widely used in provider countries to cover foreign student education in relation to consumer protection, recruitment protocols, administration of fee payments, academic standards, and student welfare practices. How effective such voluntary codes are is a matter of debate. There have been no studies of the extent or the effectiveness of compliance.

As international movement grows, the need for standardized regulation grows with it, and at the highest possible level of aggregation. Assessing qualifications and accreditation procedures on a case-by-case basis is resource intensive, the more so when provider institutions are dealing with students from fifty or more countries. However much they might support the principle of university autonomy on their own turf, institutions negotiating with foreign education systems find it more effective to deal with one national agency than with a multitude of institutions. The momentum for a worldwide system is driven by efficiency and flexibility. What is needed across all countries is a regulated process for determining student and institutional standing with a minimum of duplication.

Provider Institutions in Foreign Countries

Provider institutions enter foreign higher education systems in several ways. First, in "twinning" arrangements, the first part of a study sequence is provided in the foreign country by a partner institution and the subsequent part by the provider institution in its home country. The syllabus, assessment, and quality assurance procedures that are used in the first stage are normally subject to the foreign provider. The two stages must articulate effectively, creating a tendency to quality control. Second, through a "franchising" arrangement, a partner institution located in a foreign country provides the whole of a study sequence on behalf of the provider institution, while subject to the provider in syllabus, assessment, and quality assurance. In this manner it is possible to achieve a British, U.S., or Australian degree without dealing directly with the university, let alone seeing the parent campus. Under franchising arrangements, the fuller discipline created by twinning-style articulation is absent. Third, provider institutions may set up a branch campus in a foreign country. A number of U.S., British, and Australian institutions have established campuses on foreign soil, mostly in Southeast Asia and Western Europe. For example, the University of Phoenix is in Rotterdam. Several U.S. business schools have set up in Singapore with local government support. Australia's Monash University has established campuses at Kuala Lumpur in Malaysia and Johannesburg in South Africa, and plans more offshore sites.

Twinning, franchising, and branch campuses each pose somewhat different problems of governance. There is a varying degree of integration between provider country curriculum and foreign country curriculum, while in all three cases, foreign country requirements must be taken into account, and these (which vary by mode of education and by country) tend to cut across the norms of internal governance in the provider country. How can boards ensure that foreign operations are sufficiently similar to home country operations to guarantee the validity of the degree—or is homogeneity the wrong approach to the international setting, in which more than one culture must be taken into account? Is quality assurance sufficient to deal with these issues, or is tighter regulation required? How and to what extent do provider country faculty and boards become involved in decisions about franchised degrees? In a country such as Malaysia, is provider faculty approval needed for a curriculum offered by a branch campus operating on foreign soil, for foreign student nationals, subject to formal Malaysian requirements to provide Malay Studies and Islamic Studies?

Some foreign governments bar or severely restrict the entry of extranational providers, especially private providers and for-profit providers. Greece and Israel almost totally prohibit nonnational providers in the national system and refuse to recognize their qualifications. On the other hand, countries such as Malaysia, Singapore, and Hong Kong encourage foreign providers on the grounds that national system capacity is inadequate (Malaysia) or that there are advantages to be derived from the location of leading global universities on home soil (Singapore). In many other countries the requirements governing national higher education limit the capacity of foreign providers to operate successfully. For example, Australia has adopted protocols for use of the title *university*, including the provision of teaching and research across a broad range of disciplines, academic freedom, and a governing body independent of commercial or state interest, that make it very difficult to set up a new university whether foreign or domestic, especially a for-profit university—though the titles *college* or *institute* are not so restricted (MCEETYA 2000). Many of the same kinds of requirements restrict the potential for foreign and commercial universities in certain of the accreditation regions in the United States. South Africa has a prima facie bias in favor of confining the title *university* to national providers.

Provider countries have developed voluntary codes of conduct in relation to offshore activities: for example, the U.S. regional accrediting commissions in *Principles for United States Accreditors Working Internationally: Accreditation of Non-United States Institutions and Programs* (CHEA 2001) and the Australian Vice-Chancellors Committee's voluntary *Code of Ethical Practice in the Provi-*

sion of Offshore Education and Educational Services by Australian Higher Education Institutions (AVCC 1995). However, the transparency of offshore provider activities is limited. Compliance with voluntary codes of conduct is more readily scrutinized in the provider country than outside it, while provider governments are less interested in tracking offshore activities. Only the UK—mindful of the market advantage—has so far developed a strong regulatory regime for offshore activities, expressed in its *QAA Code of Practice for the Assurance of Academic Quality and Standards: Collaborative Provision* and enforced through an audit program.

In fact, it is likely that cross-national education that is provided outside the home country will fall outside regulation altogether, with negative implications for academic quality and resulting in the exploitation of the developing world. For example, the importing country might delegate regulatory judgments to the quality assurance and accreditation systems of the provider country. At the same time, the provider country may take the view that regulation is the responsibility of the host country, on the grounds that the exporter cannot legislate extraterritorially. The provider country government or cross-institutional agency also may be simply unwilling to engage in the cost of monitoring the offshore activities of its own provider institutions or to interfere with their capacity to do business and generate export revenues. This points to the need for a global regime that can police such gaps in the regulatory framework.

Cross-Border, On-line Learning

Electronic distance (on-line) learning, the most global of the modes of higher education, generates a novel set of problems for regulation. It falls outside the terms of the modern university and its principal regulatory incubator, the nation-state. The inherited systems of national and regional regulation were formed on the basis of exclusive sovereign control over geographical territory. On-line education readily crosses such boundaries. It has eluded comprehensive regulation so far. Aside from its novelty and lack of fit with conventionally regulated space, there are three other reasons for this. First, as Collis expands upon in the next chapter, the development of e-learning in general and e-distance learning in particular is largely driven by technological change and the corporate sector rather than educational change and government policy. In countries such as the United States with a prima facie bias in favor of corporate freedom, e-learning enjoys tolerance and a measure of official encouragement. Second, because the potential of the technologies is open-ended there is genuine uncertainty about how to define the field, the more so because those who make policy rarely practice the technologies; this is coupled with a reluctance to intervene too early, given that many interests, universities, and companies have staked claims. Third, policies on internationalization are rarely articulated with policies on distance learning and policies on educational technologies.

Cross-border, on-line learning varies considerably in mode, medium, pedagogical forms, provider character, and student take-up. Electronic delivery is in some continuity with print and broadcast modes of distance learning, and it can be supported by one or both but is largely new. At the most basic level it takes in Web-based communications such as e-mail. It may involve student administration (enrollment, the dispatch and marking of assignments and tests, etc.) via the Web and the retrieval of materials posted on a Website. It may take in video conferencing, CD-ROMs, and other multimedia. Increasingly, it requires interactivity on the Web, through the asynchronous posting of work and sharing of comments, real-time chat, or tests. Within these different media there is scope for much variation in pedagogies, and e-learning varies in the degree of support by face-to-face student administration, teaching, and study assistance. Most e-learning includes at least some bricks-and-mortar support, such as tutoring assistance provided in study centers. For example, the 1999 survey of offshore Australian education by Davis et al. (2000, p. 42) classified few programs as "independent distance" and found that only 1 percent of programs were exclusively on-line. There is much mixing of modes. Some face-to-face students on offshore campuses had distance-style contact with the parent university. "Off-campus distance" students enjoyed staff assistance, including teaching in partner institutions or dedicated centers.

On-line learning is associated with extreme claims about its potential to replace or transform conventional higher education, mostly emanating from the industry itself. However, the early student take-up has not met these expectations. Solely on-line education is relatively unpopular, except with certain students who are working or in remote locations. There is more scope for the development of mixed modes of delivery than for the substitution of e-learning for face-to-face. In the developed world, the often formidable outlays on communications grids, hardware, and courseware have failed to generate the expected outcomes. For example, Western Governors University has fallen well short of enrollment and financial expectations. Policies based on e-learning as a cheap expansion of access have faltered. Proper on-line learning costs at least as much as face-to-face learning and requires similar staffing ratios. Foreign students place a lower value on distance education and on franchised degrees at home, compared with face-to-face education in the provider country. Despite these limitations, on-line learning will expand as a distinctive distance learning mode and as an aspect of face-to-face learning.

Can Internet-based activities be regulated at all? Statements that national governments cannot affect cross-border electronic traffic are not strictly accurate. The Chinese government has erected a "firewall" around the country, and Singapore, Saudi Arabia, and South Korea also filter and censor some Internet content. However, these moves are at the cost of free data exchange and free trade, disrupting national capacity at the global level. More significant is the emergence of geo-location technology, which enables Websites to direct content on the basis of place, 70 to 90 percent of the time (The Internet's new borders 2001). If Websites can do this, then laws can direct them when and where to do it. In future it may be possible to control a would-be educational provider without overturning the whole basis of the Internet. Governments would be able to collaborate in a regulatory regime. We are not in that situation yet.

On-line learning is problematic for governance at both the macrolevel and the local level. At the macrolevel, where on-line learning is supplied by a commercial provider without institutional roots in higher education, it is very difficult to regulate. Where the commercial provider needs formal accreditation to sustain market position, regulation has a way in. On-line education provided by bona fide universities is more readily regulated, but in cases in which there is no geographic presence and no local partner, importer countries must depend on the willingness of exporter providers to conduct quality assurance. Importer governments rarely seek to regulate distance learning by controlling electronic communications. For example, in Singapore, approval is not required for cross-border delivery through courses that have no local presence (Ziguras 2001). However, India is likely to require all foreign universities offering distance education to register (Middlehurst 2001). Among provider nations, practices vary. Some U.S. accrediting agencies regulate the quality of international operations, though in some cases the template is the same as that used for local face-to-face operations. This means that neither the particular character of distance learning nor the particular character of international operations—let alone the needs of the importing country—are fully incorporated into the process of accreditation.

Within institutions, on-line learning is the extreme case of the more general tendency: the empowerment of executive leaders in the shaping of cross-border education, and the partial exclusion of faculty from key decisions. Faculty have input but lose control. On-line education depends on big-budget decisions on hardware and operating systems that are made centrally and are subject as much to executive judgments about strategic development as to pedagogical imperatives. Much of the development of new learning technologies is carried out by nonfaculty staff, and much of the teaching in new modes of delivery is carried out by part-time faculty who are outside the tenured core and less able to exercise academic freedom or academic veto (Rhoades 1998). Despite the high risks involved in expenditures on IT systems and Web development, the technical character of on-line learning makes it hard for boards to scrutinize.

The particular difficulties posed by the regulation of on-line, electronic learning will have to be confronted. It is important that the higher education sector and the public agencies lead this process. Otherwise e-learning, spinning off from mainstream provision, will become driven by the industry itself without much reference to the core national and global regulatory issues governing face-to-face higher education. In the long run it would be highly damaging for higher education if one set of values premised on public good were applied to conventional face-to-face learning and another commercial set of values were applied to distance learning.

Thus if, as Neil Hamilton cogently argues in chapter 3, faculty need to be more involved at a state level, the same can be said, if not more so, for faculty involvement at a global level. Contreras notes the trend to bogus e-degrees and all-but-bogus electronic institutions: "International quality control of degrees is becoming a major issue as more diploma mills are flushed out of the United States or appear spontaneously in countries with little oversight of private colleges. Some of these entities send out bulk e-mails offering 'prestigious unaccredited degrees' for a fee, no questions asked, no work required. Others require nominal work or a one-month residency on some tropical isle in order for the degree to be awarded" (2001, p. 5).

In a borderless electronic environment, quality assurance is only as strong as its weakest link. This raises the question of the extent to which existing approaches to quality assurance are translatable into distance education and to what extent we should be developing new approaches (Van Damme 2000, p. 15). The claim that e-learning and conventional delivery are converging or are essentially similar is a demand for equality of status dressed up as a claim for identity of mode. However, though the full potential of electronic learning is as yet unclear, it is already clear that there is a sharp educational-pedagogical distinction between learning primarily conducted on a face-to-face basis and learning that is not. The World Bank's senior adviser on higher education, Jamil Salmi, notes: "At the institutional level, it is doubtful that without significant adjustments, the principles and standards to evaluate campus-based programs can be used to assess the quality of on-line courses. At the national level, countries need to develop information systems and participate in international networks to be able to evaluate the quality of the foreign programs available to their students" (Salmi 2000, p. 2).

The tendency to read quality and quality assurance in distance learning through the prism of face-to-face education is a principal weakness in many systems of quality assurance and has retarded the evolution of instruments specific to electronic distance learning. It is the easy way out, but it will not serve. The e-learning industry presents e-learning as pedagogically equivalent while subject to a distinctive mode of governance through trade policy rather than the public good. The axes of difference and sameness (Marginson and Mollis 2001) should be reversed. E-learning should be understood as pedagogically distinct, while at the same time it is brought into a common global regulatory regime that encompasses all of the modes of higher education.

Cross-Border Partnerships and Consortia

Cross-national collaboration between individual institutions not only encourages convergence and homogenization across the globe; it also, by posing novel problems of regulation, is one of the precursors of a future global regulatory regime. Various cross-national groups have emerged, spanning the English-speaking world, Western Europe, and some Asian countries. The purposes of these consortia vary, but common goals include staff and student exchange, research collaboration, cross-national quality assurance and auditing and validation of courses, and the commercial development of e-learning platforms and prototypes. There is potential for joint "badging" of degrees, joint curricula, and global work experience programs during courses. One such grouping, Universitas 21, includes leading institutions in Australia, New Zealand, Singapore, Hong Kong, and mainland China: the Universities of Lund and Freiburg in Europe; British universities including Edinburgh, Glasgow, Birmingham, and Nottingham; and the University of Virginia.

Eckel (2002, p. 16) notes a range of cross-border partnerships involving U.S. institutions. Some universities have a minority interest in corporate parents located in another country, and there are joint programs between paired U.S. and international universities. Johns Hopkins University and the National University of Singapore are developing a joint doctoral program in basic sciences and a masters program in clinical research. Green et al. note that cross-border partnerships tend to force changes in academic governance: "Because these new programs and delivery systems extend beyond a single institution, individual academic governing bodies' expectations and traditions may be called into question. The alliance might make decisions that traditionally fell under the domain of campus academics. Decisions that remain within the traditional governance structure may need to be addressed by faculty governance bodies across multiple institutions, each of which has its own traditions, standards, and expectations for academic decision making . . . To what extent can existing decision-making structures cope with the new environment?" (Green et al. 2002, p. 20).

Further, as James Duderstadt touches on in chapter 5, the monitoring and auditing of commercial partnerships can pose a difficult challenge for boards, especially when the institution lacks a controlling interest. In Europe international university networks have been facilitated by mobility frameworks such as ERASMUS and SOCRATES. There are also larger, looser networks such as the European University Association (EUA) and the International Association of University Presidents (IAUP). Eaton (2001) points to the potential for collaboration among accrediting agencies, as already takes place on a voluntary basis at the national level in the United States. Van Damme (2000) highlights voluntary codes of practice in quality assurance. Such initiatives are often dispersed: the foundation of the International Quality Review Process (IQRP) in 1995, jointly shaped by the OECD's Institutional Management of Higher Education (IMHE) and the Academic Cooperation Association (ACA) and focused on the internationalization activities of universities, was an important development.

Global Professional Associations

The growing mobility of skilled labor within particular professions poses the need to facilitate the international transferability and recognition of qualifications. Strict national regulations concerning the recognition of qualifications protect the interests of nationals against competition from foreign labor without regard to the quality of the work. There is "an often unrealistic appreciation of the quality of domestic degrees, not checked by a truly comparative understanding of the value and diversity in foreign degrees" (Van Damme 2001,

p. 8). Nevertheless, part of the problem is that the immense diversity between countries in degree structures and training regimes, length of study and indenture, and the balance between national and universal course contents naturally lends itself to complex bureaucratic procedures. The facilitation of global mobility requires simplification and convergence of procedures. Little progress has been made on these issues within educational policy; rather, existing barriers have had to be circumvented by policies regarding professional mobility in both the European Union and the North American Free Trade Agreement (NAFTA).

Here certain globally organized professional associations have emerged as a powerful force for internationalizing and part-harmonizing curricula and accreditation. The engineering (Johnson 2001), medical, and legal professions have been active in relation to the content of teaching programs, quality assurance, international minimum standards, and criteria of professionalism. In engineering, the Washington Accord of October 28, 1997 was endorsed by engineering accrediting authorities from the United States, the UK, Australia, Canada, Ireland, New Zealand, Hong Kong, and South Africa. This agreement set criteria, policies, and procedures for accrediting academic engineering programs. The signatories agreed to accept each other's accreditation decisions and to monitor each other's accreditation programs.

Toward a Global Framework for Governance

The global dimension is transforming the internal and external governance of higher education in two ways. First, it is *relativizing* national, regional/state, and local regulatory and policy frameworks. It brings a new set of elements and problems to the state settings, in particular, which Terrence MacTaggart considers in chapter 4. The larger consequences are yet to become apparent, but it is clear that these elements and problems cannot be excluded or fully controlled within traditional internal and external mechanisms. Second, the global dimension has posed the need for a stable *global framework for governance* in higher education to enable the flexible regulation of cross-border dealings in higher education, which are bound to increase.

What should be the principal elements of such a framework of governance at the global level? Van Damme (2001, pp. 8–10) suggests that it would include, at a minimum:

- an international understanding of common concepts and terminology;
- rules governing the use of basic labels such as *university, doctorate, professor,* etc.;
- standardized registration procedures;
- elements of a professional code of good practice;
- protocols for consumer protection;
- the removal of barriers to student and staff mobility;
- a comprehensive system for the international transferability and recognition of qualifications and course credits;
- an international approach to quality assurance and accreditation of providers.

Such a framework would not be top-down or prescriptive. It would be designed to facilitate relations among autonomous institutions and among sovereign nations. Rather than subordinating internal and external governance, it would join more effectively the different local governance regimes, and the state and national policy sites, across the world.

As noted, the global strength of U.S. higher education has retarded its encounter with relativization. For example, U.S. influences in German higher education are felt much more keenly than German influences in U.S. higher education (in contrast with the situation 150 years ago). At the same time, U.S. institutions are more engaged in more national settings than the institutions of any other country. In contrast with the situation elsewhere, the main driver of globalization in U.S. higher education will be activities offshore and the need to reconcile the international and domestic agendas. The old separation between these two spheres—which enabled domestic isolationism to coexist successfully with imperial adventure—is no longer viable. That separation is one of the casualties of the global era.

The nation—or, in the case of the United States, the subnational state/region—remains the principal site of external governance in higher education. Nevertheless, institutions of governance operating at this level are increasingly required to take account of higher education institutions and policies in other nations. Problems of cross-national mobility, recognition, and accreditation have to be addressed. Decisions have to be made about cross-border, on-line learning. In many countries, external governance at the national level is also directly affected by global agencies such as the World Bank/IMF, the OECD, and UNESCO. It is not that the formal authority of traditional external governance has been interrupted. Rather, traditional authorities no longer have sole control of their own agendas. Issues arise from outside their territory as well as within. Inside their territory, the globally mobile students, faculty, and institutional entrepreneurs have become their own constituency with a prima facie interest in reducing the regulatory barriers to mobility. National policy makers and local institutional leaders may not always share this admiration for mobility, but it is hard to resist. Institutions that set themselves against global mobility stand to lose income, intellectual capital, and educational prestige. Unless an institution's ambition is highly parochial, this is not a realistic strategy.

The crucial issue is how to factor this global dimension into governance without jeopardizing local self-determination. Our original state of being is a Hobbesian international order in which the respective national regulatory regimes are "public," but the common space in which they are all located becomes defined as an unregulated zone in which all activity is "private." As noted, public universities operating outside their own country become seen as private providers. In the absence of any other element this creates an apparent bias to one kind of global regulatory regime, that of trade policy, and the debate about regulation becomes dichotomized between those who support free trade for economic reasons and those who want to protect the existing local or national character of higher education. This debate is not played out on a level playing field. As noted, developed countries are in a much stronger position to assert the character of their educational traditions than are developing countries. This suggests the need for new global mechanisms that will enable the "global public good" to be defined and regulated and allow trade policy to be brought into conjunction with policies designed to sustain national identity and educational quality—policies able to account for the multiple and complex character of cross-border relations in a networked world. In this manner we can begin to move beyond the limits of a Hobbesian international order.

The common interest lies in speed of passage and free educational exchange. The primary issue is not the liberalization of commerce for the sake of commerce, it is the cultural benefit of free and open collaboration (Sen 1999b). Trade is not the highest good; it is one aspect of human exchange. From time to time, the requirements of a trade regime in higher education will need to be modified, to sustain the local or national identity and viability of academic programs, strengthen the contribution of higher education to nation-building, and provide an equitable framework of social opportunity in each country, especially in the developing world (Singh 2001).

A sustainable framework for international and global governance in higher education will need to be comprehensive, encompassing the extensive role of national governments in most countries as well as the traditional public and nonprofit private schools to contain all forms of transnational provision, including for-profit education and on-line learning, and to accommodate the interests of students and the burgeoning demand for knowledge (Van Damme 2001, p. 6; World Bank 2002, p. 66). This means, on one hand, reducing regulation that interrupts the flow of people, money, and ideas in higher education, and, on the other hand, establishing new regulatory structures that function like communication and transport systems by linking higher education around the world. The essence of building a global framework lies in this double movement, in which selective deregulation is combined with new globally attuned regulation.

In economic terms, such a global framework for the governance of higher education constitutes a global public good (Kaul et al. 1999; World Bank 2001) that provides more favorable conditions for the creation of national and local public and private goods in and through higher education. Basic research and, after a time lag, all forms of knowledge are natural public goods whose benefits are not exhausted by one user but can be drawn on by all. The teaching and community service functions of higher education also have substantial collective benefits beyond those appropriated by individuals in the form of enhanced earning power. These collective benefits flow across borders as well as within them. A global regime for governance will enable such public good benefits to be maximized. "International regimes provide the basis for many other intermediate products with global public benefits—such as international surveillance systems, international infrastructure, international aid programs ... The benefits of global regime building are enhanced predictability in international relations and trans-border activities, which reduce the risk of conflict and misunderstanding. As a result transaction costs are reduced, encouraging cooperation and improving efficiency" (Kaul et al. 1999, pp. 13–14).

It must be emphasized that the global dimension of governance would *not* replace local, regional/state, and national modes of governance. It would be merely a framework for these activities. We are not talking about global governance from above but rather a global framework in which governance at every level takes place. Nations and institutions have no intrinsic obligation to each other, and any attempt to impose a global system from above—for example, regulation by a supranational agency—would fail. Nor would it be desirable. The many national and local differences in higher education are of common potential benefit, providing that they are made accessible to all (making diversity more accessible to all is one of the potential public goods offered by a global framework). Some educational variations between nations might be targeted for long-term reduction, for example, those that inhibit structural articulation between national systems, or the disparities between nations in educational resource levels and participation rates (Guadilla 2000). Other variations, such as certain forms of diversity in pedagogical and curriculum contents, might be encouraged. Such variations not only constitute public goods in the nation concerned, they enable that nation to make its own distinctive contribution to world higher education.

In the United States, the establishment of a global framework would not jeopardize the accrediting power of the states or compromise the role of the regional accrediting associations within the country. Rather, it would provide a systematic set of protocols for managing certain kinds of accreditation decisions that are currently tackled in a fragmented and inconsistent manner, or not tackled at all—for example, decisions about U.S. institutions operating offshore, foreign providers operating in the United States, cross-border e-learning, and joint cross-country programs. Such protocols would take into account established accreditation and quality assurance regimes operating outside the United States, such as those of the UK and the European Union. States and institutions would remain free to modify their interpretation of these protocols as they see fit. The global dimension is with us for the foreseeable future; the question is how best to deal with it. Formalizing the global dimension in governance would not add another layer of regulation as such, another set of bureaucratic steps to undergo. Instead it would enable existing problems of governance to be handled more speedily and effectively.

Nevertheless, the development of a global framework for the governance of higher education, as a global public good, raises some difficult issues. One such issue is that of who pays the costs, a problem posed by all global public goods (Kaul et al. 1999). Though the gaps in the framework of national regulation may detract from the potential for a global framework, filling those gaps does not necessarily meet the felt needs of the nations concerned. It will not be immediately evident to national authorities that they should bear the cost of their part of providing the global public good. Part of the process of moving toward a mutually beneficial global framework is to establish an appropriate policy climate in which those common benefits are more readily imagined, and national governments and regional authorities—and perhaps leading universities—can commit to the "internalization" of the economic externality. Once global practices reach a threshold level of operation so that it becomes more advantageous to be inside the emerging framework than outside it, the framework gains enough authority to become determining. In the last analysis, a global framework of governance depends on voluntary cooperation that is sufficiently comprehensive to penalize those that remain outside the framework.

A second, more difficult issue is how to manage the unevenness of resources and status between countries' higher education systems. All countries outside the United States are concerned at the potential for Americanization in a more facile global environment. This is true of developed nations as well as developing ones. In 1999 the former education minister for France, Claude Allegre, warned that higher education in Europe was at risk of being dominated by "American values" as a result of U.S. universities setting up branches and degree programs in Europe. He stated that "if Americans install their universities all over the world, all on the same model, with the same curriculum, it would be a catastrophe"; and he called on Europe to maintain its "national specifics." Likewise in the developing world, African faculty refer to the "recolonization" of their universities via the imposition of U.S. quality assurance rather than a partner approach to quality (Hayward 2001, pp. 3–5).

If the capacity for national and local diversity is to be preserved and enhanced, this will require a global regime based on reciprocity and mutual respect, rather than "might is right." This again illustrates that there is more at stake than trade. The system of governance should facilitate trade, but at the same time it should operate as a counterweight to the negative effects of economic exchange, such as enhancing global inequalities and cultural domination by the stronger trading nations. For example, when an U.S. or Australian university provides distance learning in, say, India, it should not be enough for that program to be quality assured in the exporting country, in terms of its cultural and educational norms. The program should be quality assured also in India. Recalling Amartya Sen's point, in a plural world, multiple partners require multiple accreditation procedures and multiple lines of accountability. In addition a global framework requires negotiating structures capable of dealing with highly sensitive national and local issues.

Steps to liberalize trade and mobility in education and to introduce common approaches to quality assurance and standards will be unsuccessful if they fail to address adequately the concerns of home-country governments (McBurnie and Ziguras 2001). While cross-national education offers enhanced opportunities to students, it does not automatically address the academic, professional, or skill requirements of the national infrastructure. Further, there are possible negative effects on the home-country system: both students and staff may be drawn away, so that the home system is "hollowed out," and some international educational practices have the potential to undermine national policy objectives. National government concerns may include language issues (for example, the role and status of the language of instruction, the national language, and ethnic minority languages); the preservation of local culture, history, and practices in balance with globalizing factors; and the equity effects of fee-charging foreign institutions.

A third, fundamental issue lies in the respective roles of autonomous institutions and state and national governments. In many countries there is a discernable movement toward the Anglo-American model of institutional autonomy and self-regulation and the growing regulatory or quasi-regulator role of nongovernment bodies derived from higher education itself, such as consortia for quality assurance. At the same time, in most countries, national government will continue to be a powerful site of regulation. A stable global regime cannot be created simply by agreement between nation-states, nor can it rest solely on the free cross-border association of institutions themselves. Nevertheless, precisely because global relationships now partly have escaped the capacity of nation-states to control or even to monitor them, in the longer term the general move toward U.S.-style systems of self-regulation will enhance the potential for a worldwide framework enabling the benefits of higher education to be maximized—always provided that non-U.S. nations and their institutions can sustain their distinctive identities within such a regime. In the medium term, a global regime needs to be sufficiently loosely coupled to allow significant structural differences to coexist.

I now consider three spheres in which the potential for a global regime is being explored in practice—the World Trade Organization negotiations on trade in services, the development of a "common higher education space" in the European Union, and the growing international collaboration in relation to quality assurance—and offer a conclusion.

The General Agreement on Trade in Services

In negotiations over the General Agreement on Trade in Services (GATS), the World Trade Organization aims to liberalize trade in services such as education by providing member countries with legally enforceable rights to such trade. Nations are asked to make commitments to two principles: market access (governments should not discriminate between incumbents and new entrants to a market) and national treatment (governments should not discriminate between domestic and foreign service providers). By 1998, twenty-three countries had made specific commitments on higher education services: Australia, Austria, Belgium, Canada, Czech Republic, Denmark, Finland, Germany, Greece, Iceland, Ireland, Italy, Japan, Korea, Mexico, New Zealand, Norway, Portugal, Spain, Switzerland, Turkey, the UK, and the United States. Not every nation has committed to all items. For example, Australia has committed to full market access and national treatment in relation to foreign providers of cross-border distance education, but in relation to commercial presence (foreign providers teaching in Australia) has committed to market access but not national treatment. This allows the Australian government to subsidize local producers without funding foreign producers, a de facto discrimination. Australia pursues a trading double standard familiar also to Americans—full trade liberalization in importing nations while protecting the domestic higher education system.

Meanwhile the United States is arguing that while "education to a large extent is a government function," the development of "supplementary" commercial markets in higher education, adult education, and industry training is desirable. This would be facilitated by national commitments on market access and national treatment (Delegation of the United States 2000). While avoiding a direct confrontation with the nonprofit sector and the accreditation industry on home turf, the United States wants to free up opportunities for U.S. exporters, with other national governments taking the local political flak.

Again, the logic is that the education system should provide public good at home but private good abroad. As befits a Hobbesian order, this would enable imperial domination by a small number of English-language providers. This kind of globalization might enhance economic freedom but does so at the expense of cultural identities and will be continually resisted. Altbach remarks that "any WTO-style treaty would inevitably harm the emerging academic systems of the developing countries, unable to compete economically against the major exporters, that are indifferent to nation-building in the importer countries. Even in the developed countries, the idea that the university serves a broad public good would be weakened, and the universities would be subject to all of the commercial pressures of the marketplace—a marketplace enforced by international treaties and legal requirements" (Altbach 2001, p. 4).

On September 28, 2001, four organizations—The Council for Higher Education Accreditation (CHEA), the American Council on Education, the Association of Universities and Colleges of Canada, and the European University Association (EUA)—signed a joint declaration opposing the inclusion of higher education services in the GATS negotiations. The declaration stated that "higher education exists to serve the public interest and is not a 'commodity,'" that "authority to regulate higher education must remain in the hands of competent bodies as designated by any given country," and that there must be appropriate quality assurance mechanisms, under competent bodies, to ensure that quality is not compromised, regardless of the method of delivery (EUA 2001). At the same time, the signatories supported global mobility: "The signatory organizations however express their members' own commitment to reducing obstacles to international exchange and cooperation in higher education using conventions and agreements outside of a trade policy regime. This commitment includes, but is not limited to improving communications, expanding information exchanges, and developing agreements concerning higher education institutions, programs, degrees or qualifications and quality review practices" (EUA 2001).

A trading regime does not encompass these broader strategies of liberalization. What is required is political negotiations grounded in a common sense of mutual rights and obligations, in which the facilitation of trade in selected areas is a subordinate element.

The European Union and the Common Higher Education Space

A richer potential for global frameworks lies in the current negotiations in the European Union to create a distinctively European higher education space, which is constituted by a fecund combination of elements: the will to cooperate within transparent common systems, national sovereignty and national diversity, and institutional autonomy and external accountability.

The subsidiarity principle implies that European policy will be developed only in those areas where national policy making is insufficient, and Article 126 of the Maastricht Treaty specifies full respect for the member states in relation to "the content and structure of their educational systems and their cultural and linguistic diversity" (European Ministers of Education 1999). Nevertheless the Bologna declaration embodies a substantial commitment to mutual transformation. It commits European countries to measures to strengthen educational and workforce mobility and to promote a European approach to cross-national education; it also involves selective reforms to establish harmonization. In summary, the Bologna declaration foreshadows the adoption of a single system of recognizable and comparable degrees; the creation of a European-wide system of credits; European-wide access to student services and recognition of teachers, researchers, and administrative staff; interinstitutional cooperation and mobility; the introduction of European elements in curricula; and the promotion of methods of quality assessment.

Cross-national governance mechanisms can only work without the violation of national sovereignty, if the linkages are sufficiently flexible. The April 1997 Lisbon convention on the recognition of higher education qualifications replaced the former notion of "equivalence" of diplomas and degrees with the concept of "recognition." This depends on a common trust in the procedures for accreditation and quality assurance in each country. At the same time, portability is enhanced within standardized structures. There has been some progress toward a common system of first and second degrees based on the Anglo-American norm; for example, Germany and Austria have introduced new bachelors/masters curricula alongside the extended masters programs traditional in both the Germanic countries and Scandinavia (Van Der Wende 2000). The quality assurance systems used in EU countries encompass a variety of processes for minimum quality control, detailed summative audit, and formative audit primarily directed to improvement. The European approach adds to rather than replaces national quality assurance. It is unlikely that a single European-wide system of quality assurance will be adopted; more likely there will be a common framework for validating quality assurance and accreditation decisions made by national authorities, institutions, academic disciplines, and professional bodies (EUA-CRE 2001, p. 10). Continued implementation of the Bologna declaration depends on national and interinstitutional cooperation. The European Commission gained no extra authority for implementing the European higher education space. "Subsidiarity" remains primary.

Though EU-member countries are currently preoccupied with the processes of Europeanization, their ultimate purpose is global. The June 1999 Bologna declaration states: "We must look with special attention at the objective to increase the international competitiveness of the European system of higher education. The vitality and efficiency of any civilization is measured, in fact, by the attraction that its cultural system exerts on other countries. We need to ensure that the European system of higher education acquires in the world a degree of attraction equal to our extraordinary cultural and scientific traditions" (European Ministers of Education 1999).

In the other metanational regional associations, including NAFTA, the Association of Southeast Asian Nations (ASEAN), the Asian-Pacific Economic Cooperation (APEC), and the Southern Common Market (Mercosur) in South America, the common agendas are more limited than the EU's and are focused primarily on economic integration and national security. Mercosur has established agreements about mutual recognition of primary and junior high school qualifications (other than technical studies) and has proposed a regional technical commission of officials from each ministry of education to establish equivalencies of degrees and certificates.

Accreditation and Quality Assurance

Eaton (2001) notes that in 1999, thirty-four of the fifty-five regional, national, and specialized accreditors affiliated to the U.S. CHEA were engaged in international activity. Together the CHEA organizations were accrediting 355 programs or activities in sixty-five different countries. The growing international collaboration concerning quality assurance is driven by the rise of cross-border education, the global activities of professional associations, and awareness that these activities might become a primary medium for global-level exchange in governance. Though quality assurance systems evolved in the 1990s within national boundaries, these processes can be turned to cross-national integration:

> We have come to the point where the international mobility of students and the broader processes of internationalisation in higher education can no longer avoid the confrontation with issues of quality and quality assurance. When increasing numbers of students seek to study abroad and demand their foreign credits and degrees recognised and validated in their home country or elsewhere, when transnational education will become an economic reality where students move to places and institutions where they perceive to be served best, the formalism, voluntarism and mutual confidence of, for example, the European Credit Transfer System will not suffice any longer. The issue of quality and quality assurance

will become of crucial importance to internationalisation policies. (Van Damme 2000, pp. 10–11)

Nevertheless, there are formidable challenges in attempting to align national systems of accreditation and quality assurance. "The readability and transparency of these quality assurance and accreditation systems to other countries, foreign institutions and international students is low" (Van Damme 2001, p. 9). Accreditation can be understood as a formal statement by an external body, resulting from a quality assurance procedure, that agreed standards have been met by the institution or its program. There is great variety in the conceptions and measurement of standards, and national approaches to quality assurance vary from self-assessment to external audit, as well as many different mixes of the two, and from discipline-based assessments to whole-of-institution approaches driven more by management criteria than by academic values (Harman 1998). The role accorded to students, employers, and professional associations varies. As noted, sometimes accreditation is used to encourage mobility and open up systems to new providers; sometimes it is used to protect the domestic higher education market. Above all, there is variation in the role of the nation-state in accreditation and quality assurance.

Initial steps toward better cross-border collaboration include the improvement of communication between national quality assurance agencies, the development of agreed protocols for validating quality assurance and accreditation agencies themselves, and the instances of metanational accreditation. Though a comprehensive global accreditation regime is out of reach at this time, it is possible to make real progress in selected areas, as demonstrated by the Washington declaration in engineering. Currently, the crucial part of the puzzle is the relationship between North America and Europe. The United States / NAFTA and the EU are the most influential global prototypes, the largest blocs of world-leading institutions, and the largest worldwide attractors of international students and faculty expertise. The United States and the EU also embody a considerable diversity in systems of governance. If these two blocs can be brought into a loose and productive conjunction taking in accreditation, quality assurance, and other mechanisms for the facilitation of mobility and exchange, their association would affect other world regions. It would significantly advance the potential for a global framework that is fully sensitive to state/national and local governance.

REFERENCES

Adam, S. 2001. *Transnational Education Project: Report and recommendations.* Brussels: Confederation of European Union Rectors' Conferences.

Altbach, P. 2001. Higher education and the WTO: Globalization runs amok. *International Higher Education* 23:2–4.

Australian Vice Chancellors' Committee (AVCC). 1995. *Code of Ethical Practice in the Provision of Offshore Education and Educational Services by Australian Higher Education Institutions.* Canberra: AVCC.

Castells, M. 2000. *The information age: Economy, society and culture.* Vol. 1, *The rise of the network society.* 2d ed. Oxford: Blackwell Publishers.

Council for Higher Education Accreditation (CHEA). 2001. *Principles for United States accreditors working internationally: Accreditation of non-United States institutions and programs.* Washington, DC: CHEA.

Contreras, A. 2001. International diploma mills grow with the internet. *International Higher Education* 24:5–6.

Davis, D., A. Olsen, and A. Bohm, eds. 2000. *Transnational education providers, partners and policy: Challenges for Australian institutions offshore.* Brisbane, Australia: IDP Education.

Delegation of the United States. 2000. *WTO Council for Trade in Services Special Session, Communication from the United States: Higher (tertiary) education, adult education and training.* December 18. GATS 00–552. Available from www.wto.org.

Dow, S. 1990. Beyond dualism. *Cambridge Journal of Economics* 14:143–57.

———. 1996. *The methodology of macroeconomic thought: A conceptual analysis of schools of thought in economics.* Cheltenham, England: Edward Elgar Publishers.

Eaton, J. 2001. American accrediting and the international environment. *International Higher Education* 23:13–15.

Eckel, P. 2002. Governing entrepreneurial strategic alliances that capitalize on the curriculum. Working paper. Washington, DC: American Council on Education.

Engberg, D. 2001. Attitudes about international education in the United States. *International Higher Education* 22:8–9.

European Association of Universities (EUA-CRE). 2001. *Towards accreditation schemes for higher education in Europe?* Final project report, CRE Project, co-funded by the SOCRATES Program (Complementary Measures for Higher Education). Brussels: European Association of Universities.

European Ministers of Education. 1999. The Bologna Declaration of 19 June 1999. Retrieved September 15, 2003, from www.udg.es/udgeuropa.

European University Association (EUA). 2001. *GATS (WTO) and the implications for higher education in Europe.* Retrieved from www.unige.ch/eua.

Green, M., P. Eckel, and A. Barblan. 2002. *The brave new (and smaller) world of higher education: A transatlantic view.* Washington, DC: American Council on Education.

Guadilla, C. 2000. *Comparative higher education in Latin America: Quantitative aspects.* Caribe, Caracas: UNESCO / Instituto Internacional para La Educacion Superior en America Latina y Le.

Harman, G. 1998. Quality assurance mechanisms and their use as policy instruments: Major international approaches and the Australian experience since 1993. *European Journal of Higher Education* 33 (3): 331–48.

Hayward, F. 2001. Finding a common voice for accreditation internationally. Washington, DC: Council for Higher Education Accreditation. Retrieved from www.chea.org /international/comon-voice.html.

Held, D., A. McGrew, D. Goldblat, and J. Perraton. 1999. *Global transformations: Politics, economics and culture.* Stanford: Stanford University Press.

The Internet's new borders. 2001. *The Economist,* August 11, pp. 9–10, 17–20.

Johnson, J. 2001. *The globalisation of science and engineering education.* Paper presented at the conference on Globalisation and higher education—Views from the South, March, University of Capetown. Arlington, VA: U.S. National Science Foundation.

Kaul, I., I. Grunberg, and M. Stern. 1999. Global public goods: Concepts, policies and strategies. In *Global public goods: International cooperation in the 21st century,* ed. I. Kaul, I. Grunberg, and M. Stern. New York: Oxford University Press.

Marginson, S. 2002. Towards a politics of the enterprise university. In *Scholars and entrepreneurs: The universities in crisis,* ed. S. Cooper, J. Hinkson, and G. Sharp. Melbourne, Australia: Arena Publications.

Marginson, S., and M. Considine. 2000. *The enterprise university: Power, governance and reinvention in Australia.* Cambridge: Cambridge University Press.

Marginson S., and M. Mollis. 2001. "The door opens and the tiger leaps": Theories and reflexivities of comparative education for a global millenium. *Comparative Education Review* 45 (4): 581–615.

Marginson, S., and G. Rhoades. 2002. Beyond national states, markets and systems of higher education: A global agency heuristic. *Higher Education* 43 (3): 281–309.

McBurnie, G., and C. Ziguras. 2001. The regulation of transnational higher education in Southeast Asia: Case studies of Hong Kong, Malaysia and Australia. *Higher Education* 42:85–105.

Middlehurst, R. 2001. *Quality assurance and accreditation for virtual education: A discussion of models and needs.* Paper presented at the UNESCO Expert Meeting, September, Paris.

Ministerial Council for Education, Employment, Training and Youth Affairs, Australia (MCEETYA). 2000. National protocols for higher education approval processes. Retrieved from www.dest.gov.au/highered/mceetya.

Mollis, M. 1999/2000. The Americanization of the reformed university in Argentina. *Australian Universities Review* 42 (2), 43 (1): 38–43; 45–52.

Mollis, M., and S. Marginson. 2002. The assessment of universities in Argentina and Australia: Between autonomy and heteronomy. *Higher Education* 43 (3): 311–30.

Organization for Economic Cooperation and Development (OECD) 2001. *Education at a Glance.* Paris: OECD.

Rhoades, G. 1998. *Managed professionals.* Albany, NY: SUNY Press.

Salmi, J. 2000. Facing the challenges of the twenty-first century. *International Higher Education* 19:2–3.

Sen, A. 1999a. Global justice: Beyond international equity. In *Global public goods: International cooperation in the 21st century,* ed. I. Kaul, I. Grunberg, and M. Stern. New York: Oxford University Press.

———. 1999b. *Development as freedom.* New York: Anchor Books.

Singh, M. 2001. *Re-inserting the 'Public Good' into higher education transformation.* Paper presented to a conference on Globalisation and higher education—Views from the South, University of Capetown, March. Discussion Series, No. 1. Pretoria: South African Council on Higher Education.

Tremblay, K. 2002. Student mobility between and towards OECD countries: A comparative analysis. In *International Mobility of the Highly Skilled.* Paris: OECD.

Van Damme, D. 2000. Internationalization and quality assurance: Towards worldwide accreditation? *European Journal for Educational Law and Policy* 4:1–20.

———. 2001. The need for a new regulatory framework for recognition, quality assurance and accreditation. Paper presented at the UNESCO Expert Meeting, September, Paris.

Van Der Wende, M. 2000. The Bologna declaration: Enhancing the transparency and competitiveness of European higher education. *Higher Education in Europe* 25 (3): 305–10.

Woodcock, M. 2000. The place of social capital in understanding social and economic outcomes. In *The contribution of human and social capital to sustained economic growth and well-being,* ed. J. F. Helliwell. International Symposium Report. Human Resource Development Canada and OECD. Available from www.hrdc-drhc.gc.ca.

World Bank. 2002. *Constructing Knowledge Societies: New challenges for tertiary education,* ed. Richard Hopper. Education Group, Human Development Network. Washington, DC: World Bank.

Ziguras, C. 2001. *The effect of GATS on transnational higher education: Comparing experiences of New Zealand, Australia, Singapore and Malaysia.* Paper presented to the annual conference of the Australian Association for Research in Education, December, Fremantle. Retrieved from www.aare.edu.au.

CHAPTER TWO

The Paradox of Scope

A Challenge to the Governance of Higher Education

David J. Collis

The governance of our institutions of higher education has always been problematic. Over hundreds of years, power has shifted from the academic guild of British universities in the Middle Ages, to the trustees that initially established universities in the United States, to the heroic U.S. university presidents in the late nineteenth and early twentieth centuries, to the faculty, and perhaps even the students, by the end of the last century (Kauffman 1993; Kerr 2001, p. 137; Glaeser 2002; Jencks and Reisman 2002). The crown has always sat uneasily on each head. The essential problem, as Clark Kerr has identified, was that each of the multiple constituencies of the "multiversity" always had, if not decision-making authority, at least veto power. And, as Kerr notes, the only choice that cannot be vetoed is the status quo (Kerr 2001, p. 134). While the resulting conservatism in the governance of higher education may have contributed to the longevity of many institutions,[1] it has always acted as an obvious constraint on their ability to respond to exogenous change.

In this chapter I argue that circumstances today are conspiring to expose the inherent weaknesses in the governance of higher education. The argument extends Simon Marginson's thesis by recognizing that the external environment of universities and colleges is undergoing profound change. Globalization, technology, the massive growth of tertiary education, the emergence of the knowledge economy, and the intrusion of market forces into the sector, among other forces and trends, all threaten to disrupt the hallowed halls of academia in new ways (Collis 1999 and 2001; Newman and Couturier 2001; Kirp 2002). If universities and colleges are to successfully adapt to these unavoidable societal trends, they must develop, communicate, and implement clear and concise strategies. The hallmark of those strategies will be a willingness to make difficult choices among very different alternatives (Porter 1996). Yet, as James Duderstadt, George Keller, and others in this volume contend, it will be the governance structure of universities that ultimately impedes their ability to make those hard choices. Therefore, it is governance that requires the most careful analysis, evaluation, and improvement.

The bulk of the chapter explains why the governance of higher education is more problematic than ever before by drawing on recent research in the strategy field that has identified "the paradox of scope" (Sawhney 2002; Gulati, Huffman, and Neilson 2002). This phenomenon examines and explains the blurring boundary of the business firm today by noting that two opposing forces are operating simultaneously. The traditional core of many companies is shrinking as activities such as IT, logistics, and even manufacturing are outsourced, while at the same time, firms' peripheries are expanding through the proliferation of alliances, joint ventures, partnerships, and other long-term contracts. Whether the contemporary firm is larger or smaller than twenty years ago is impossible to measure, since on some dimensions (full-time employees) it might be smaller, while on others (market sales and share) it is larger.

The firm still has the same scope of responsibilities—making the product, delivering it to customers, and so on—but its authority over those activities has been reduced. No longer are activities performed within the hierarchy and subject—within a zone of indifference—to the fiat of the employment contract that distinguished the traditional boundary of the firm (Grossman and Hart 1980). Instead, executives have to deal with an additional set of relationships, none of which are subject to traditional hierarchical modes of control. Achieving change when dealing through and with multiple partners, all of which have their own vested interests, becomes increasingly problematic, as Marginson has cogently noted in chapter 1.

The argument has been made that exactly the same phenomenon is occurring within universities and colleges (Clark 1993; Zemsky and Massy 1995; Geiger 1993). I present data that demonstrate how the traditional core of the university—full-time faculty, liberal arts and scientific education, student services that act in loco parentis, the library—is declining, in some cases in absolute terms, in others cases relatively, while at the same time the periphery of the institution—outsourcing partnerships, corporate training, vocational courses, sponsored research, license and patent activity, discrete research institutes and centers—is expanding.

While not necessarily an inappropriate response to the societal pressures outlined above, the operation of this "paradox of scope" within higher education extends the set of constituencies that must be managed by every institution, while shrinking the share of activities with which participants in governance are acquainted or capable of administering. The result is likely to be an even more conservative institution, frozen in panic before the oncoming educational revolution.

Having explained the increasing inability of current governance structures to respond to external events, the chapter concludes by proposing recommendations for improving those structures. Many of these ideas are derived from the experience of the private sector as it too struggles to reconcile the "paradox of scope." There are obviously important differences between higher education and industry, not least the existence of a single objective—shareholder value maximization. Within business, the efforts of bodies such as the Cadbury committee in the UK, reformers like the California Public Employees' Retirement System (CalPERS) in the United States, and self-examination by companies like General Motors provide valuable benchmarks and principles for higher education to consider.

Governance in Higher Education

Governance in higher education, as George Keller expands upon in chapter 6, has been defined as "the structure and processes of decision-making" (Carnegie Commission 1973) and "the establishment of policies to guide (the work of the institution)" (Kauffman 1993, p. 224), as opposed to the daily management or administration of the institution (Ehrle and Bennett 1988). More specifically, Balderston (1995, p. 58), Kauffman (1993, p. 226), and others (Nason 1982; Fisher 1991, pp. 93–105) follow the spirit of the original Carnegie Commission report (and before that the 1966 description of responsibilities laid out by the AAUP) in identifying a list of between six and thirteen functions that governing boards fulfill, which includes:

- to safeguard, or hold in "trust," the institution's mission and long run welfare;
- to buffer the university from its external constituencies;
- to oversee fiscal integrity and financial solvency;

- to stand as final arbiter of internal disputes among stakeholders;
- to act as an "agent of change" by enunciating major policy standards and long-range plans;
- to select, monitor, and review the president and the overall administrative structure of the institution.

For our purpose, which is to draw on analogies from the private sector to generate insight and prescriptions, governance is interpreted as "setting the strategy for the institution." While somewhat narrower than the definitions implied above (and equally vulnerable to differing interpretations) and narrower than the function served by the board of directors in a publicly quoted firm, this definition is useful for the connotation of setting long-term direction for the institution—the task that is perhaps most difficult for boards of trustees to perform today, as James Duderstadt discusses in chapter 5.

This definition downplays the important task of governance with respect to the internal coherence and harmony of the institution (which was the major concern of the Carnegie Commission as it struggled to resolve the internal dissension that had driven universities in the 1960s) by stressing the nature of the fit of the institution with its external environment. However, it is exactly the outward-looking aspect of governance, of steering an institution in the difficult interplay between the entity and its environment, that is the challenge for universities and colleges today.

In fulfilling this function, governance has always been a major concern of universities and colleges. Despite that the Carnegie Commission saw the governing board as an "agent of change," this concern can best be expressed as a worry that the structure of governance in higher education has resulted in an essentially conservative institution (Zemsky and Massy 1995). While conservatism may have contributed to the longevity of the institutional form (Kerr 2001, p.175; or see the claim in Rothblatt and Wittrock [1993] that the university is the second-oldest institution in the Western world after the Catholic Church), throughout history the resulting inertia has been viewed as a liability by contemporary observers. They fear it might cause the institution to break under the stress of adapting to external trends and forces. Kerr (2001, p. 126), for example, saw the university reforms of the 1960s killed by a conservative faculty.

It has always been recognized that the governance of higher education is problematic (Gumport and Puser 1997, p. 18). Indeed, there are at least five reasons why governance in this sector should be less effective than in the private sector, with which it is often contrasted.[2]

First, lacking the unidimensional goal of shareholder value maximization that drives firm behavior (Jensen 1989), universities and colleges simultaneously pursue multiple goals. Every participant in higher education has to balance demands for research, teaching, and public service, to name only the three most commonly identified objectives of higher education. Even if there was consensus on the weight to attach to each objective, managing the tradeoff among those goals is complicated by uncertainty about whether the various outputs are substitutes or complements (Zemsky and Massy 1995).

Second, and again in contrast to the clarity of the output measure in the private sector,[3] it is extraordinarily hard to evaluate the output of the higher education sector. Even if we can measure the absolute number of graduates or academic articles written, the absence of uniform quality metrics makes the interpretation of quantitative measures impossible. Has the quality of undergraduate learning gone up or down over the past twenty years? At Harvard grades have certainly gone up—to the extent that more than 90 percent of graduates receive honors—but has learning, or the quality of the graduates, improved? In the absence of a universal graduate test such as the SAT, or even the British use of external examiners to ensure consistency across institutions, how can we know the answer to that question? And if we cannot measure outputs, how can those charged with governance know the answer to the basic question, "How well is my institution performing?"

In the absence of adequate output measures, administrators have instead been forced to manage inputs. Following the maxim that "we can only control what we can measure" (Simons 1995), administrators are monitoring faculty teaching hours, or even, in the recent case of Boston College, the time faculty spend in their offices! Managing inputs is inferior to managing outputs (Donaldson 1995), and the penalties of trying to directly control faculty time are enormous. However, without accurate output metrics, administrators fulfilling their obligation to oversee the use of resources have no viable alternatives.

Third, multiple conflicting constituencies within academic institutions are represented in the various governing bodies of those institutions (Kerr 2001). Each of the stakeholders—faculty, administrative staff, students, alumni, the surrounding community, recruiting firms, public funding agencies, and so on (the list can be endless)—have their own agendas and vested interests. While alumni might be obsessed with "the remembrance of things past" (Kerr 2001, p. 72), particularly athletics, faculty are more concerned with research and the tenure process, while students care more about the classroom experience and (perhaps most) about the residence halls and campus social life. The resulting "goal divergence" (Richman and Farmer 1976, p. 214) among constituencies is problematic, but not uncommon in many other organizations. That all of these constituencies are, to a greater or lesser extent, represented on the governing bodies of universities and colleges does however lead to "multifractionated governance" (Kerr 2001, p. 144) that impedes governance decisions.

Indeed, the normal divergence of interests among constituencies is exacerbated by the fourth weakness in higher education governance structures—that certain constituencies, to some extent, have been given veto power, or, as Kerr observes, "each identifiable group (has) not only a voice but a veto" (2001). This arises for two reasons. The first is that many governing bodies have a tradition of consensus decision making that values unanimity and so gives effective veto power to any reasonably determined voting bloc. More fundamentally, and less easy to amend, certain groups, such as the faculty, are not subject to sanction by the administration. As a result, even if they cannot block an initiative within the formal governance process, they can exercise effective veto power simply by choosing not to implement the governing body's agenda.

Finally, the absence of hierarchical control within universities and weak faculty incentives leave administrators little scope for dealing with malefactors or malingerers. As described above, this inevitably leads to difficulties implementing a governing body's directives, and so those bodies are less likely to initiate changes they know will meet faculty objections. The authority of those charged with administering policies set by the governing body is easily subverted because they do not have the ultimate recourse to terminate employment. In the private sector, in contrast, where all employees are subject to traditional contracts, those who do not accept the direction or the values of the firm are relatively easily removed. In fact, Jack Welch was very clear that one of the keys to his success as CEO of General Electric (GE) was his willingness to "take behind the woodshed and shoot" (Welch and Byrne 2001) executives who did not buy into his values—even those who were otherwise high performers. Imagine a university president proudly pointing to actions like that! Faculty are not employees in the traditional sense (Cleman 1973), and it is the resulting absence of the ultimate discipline to which Kerr attributed the ending of the heroic academic presidency (2001).

Administrators are even limited in their ability to use less draconian measures, such as incentive compensation, to implement initiatives. There are constraints on how differentiated faculty compensation can be as a result of rewarding desirable behavior and punishing unsatisfactory performance. The lack of instruments with which to influence and persuade a key constituency to adhere to institutional initiatives will always undermine governance in higher education.

These deficiencies in governance are true regardless of institutional type. There are obviously important differences in the structure of governance between public and private institutions (see Simpson and Frost 1993, pp. 75, 76), between for-profit and not-for-profit schools, among states, and across Carnegie Commission tiers.[4] I do not want to diminish those differences. However, the above arguments are generally applicable to all institutions. Similarly, although the focus of this paper is on the United States, the arguments would be valid in most countries, even if the specific deficiencies varied among countries.

The predictable outcome of such a governance structure is that it is conservative—perhaps more conservative than effective. The inability to define clear goals or measure progress toward the achievement of those goals, the existence of multiple constituencies with conflicting objectives, and the absence of effective sanction against groups with veto power all suggest the enormous difficulties of fulfilling the key governance task of "change agent." While some scholars have noted the value of preserving the status quo in terms of the longevity of the institution, others point to conservatism as an inevitable source of decline (Hannan and Freeman 1977). When faced with considerable environmental change and uncertainty, an inability to adapt can be fatal.

Threats to Higher Education

The vulnerability of any institution depends on the degree of environmental change. When the external context alters rapidly, organizations must adapt or run the risk of being surpassed or becoming outmoded. That adaptation takes the form of making choices among trade-offs (Porter 1996). While it would be wonderful if universities and colleges could be all things to all people, the reality is that providing more of one thing requires us to provide less of another. As the demand for universities to become more customer sensitive, to cater to new and differentiated audiences, to seek out new sources of funding, to respond to new competition, and so on increases, it becomes critical to make those trade-offs—to choose a strategy (Collis 1999, 2001). Yet because a strategy requires the institution to make choices, current governance structures will become a real liability.

This is the case in higher education today. The number and extent of changes to the industry in the next decades is likely to force institutions to make some fundamental choices.

While every generation appears to believe that society is changing at a faster rate than ever before (and there have been profound changes in higher education since World War II, particularly in the 1960s and 1970s),[5] over the next twenty years the industry will undergo dramatic alterations. I do not wish to reiterate what those changes will be nor detail an explanation of their impact. Rather, it is sufficient here to partially list the forces at work and refer the reader to the several existing papers that more fully make the argument (Collis 1999, 2001; Newman and Couturier 2001; Kirp 2002).

In brief, domestic demographics are working to increase dramatically demand for higher education as the echo of the baby boom reaches college age. While the absolute number of high school graduates will increase by 25 percent to peak in 2008 (U.S. Department of Education 1996), demand will increase proportionately as participation rates also increase. In 1995, 65 percent of high school graduates went on to college, up from only 49 percent in 1980 (U.S. Department of Education 1996).

Partly facilitated by the convenience of new technologies but also driven by the widening income gap between college graduates and those with high school diplomas—now up to more than 65 percent (U.S. Census Bureau 2001)—adults are becoming students in record numbers. Already 43 percent of all postsecondary enrollments, students over the age of twenty-five will soon be in the majority (ThinkEquity 2002), and yet only a quarter of the U.S. population over the age of twenty-five has a bachelor's degree. As the knowledge economy continues to require a better trained and educated workforce, these trends toward the expansion of higher education will continue.

Indeed, there is already a massive parallel education system in place—the corporate training market (at least a quarter the size of the formal higher education market [Moe and Blodget 2000]). Adelman, for example, estimates that close to 2 million certificates have been granted in the past decade, which are perfectly satisfactory credentials for most companies (Adelman 2000; Christianson and Fajen 1999). As lifelong learning becomes an integral part of the employment experience, this sector will continue to grow at historically high rates—11 percent per year (Moe and Blodget 2000).

Technology, particularly the Internet, is changing the face of higher education, as Marginson pointed out in chapter 1. While the immediate impact of e-learning frequently has been overstated, within a decade of its initial adoption, nearly 90 percent of all colleges and universities will offer some form of it (International Data Corporation 2001). Similarly, although electronic usage is higher within the broadly defined corporate training market (Collis 2002), more than 2 million degree-oriented students will be enrolled in online courses by 2004, and the rate of growth is more than 30 percent per year (International Data Corporation 2001).

Drawn by the huge increase in demand, and with entry facilitated by the shift in the nature of that demand from traditional residential undergraduate education to part-time nonresidential lifelong learners, the private sector is beginning to intrude on the hallowed halls of academia. While publicly listed for-profit companies today account for only 2.2 percent of enrollments and 1.1 percent of total higher education expenditures, they are growing at 20 percent per year (ThinkEquity 2002). Indeed, 15 percent of the *Business Week* top sixty "hot growth" companies in 2002 were involved in the higher education market ("Hot Growth Companies 2002" 2002).

Finally, the higher education sector is poised to undergo a rapid period of globalization. Whereas there are 84 million students currently enrolled in tertiary education around the world (World Bank 2000, Table B), that number is expected to double over the next twenty-five years (ThinkEquity 2002). Yet tertiary enrollment rates in many developing countries, including China and India, are still only around 5 percent (World Bank 2000, Table B).

Whatever the ultimate drivers of change in higher education, and whatever manifestation that change actually takes, it is clear that in the face of this set of societal forces, universities and colleges must make some basic strategic choices. Should they retreat to serving the traditional eighteen-year-old, residential liberal arts student, or should they embrace the nontraditional student market? Should they respond to private sector entry by trying to cut costs and compete on price, or by improving quality and the differentiation of degree offerings even at the expense of a widening tuition price gap? Should they seek customers (students) beyond their traditional geographic market or retain a local market focus? While the appropriate strategic choice will differ among institutions in the various tiers of higher education, each of which comes with a different heritage and is motivated by a different mission, all face hard choices.

Fundamental questions like these cannot be avoided, nor can they be compromised. Each involves a choice among different strategies which require different and incompatible policies and allocation of resources to implement (Collis 1999, 2001). In responding, inaction and indecision is worse than almost any action. Being "stuck in the middle"—trying to satisfy all markets equally, without satisfying any effectively—is a recipe for disaster (Porter 1980). Yet the traditional governance structure of these institutions most likely will lead to exactly that outcome. In a context where not acting decisively has far more detrimental consequences than acting in a(ny) clearly chosen direction, the governance of higher education that is designed either to preserve the status quo or to satisfy all constituencies equally becomes a real liability.

The last time universities and colleges faced such substantive change was during the original expansion of higher education in the 1960s and 1970s. The difference between then and now is that change in the 1970s was in response to a coherent and agreed-upon policy mandate to expand the scope of higher education. Today, change is not happening in response to such clear top-down direction but is being led by the disruptive and unpredictable market and technological forces that Marginson discusses in chapter 1. Whereas the higher education sector was controlling its own fate in the 1960s and 1970s—it was in fact responding to a coherent strategy—today it is being buffeted by exogenous trends and new and unknown competitors.

It is also important to note that the cause for concern for colleges and universities is not just the unwarranted and unwanted intrusion of market forces into academia and the resulting emergence of "academic entrepreneurialism" (Slaughter and Leslie 1997; Kirp 2002). Colleges and universities always faced a cash constraint and still had to obey the laws of supply and demand. Rather, the impact can best be interpreted by, and encapsulated in, the notion of the "paradox of scope."

The Paradox of Scope

Shifts in the external environment are causing an essential problem for the governance of universities and colleges, known as the "paradox of scope" (Sawhney 2001; Gulati, Huffman, and Neilson 2002). This phenomenon refers to the blurring of the traditional boundary of the firm.[6] Fifty, possibly even twenty years ago, it was very clear what activities were inside and outside the firm. It almost did not require explanation, since the employment contract clearly identified those who worked for the firm and those who did not. Today, the contractual nexus (Grossman and Hart 1986) of the firm is more complex and its boundary correspondingly diffuse.

In fact, the boundary of the firm is becoming increasingly indistinct as traditional core activities are outsourced or supplied by part-time or temporary workers, while at the same time, the scope of activities the firm must manage expands through its relations with a network of alliances (Gulati, Huffman, and Neilson 2002).

In the heyday of corporate America, manufacturing firms were more or less completely vertically integrated and performed nearly all the activities necessary to produce, sell, deliver, and service a product for customers. Even if all companies did not go as far as Ford at the River Rouge plant, where iron ore and sand went in one end and Model T cars came out the other end (Chandler 1990), most companies designed the product they sold and manufactured many of its components. They certainly assembled the product themselves and marketed the product direct to consumers, usually delivering it and then providing service to their customers. Today a company like Dell, the world leader in personal computers, does no manufacturing, delivery, or servicing of its product, nor does Nike perform any manufacturing or operate its own supply chain logistics. The explanation is that companies can maximize shareholder value by concentrating on their "core competence" (Prahalad and Hamel 1990) and outsourcing every other activity. Only in those functions in which the firm has a set of unique or advantageous resources (Wernerfelt 1984; Barney 1991) can it earn economic profits.[7]

Indeed, outsourcing today is a trillion-dollar business (Dun and Bradstreet 2001) that is motivated equally by a desire to save cost and to focus on core competencies (Corbett and Associates 2001). Even activities that were traditionally considered central to a firm's operations are being outsourced. For example, contract manufacturers like Flextronics, with revenues in the billions, now assemble the bulk of personal computers rather than the name-brand companies from which consumers actually buy. In fact, 21 percent of the Fortune 3,500 outsource some amount of manufacturing, and a similar percentage outsource parts of the human resources function (Ross et al. 2001). Even a research-based giant like the pharmaceutical company Merck recognizes that it cannot cover all possible scientific developments itself and is looking to spend 20 percent of its research and development budget through outside entities (Pisano and Slack 2001).

When a company outsources an activity, however, it cannot abdicate responsibility for the performance of that activity. The customer still holds Dell accountable for the activities that come bundled with the product. Dell, therefore, has to structure and manage its relationship with its third-party vendor of services as carefully as if it operated that activity itself. Outsourcing merely substitutes one managerial headache—managing a workforce—for another administrative concern—managing an arm's-length relationship with a third party. Contracts alone cannot manage the relationship, and so the firm has to learn new skills and acquire new capabilities to function adequately with these new organizational arrangements.

In addition to outsourcing, increasing competition and globalization are forcing companies to look beyond the traditional advantages of size and market scope. Instead, they seek to combine the scale of a large firm with the speed of a small firm, the access of a global footprint with the flexibility of a local presence. Attempts to build this "boundaryless organization" require maximizing access to markets and technologies while minimizing bureaucratic fixed-asset investments. This can best be achieved by leveraging the capabilities of partners through alliances.

Indeed, alliances are increasingly important to the private sector. In 1980 only 1 percent of the revenue of the Fortune 1,000 firms was accounted for by alliances. By 1995 that share had risen to 15 percent (Doz and Hamel 1997). While alliances were being formed at the rate of 2,000 per year in 1990, by the turn of the millennium, the rate was up to 5,000 per year (Thomson Financial 2001).

This chapter is not about the operation of the paradox of scope in the private sector, but the appendix outlines the argument that explains why it is blurring the boundary of the firm. In summary, no company illustrates the paradox of scope better than the most widely admired firm of the past twenty years—General Electric (GE). In 1980, GE had sales of $25 billion generated by 402,000 employees. Today, GE has sales of $128 billion generated by only 313,000 employees. Adjusting for inflation, its revenue per employee has gone from $62,000 to more than $200,000. While productivity growth accounts for some of that increment, a substantial part of the increase is a result of the expansion of the scope of the company through nonhierarchical organizational arrangements.

The Paradox of Scope in Higher Education

The argument that the paradox of scope is at work in higher education is in many ways not a new observation. Rather it is a confirmation of what others have identified. Clark, for example, observes increasing complexity in higher education (1993). Zemsky and Massy note that colleges and universities grow by addition, not substitution (to quote Stanford's President Donald Kennedy, like "elements in the periodic table"), so that, "taken as a whole, the 1980s and 1990s can be seen as a time of growing perimeters and contracting institutional cores" (1995). Similarly, Geiger notes "a shift in the balance of activities in universities away from the center and toward the periphery" (1993, p. 74), leading to fragmentation, to the extent that "the very notion of a core might be called into question" (p. 75). Slaughter and Leslie interpret the change as a "paradox of power," with the center wanting centralized powers to achieve change and deal with external agents, while the pressure within the "entrepreneurial university" is for budget devolution and the decentralization of power so that every tub can stand on its own bottom (Slaughter and Leslie 1997).

Rather than replay the explanations for the phenomenon, I want to document the extent to which the paradox of scope is happening within higher education by presenting data on the shrinking core and the expanding periphery of colleges and universities within six categories:

- student composition,
- course offerings,
- funding sources,
- expenditure categories,
- staff mix,
- outsourcing activities.

But first, as a benchmark, we must characterize the traditional core of the university or college, as it was perhaps only thirty years ago.[8]

I have in mind the idyllic university or college of our common memory. The students are eighteen-year-olds, fresh out of high school, for whom a large part of the undergraduate experience is the personal growth that accompanies living away from home for the first time. The residential campus they attend, therefore, comes complete with a full set of facilities for living, social, and physical activities, all provided by the university itself. The academic experience is designed to educate the student in the broadest sense and so provides a liberal arts degree that stresses that "learning to learn" is more important than the specific content of any knowledge that is imparted. Teaching is conducted by full-time, tenure-track faculty who use the classroom and the blackboard as primary vehicles for transmitting information. These faculty spend their entire

Table 2.1. Students 55 and Under Participating in Adult Education (percent during the year)

	1991	1995	1999
Rate	33	40	45

Source: Digest of Education Statistics 2001, Table 359

year at the institution, either teaching or conducting research, and define their primary loyalty as to that institution. Funding for the school comes primarily from tuition, which is paid for by family contributions and is supported either by the endowment or by the state, while research is block grant funded by the state.

It is this harmonious and self-contained world that has been disrupted by the paradox of scope over the past thirty years and that will be further transformed over the next thirty years.[9]

Student Composition

There are many dimensions on which the composition of the student body has seen a contraction in the core and expansion of the periphery (Tables 2.1 and 2.2), but perhaps the one statistic that best represents the phenomenon is that only 27 percent of those in higher education are now full-time students who have gone straight from high school and are supported by parental contribution, that is, the archetypal undergraduate of yesteryear (Digest of Education Statistics 2001). The traditional core is down to one quarter of the market. Indeed, the number of full-time students under the age of nineteen has grown by only 12 percent in absolute terms since 1970 (Digest of Education Statistics 2001, Table 208).[10]

Part of the explanation for the relative contraction of the core is that participation in secondary education beyond full-time enrollment in credentialed programs—so-called adult education—has increased substantially. Even over the past decade, the share of the population attending some sort of adult education during the year has increased from one-third to nearly half.

But even among students enrolled for degrees, the share that attends full-time has shrunk below 60 percent, and the share over the age of twenty-four has risen to 40 percent (see Table 2.2). Partly as a result of this aging of the student body, even among those full-time students, only 30 percent dedicate themselves exclusively to study without working some hours of the week to support themselves (American Council on Education 2002). The periphery of the uni-

Table 2.2. Enrollment in Degree-granting Institutions (number and percent)

	1970	1980	1990	1999
Full Time	5,816	7,098	7,821	8,786
	67.8%	58.7%	56.6%	59.4%
Part Time	2,765	4,999	5,998	6,005
	32.2%	41.3%	43.4%	40.6%
< 24 Years	6,196	7,561	8,032	8,981
	72.2%	62.5%	58.1%	60.7%
> 24 Years	2,384	4,535	5,788	5,811
	27.8%	37.5%	41.9%	39.3%
Full Time and	5,175	6,088	6,193	7,001
under 24 Years	60.3%	50.3%	44.8%	48.8%
Men	5,044	5,874	6,284	6,491
	58.8%	48.6%	45.5%	42.1%
Women	3,537	6,223	7,535	8,301
	41.2%	51.4%	54.5%	57.9%

Source: Digest of Education Statistics 2001, Table 208

versity and college—the nontraditional student—has, therefore, expanded dramatically since 1970.

The student body is also becoming increasingly international as more foreigners attend school in the United States. At the doctoral level, for example, U.S. citizens now constitute less than two-thirds of those completing their degrees, down from nearly 85 percent in 1967 (U.S. Department of Education 1996). Many more schools than ever before now have international operations or partnerships with foreign schools, to say nothing of the international students they have enrolled through distance-education programs. Thus even the geographic scope of the study body is expanding.

Course Offerings

Changes in the courses in which higher education students are enrolled mirror this shift in demand away from the traditional four-year liberal arts bachelor's degree. In the first instance is the huge expansion in corporate training. As mentioned earlier, this is now a $64 billion market, or about a quarter of the size of the entire higher education market, growing at about 11 percent per year (Moe and Blodget 2000). Although a large part of this activity is conducted outside colleges and universities in companies' own corporate universities (of

Table 2.3. Type of Degree Conferred (percent)

	1970–71	1980–81	1990–91	1999–2000
Associate's	19.1	23.8	23.5	23.7
Bachelor's	63.5	53.4	53.2	52.0
First Professional	2.6	4.1	3.5	3.4

Source: Digest of Education Statistics 2001, Table 260

Table 2.4. Enrollment by Type of Institution (percent)

	1970	1980	1990	1999
Two Year	27.0	37.4	37.9	37.8
Four Year	73.0	62.6	62.1	62.2

Source: Digest of Education Statistics 2001, Table 179

which there are now more than 2,000 [Meister 1998]) and by private firms, many institutions are now developing this market in the guise of company-sponsored courses and certificate training. As Adelman has documented, between 1.5 and 2 million certificates were awarded in the United States in the 1990s (2000), and several prominent providers are universities and community colleges.

Second, there has been a shift toward two-year institutions and to associate's rather than bachelor's degrees (Tables 2.3 and 2.4). Enrollments at two-year colleges now make up nearly 40 percent of all degree students, up from 27 percent in 1970–71, and nearly a quarter of all degrees are now associate's degrees, up from less than 20 percent in 1970–71. How much of this change has been accompanied on campus by an increase in remedial courses or in English as a Second Language (ESL) courses is harder to document. While much of this shift reflects the relative growth rates of different institutions, rather than changes within every institution, the fact that the market is moving in that direction puts pressure on all institutions to consider providing those services, even if only indirectly.

Even at the degree level, there has been a profound change in fields of study, which Steve Brint has referred to as the "rise of the practical arts" (2002). In 1970–71, the majority of students were still graduating in the traditional arts and sciences disciplines (Table 2.5). Yet, "occupational" disciplines, such as business, protective services, and communications, increased from 47 percent in 1970–71 to close to 60 percent of all degrees conferred by 1980–81, and they still account for 58 percent of those conferred. Indeed, there has been a prolifera-

Table 2.5. Field of Bachelor's Degrees Conferred (percent)

	1970–71	1980–81	1990–91	1999–2000
Arts and Sciences	52.5	41.7	43.7	42.2
Occupational	47.5	58.3	56.3	57.8

Source: Digest of Education Statistics 2001, Table 255
   Note: Arts and Sciences include area, ethnic, and cultural studies; biological sciences/life sciences; engineering; engineering related technologies; English language and literature/letters; foreign language and literatures; law and legal studies; liberal arts and sciences, general studies, and humanities; library science; mathematics; multi/interdisciplinary studies; philosophy and religion; physical sciences and science technologies; psychology; social sciences and history; theological studies/religious vocations. Occupational are all other disciplines.

tion of new degree courses in fields like "precision production trades" which would never have sullied academia thirty years ago.

While some disciplines, such as computer and information sciences, might be hard to categorize as purely occupational disciplines, it is useful to list only those that have more than doubled in enrollment over the past thirty years and compare them with those that have shrunk in absolute numbers. The former includes business; communications; health professions and related sciences; parks, recreation, leisure, and fitness studies; and protective services, which now comprise collectively 35 percent of all degrees, up from only 18 percent in 1970–71. The latter include English language and literature; foreign language and letters; mathematics; physical sciences and science technologies; and social sciences and history, which collectively are now represented by only 18 percent of all degrees, down from 34 percent of degrees in 1970–71. And remember that these fields, which encapsulate the essence of the liberal arts, have shrunk in terms of the absolute number of students since 1970! There can be no more compelling data on the shift away from the traditional core of higher education than in this almost exact switch between fields of study over the past thirty years.

There have been similar changes at the graduate and even the doctoral level. About two-thirds of postgraduate degrees in 1970–71 were in "practical arts," but now nearly 80 percent of those degrees are in such fields (Brint 2002, p. 4). MBAs alone have gone from 11 percent of the master's degrees conferred in 1970–71 to a quarter of all such degrees today (Digest of Education Statistics 2001, Table 256). At the doctoral level, fields directly related to a profession rather than basic science or humanities have also increased from 52 percent to 65 percent of all degrees granted over that same period (U.S. Department of Education 1996).

Table 2.6. Source of Revenue for Degree-granting Institutions (percent)

	1969–70	1980–81	1990–91	1995–96
Federal Government	19.2	14.9	12.2	12.1
State Government	27.3	30.7	26.4	23.1
Local Government	3.6	2.7	2.6	2.8
Tuition and Fees	20.5	21.0	25.0	27.9
Private Gifts and Grants	5.2	4.8	5.6	6.0
Endowment Earnings	2.4	2.1	2.2	2.3
Sales and Service of Educational Activities	2.8	2.1	2.7	2.8
Auxiliary Enterprises	13.5	11.1	10.0	9.6
Hospitals	2.9	7.6	10.1	9.5
Other Income	2.5	3.0	3.3	4.0

Source: Digest of Education Statistics 2001, Table 334

Finally, the way that courses are taught is changing as on-line education intrudes onto the campus, with 90 percent of universities and colleges expected to offer such courses by 2005 (IDC 2001). Indeed, this is only the most dramatic measure of the digitalization of the campus, as two-thirds of all students in higher education now use computers at school, up from less than one quarter in 1984 (Digest of Education Statistics 2001, Table 430), and more than 70 percent of institutions now have Web-based course management platforms, such as WebCT (Campus Computing 2001). The result, of course, is the addition of new personnel such as Web designers and PC technicians, and the further expansion of the activities that now fall under the university's purview.

Thus, what is being taught on campuses and the way it is being taught now differs substantially from the liberal arts classes that we traditionally associate with colleges and universities. Every institution has expanded its domain to incorporate these changes and so diminished the importance of the traditional core.

Revenue Sources

Accompanying an expansion in the scope of the student body and in course offerings has been a diversification in the sources of funding for universities and colleges. Or, put somewhat differently, there has been a substantial drop in the share of revenue coming from government sources (Table 2.6).

In aggregate, federal funding of higher education has fallen from 19.2 percent of total current fund revenue in 1969–70 to 12.1 percent in 1995–96 (Slaughter and Leslie 1997, Table 3.1, p. 80). Over the latest twenty-five years for which

Table 2.7. Degree-granting Institutions General Revenue Sources (percent)

Public	1980–81	1990–91	1996–97
Government	62.2	54.3	50.5
Tuition	12.9	16.1	19.0
Gifts and Endowment	2.8	4.3	4.9
Sales and Service	22.0	25.5	25.5

Private	1980–81	1990–91	1995–96
Government	21.4	18.4	16.4
Tuition	36.6	40.4	43.0
Gifts and Endowment	14.4	13.8	14.3
Sales and Service	27.5	27.4	26.3˙

Source: Digest of Education Statistics 2001, Tables 331 and 332

data is available, total federal, state, and local government funding has fallen from 50.5 percent of total university and college revenue to only 38 percent (see Table 2.6). The shortfall has been met by tuition up from 20.5 to 27.9 percent; gifts and endowments up from 6.6 to 8.3 percent; and sales, service, and other sources up from 21.8 to 25.7 percent. In fact, voluntary support for higher education has increased from a low of 5.5 percent in 1975 to a recent high of 8.4 percent in 1999 (Digest of Education Statistics 2001, Table 348).

The shifts are even more dramatic when we examine the public and private sectors separately because there has been less of an effect among private institutions (Table 2.7). In the past fifteen years in the public sector, revenue from all levels of government has fallen from nearly two-thirds to just over half.

The implication, of course, is that the institution has a far more complex job than ever before managing these diverse revenue sources. Endowment and gift income requires the cultivation of relationships with alumni and the investment managers—some of whom may even be on the university payroll.[11] Maximizing tuition income today demands sophisticated yield management techniques similar to those employed by the airlines, while sales and service revenue takes the university into the management of licenses and new ventures. In contrast, the annual budgetary process with the state, however capricious it might be, looks simple and at least has the benefit of being the devil you know.

Within research funding the implication of the expanding role of the private sector is even more radical. Research and development funds from industry were 4 percent of federal dollars in 1970 but were already up to 13 percent by 1993 (Kerr 2001, p. 188). The increasing need to deal with the private sector, and the willingness and incentive for faculty to do so, led to a position in which, even by the mid-1980s, the majority of full professors in molecular biology had equity positions in spin-off companies and were on their boards (Slaughter and Leslie 1997, p. 6). At the institutional level, these links were such that licensing income from a set of leading universities rose from $149 million in 1991 to $655 million in 1999 (AUTM 1999). Between 1980 and 1999, those institutions reported that 2,922 start-ups were established from their campuses (AUTM 1999).

At the same time, the increasing reliance on private-sector funding has led to the proliferation of discrete ventures and research centers, with their own funding and objectives that are beyond the immediate control of the governing bodies. Geiger, for example, quoting a study by the Institute for Policy Research and Evaluation at Pennsylvania State University, noted a 42 percent increase in separate research institutes in the first half of the 1980s (Geiger 1993, p. 75). Instead of the core being able to control the campus by the judicious use of government purse strings, the entrepreneurial periphery has exploited new revenue sources to achieve an independence that allows it to further advance its own interests and agenda (Slaughter and Leslie 1997).

Expenditure Categories

It is harder to document the expansion of the periphery in higher education by tracking university expenditures because many of the new activities that are being undertaken occur below the level of the very aggregated budget line items for which data are published. What we would like to be able to show at the industry level is the increase in spending on Web designers, marketing managers, and other nontraditional jobs.

What we can document (Table 2.8) is the declining share of expenditures on some traditional core activities, such as the library—down from 2.9 percent in 1974–75 to 2.3 percent in 1995–96—and physical plant—down from 7.9 to 6.4 percent. At the same time, some of the overhead expenses, in which many of the new activities would be expected to be incurred, have increased. Administration, for example, has risen from 12.8 to 14.6 percent of total expenditures.

Unfortunately, those activities that can be more directly matched to the periphery show mixed trends. While extension and public service expenditures, which include programs supported by sponsors outside the institution, have grown from 3.1 to 3.7 percent, the share of independent operations, which in-

Table 2.8. *Degree-granting Institutions Expenditure Categories (percent)*

	1974–75	1980–81	1990–91	1995–96
Instruction, Departmental Research, and Academic Support	37.4	36.6	35.7	35.0
Organized Research	8.9	8.8	9.2	9.2
Extension and Public Service	3.1	3.2	3.5	3.7
Library	2.9	2.7	2.3	2.3
Plant	7.9	8.3	6.9	6.4
Administration and Other General Expenses	14.3	14.8	15.4	15.8
Scholarships and Fellowships	4.1	3.9	5.2	6.9
Auxiliary Enterprises	11.6	11.4	9.8	9.2
Federal R&D Centers	3.1	2.0	2.3	1.8
Hospitals	6.7	8.5	9.8	9.5

Source: Digest of Education Statistics 2001, Table 341

cludes federally funded research centers, has fallen from 3.1 to only 1.8 percent. Similarly, although the hospital, which is clearly a major burden for many institutions today, has increased from 6.7 to 9.5 percent of expenditures, other auxiliary enterprises have decreased from 11.6 percent to 9.2 percent. Clearly, expenditure data at the industry level is too aggregated to be able to support the argument we would like to make.

One other aspect of the expanding periphery that is worth mentioning, however, is the unproductive "arms race," which ratchets up university expenditures in previously unheard of categories (Massy 1996, p. 81; Winston 2001). Driven by a fear that the "winner takes all" in higher education (Frank and Cook 1995), and by the need to play the *U.S. News and World Report* rankings game, colleges are spending time and money in activities that are recognized as peripheral to their core mission (Zemsky and Massy 1995). Thus, the size and sophistication of admissions staff has increased, as has the use of outside consultants to better market the institution. Indeed, *marketing* and *branding* are terms that probably would not have been used within many colleges thirty years ago. Their widespread acceptance today only reinforces the notion that the scope of what happens on a university campus is substantially broader than it used to be.

Staff Mix

The mix of personnel on campus does, however, reflect the increasing scope of the institution.

In the first place, the ratio of administrative staff to teaching faculty has

Table 2.9. Full-time Employee Occupations in Degree-granting Institutions (percent)

	1976	1991	1999
Faculty	32.5	30.2	32.2
Instruction and Research Assistants	5.3	3.9	4.3
Administration	6.4	6.7	6.9
Nonfaculty Professional	10.5	18.6	20.8
Nonprofessional Staff	45.9	40.5	35.8

Source: Digest of Education Statistics 2001, Table 224

altered dramatically over the past twenty-five years (Table 2.9). In 1976 there were more than two faculty per administrator. By 1999, the ratio was closer to one faculty member per administrator, as the proliferation of noncore activities on campus required more managerial staff. At the same time, the share of nonprofessional staff employed by universities and colleges has also fallen dramatically, from 45.9 percent in 1976 to 35.8 percent in 1999. This drop reflects the outsourcing of activities as less-skilled workers disappear off the university payroll as their services are taken over by subcontractors.

Even within the teaching faculty two important trends capture the eroding core of the institution and highlight the question of the boundary of the institution. The share of part-time faculty has increased from 22.2 percent in 1970 to 42.5 percent in 1999, and the share of non-tenure track appointments has also increased somewhat in the 1990s to nearly one-half (Table 2.10). David Kirp observes that in the California state system half of all appointments in the 1990s were off the tenure track, and more than half of all classes were taught by "disposables" (Kirp 2002). Neither of these measures captures the extent to which undergraduate teaching is performed by TAs rather than faculty, even though horror stories abound concerning that number, rumored to be over 40 percent even at Yale University.

The question for governance raised by having half the faculty as part-time employees and half the faculty off the tenure track is: Where does their loyalty lie? And are they inside or outside the boundary of the university, given that the traditional core faculty of full-time, tenure-track employees are now in the minority (less than 44 percent of all faculty) and growing at an absolute rate of less than half of 1 percent each year?

Even the loyalty of traditional faculty is in doubt. One way to capture this is to note that academic salaries are diverging as professional schools adjust salaries

Table 2.10. Faculty Status in Degree-granting Institutions (percent)

	1970	1980	1991	1992	1998	1999
Full Time	77.8	65.6	64.9			57.5
Part Time	22.2	34.4	35.1			42.5
Tenure Track				53.9	51.5	
Non-tenure Track				46.1	48.5	

Source: Digest of Education Statistics 2001, Tables 228 and 230
   Note: Non-tenure track includes instructor, lecturer, other, and no rank. Tenure includes any "professor."

to be competitive with the outside labor market (Brint 1994).[12] Over the decade from 1983 to 1993, for example, Slaughter and Leslie noted that salaries in engineering rose 85 percent and in business schools 79 percent, while faculty in philosophy and religion only received increases of 53 percent and those in foreign languages 52 percent (1997). This adjustment of faculty salaries to reflect outside options exemplifies the increasing loyalty of academics to their discipline and the corresponding decrease of affinity for the particular institution at which they happen to work. Indeed, many faculty now define their primary affiliation as being with their profession and not with an institution (Brint 1994). If even the core faculty view themselves as being transitory members of a university or college, where does that leave those charged with governing the institution?

Finally, and common to all ranks, is the intrusion of unions into the university. This is not to imply that unionization is necessarily bad for academia, it is merely to observe that governance is complicated by the presence of unions. And those unions are seeking to represent not only the blue collar workforce. Unionization activities among teaching assistants, graduate students, medical interns, and even faculty are gaining ground (Smallwood 2002) and threatening the traditional guild atmosphere of the university. Without a loyal and subservient base of retainers—the traditional position of many staff at universities—the employee structure fragments further.

Outsourcing Activities

Finally, the growth in outsourcing confirms the shrinking core and expanding periphery, as traditional activities are replaced by alliances and contractual relationships. Lacking government data on this phenomenon, we are driven to look at previous surveys that have researched the issue.

The list of activities that universities and colleges have outsourced is long and getting longer. Today it represents nearly the complete range of an institution's activities. Peterson's 1995 "Contract Services for Higher Education," for example, listed more than one hundred such services. These included, along with individual estimates of the extent of outsourcing in 1996 (Gilmer 1997; Wood 2000; Kirp 2002, pp. B13–14): bookstores, 34–40 percent; restaurant/dining halls, 60–74 percent; health and HMOs, 12.5 percent; security, facilities maintenance, IT, library, housekeeping, parking, admissions marketing, vending, 66 percent; custodial, 31 percent; laundry, 19 percent; and even recruiting presidents—80 percent of governing boards of major public universities use outside professionals in a presidential search (Lovett 2002). Even the physical assets of the institution are now being outsourced as several campuses are privatizing housing (van der Werf 2000; Sausner 2002, p. 35; Willard and Byard 2002).

The extent of outsourcing by individual institutions is perhaps best summarized in a table (Table 2.11) reproduced from Wertz (2000). These data are supported by other surveys that show that up to one-half of all universities contract out more than five different services, and only 6 percent now do all activities entirely in-house (Kirp 2002, reporting on Gilmer 1997). Indeed, on one University of Virginia campus, fifty different services are performed by private contractors (Gumport and Pusser 1997). Outsourcing, then, is just one more manifestation of the shrinking core and expanding periphery of the university today.

Caution is required in interpreting the six sets of data presented above. First, the data refer to industry, rather than institution-level phenomena. Second, much of the change captured in the data occurred in the 1970s; since then the rate of change has slowed. Third, the data show that although the core has shrunk in relative terms since 1970, it has not necessarily shrunk in absolute terms.

Nearly all the data presented above is couched at the industry, rather than the institutional, level. While the trends observed may have been apparent in aggregate, it could, therefore, be suggested that each individual institution was not seeing a contracting core and an increasing periphery. Each institution could be staying exactly the same, with industry-level changes simply being caused by a shift in the mix among those institutions. While there is obviously some merit to this argument—the proportion of tertiary students enrolled in public two-year colleges, for example, has increased from 25.6 percent in 1970 to 36.1 percent in 1999 (Digest of Education Statistics 2001, Table 179)—many of the phenomena documented above are occurring within each and every institution.

It is true that many of the trends noted above began in the 1960s and that uni-

Table 2.11. Outsourcing Activities

Privatized by over 60 Percent of Institutions
   Travel agency; asbestos removal; vending machines; refuse and waste management;
   hazardous waste removal; video game machines; banking services; food service;
   construction projects; laundry machines; publishing; architectural and engineering
   services

Privatized by 20–60 Percent of Institutions
   Beauty salons; student loan collections; retail stores; workers compensation programs;
   retirement programs; bookstore; auditing and accounting; employee assistance programs; tuition plans; unemployment compensation; copiers; printing; trademarks and
   licensing; amusement centers; golf courses; athletics concession; physical plant financing; day-care centers; campus planning; housekeeping; energy conservation; recycling;
   real estate development

Privatized by Less Than 20 Percent of Institutions
   Payroll; law enforcement; security; employee training; health center; faculty club; press;
   grounds; health and safety services; parking; benefits administration; maintenance;
   mail services; student counseling; conference center management; recreational areas;
   arena management; cinema/theater; computer operations; housing; ID-card production; student union; career counseling; placement center; financial aid; fund-raising;
   admissions; student activities

Source: Wertz 2000, Box 1

versities and colleges have been wrestling with the paradox of scope since then.[13] However, as was argued earlier, the drivers of the phenomenon today are external and unpredictable rather than the consequence of a consciously planned and coherent policy. For this reason, the slower apparent current rate of change can be more troublesome than when change is ostensibly more dramatic.

Although it is also true that the core is not necessarily contracting in absolute terms on all measures, it is everywhere in relative decline. In many cases, such as the number of students completing traditional liberal arts undergraduate degrees, the core is in fact shrinking. Elsewhere, such as in the number of full-time tenure-track faculty, the absolute rate of increase is so tiny—less than one-half of 1 percent a year—as to be almost immeasurable. Even where growth is faster, such as in the total number of students under the age of twenty-four in full-time education, the core is still shrinking in relative terms at a substantial rate.

Even if we critically analyze the data presented above, therefore, it is hard to dispute that the phenomenon of the paradox of scope has been in operation in higher education over the past thirty years. As a result, each institution now has to reevaluate its strategy and decide whether and how to respond to those industry-wide trends. Indeed, that is the basic governance problem facing colleges and universities—how should they respond to these changes, and does their governance structure allow them to make the required changes?

Implications for Governance in Higher Education

Why does the paradox of scope matter for the governance of higher education? Even if these widely noted, if less frequently documented, changes are occurring, why do they expose the weaknesses in contemporary governance structures? The answer can be put simply as "less control over more things" (Kerr 2001). The expanding periphery and contracting core of today's colleges and universities stretches the already limited adaptive capability of governance structures to breaking point.

If anything, after close to 1,000 years of experience, the governance system that we have should be able to effectively manage the traditional core of an institution. Even if this assertion were true, however, the core is shrinking. Governance structures and processes that have accumulated out of and evolved with the hard lessons from balancing trade-offs among a limited number of constituencies are now relevant for a decreasing share of an institution's responsibilities. Parties that have learned how to manage within the constraints of the existing governance structures because they have faced off over the same issues for many years are no longer just dealing with those concerns. The comfort zone within which traditional governance has some chance of working is disappearing along with the traditional core.

However, the main challenge to governance is not the declining core of the institution but its expanding periphery.[14] It is here that the weaknesses of traditional governance are exposed.

First, as Duderstadt and Keller discuss in chapters 5 and 6, those in positions of authority within governing boards and the administration are being asked to make decisions and pass judgment in areas in which they have no expertise. It is not unusual, for example, for a dean with a background in English literature to be charged with developing an institution's policy toward intellectual property rights over the biotech research performed by adjunct faculty in the medical school with industry funding. While there is no reason to believe that ultimately the dean will not, with appropriate expert advice, be able to reach a sensible conclusion, the frequency with which such key governance figures are being asked to step outside their areas of expertise is increasing in lock step with the expansion of the periphery.

Even in the private sector, it is not expected that an executive can effectively manage every business. Conglomerates trade at a discount today for that very reason (Lang and Stulz 1994). Indeed, it is widely accepted that every manager possesses a "dominant logic" (Prahalad and Bettis 1986)—a way of thinking, a set of beliefs, and a management style—that is constructed from experiences accumulated over their careers. To the extent that these experiences are accrued primarily within one sector—consumer packaged goods, software, and so on—managers are not expected to be effective in another arena. Yet we expect university administrators and governors to become masters of a vast array of domains. Elsewhere, I have observed that the current university is responsible for more businesses than Disney or its media conglomerate competitor Vivendi (Collis 2001). Nevertheless, both companies are under capital market pressure to contract their scope of activities because that breadth of scope is viewed as unmanageable.

Second, if the art of governance is to balance competing constituencies through delicate trade-offs, careful compromises, and judicious offers of quid pro quos, the complexity of such deals is complicated by any increase in the number of constituencies. The number of linkages between n entities $[n(n-1)/2]$ increases exponentially with the number of entities. With four parties' interests to balance, there are six trade-offs to manage. With six parties (a 50 percent increase), there are fifteen tradeoffs to manage (a 250 percent increase). I always remember John McArthur, the former dean at the Harvard Business School, pulling out a chart from his desk drawer to show how he really managed the school. The chart was a matrix of sixty programs by forty constituencies. This meant he had to manage 2,400 different cells! Or, put another way, he could spend one hour a year on addressing the issues each constituency had about any program! As programs and constituencies expand, it becomes increasingly difficult to govern the sheer complexity of the institution, let alone build a consensus behind a fundamental change in strategy.

Third, governing bodies have less hierarchical control over the periphery than the core. Within the traditional activities of academic institutions, there is an employment contract. However limited the ability of the administration to prescribe the behavior of employees, particularly faculty, there is at least some recourse and some incentive structure with which to moderate actions. When it comes to the periphery, however, there is no hierarchical control, and there are substantially fewer high-powered incentives available (Slaughter and Leslie 1997). Management of the periphery is achieved through an arm's-length contract and not through an employment contract that allows for substantial discretion over behavior.

When a college or university subcontracts restaurant service or facilities maintenance, it cannot abdicate responsibility for the provision of those services, even if it no longer has any formal authority over their performance. Penalties for poor quality or failure to meet specified standards might (indeed should) be included in the contract, but ultimately the institution cannot itself intervene to remedy any failings. The only recourse is to terminate the contract, seek a new supplier, and perhaps face years of litigation. This absence of direct authority over an activity for which an entity is accountable violates one of the basic tenets of effective organization design (Goold and Campbell 2002; Thompson 1967). While outsourcing and other contractual relationships are common in the private sector, that an increasing share of the university's activities are delivered this way through contractual rather than employment relations causes real problems.

Furthermore, the expansion of the periphery increasingly takes away policy discretion from the governing body. Once a foundation has given a research grant, once a donor has contributed to build a new football stadium, the ability to change direction and decide to close the department or switch funds to residential rather than sports facilities is severely restricted. The accumulated legacy of all the commitments made to external parties at the periphery severely constrains the freedom of action of the institution as a whole. It is as if the captain at the helm can barely overcome the momentum of the ship he is charged with steering.[15]

Finally, the blurring boundary of the institution creates ambiguity and an unclear definition of roles and responsibilities. Independent decisions made at the ungovernable periphery of the institution lead it in many directions. The college or university comes to resemble a mold, gradually and inexorably spreading in random fashion over the petri dish of the higher education marketplace. Without a clear boundary that defines what is inside the institution and what is outside, what it should do and what it should not do, there continues to be what the military refer to as "mission creep," as each succeeding tier of the periphery itself pursues new directions of its own accord. In turn, this further confounds the definition of the boundary and so allows for even more blurring of the boundary. The institution embarks on a spiral of decreasing control over an ever-expanding periphery.[16]

This is the challenge for governance—to take back charge of the institution, to define a strategy that specifies the domain in which it will operate. If it fails to do so, the risk inherent in the new competitive environment is that as the institution expands everywhere in the periphery, it will be successful nowhere. A diffuse allocation of resources and an inability to prioritize among activities will lead to the failure to commit sufficient scarce resources to any one venture. In the presence of competitors, whether existing institutions or new entrants, that have made strategic commitments to certain courses of action, the university or college that is experimenting with everything will be everywhere undermined by the specialists. The ultimate threat of the paradox of scope is that the undirected expansion of the periphery weakens not only the shrinking core but the periphery itself. Yet it is precisely the operation of the paradox of scope that makes it so hard for current governance structures to fulfill the strategic task and make the hard choices.

Improvements to Governance in Higher Education

What improvements to the existing governance structure can I recommend that might mitigate these problems? At this stage, I have to confess that I am not an expert on corporate governance. As a consequence, the suggestions that follow should be taken as just that—suggestions. To the extent that they have any validity, it is because they are based on proposed improvements to governance in the private sector, which is also dealing with the paradox of scope.

Today there is a crisis in governance in the private sector. The bankruptcy of Enron and other energy trading companies; the meltdown in share values of the telecommunications giants like WorldCom and Qwest; the exorbitant compensation and termination packages provided executives, like Geoffrey Winnick at Global Crossing, whose companies have later failed miserably; and the lack of trust in the reported accounting data of nearly every major company from Tyco to GE have all thrown an embarrassing light on the state of corporate governance. Where was the board of directors in these cases?

Even before this latest turmoil, however, corporate governance had been of concern around the world for the past fifteen or twenty years, and there have been several important attempts to improve the system in different countries.

In the UK in 1992, the Cadbury Report made a number of recommendations that were then voluntarily adopted by British companies and reported to the stock exchange. Germany has rewritten tax legislation to encourage certain forms of structure (Buhner 2000). The Japanese ministry of finance has made various attempts to change the commercial code to increase corporate accountability to independent auditors and investors (Collis and Montgomery 1997, p. 194). Even in the United States, where there has been no regulatory reform until now, individual companies, under pressure from activist shareholders like CalPERS and Robert Monks, have initiated their own set of proposals. General Motors (GM), for example, in 1994 adopted a twenty-eight-point plan that defined the roles and membership of the board, importantly, giving the board itself control over the agenda (The GM Board Guidelines 1994, pp. 5-9).

However, the biggest change in the United States happened with the announcement in June 2002 by the New York Stock Exchange of new regulations defining how listed companies must structure their boards (Useem 2002, p. A15). The intent is to allow shareholders, through independent representation on the board, to regain control of the corporation from entrenched and potentially self-serving management (Byrne 2002).

Many of the specific suggestions to improve corporate governance, such as independent boards of directors, have focused on minimizing the effects of agency conflict—the inherent conflict between the principal (shareholders) and the agent (managers) (Jensen and Meckling 1976)—which, without effective governance systems, would result in executives taking actions that favor their personal interests at the expense of shareholders.[17] It is not clear that these recommendations are necessarily needed within higher education. Typically, we would assume that there is much closer goal congruence between stakeholders in a university and the president and administration. Similarly, the extrinsic motivations that appear to be so important to managers in the private sector are presumed to be much less prevalent in academia. This does not mean that we can ignore the fiscal oversight role of the governing body that features in their list of functions those described by the Carnegie Commission;[18] rather, that aspect of governance is not the object of concern.

If solutions to the conflict between principal and agent are less of an issue in higher education, we can still look to the private sector for suggestions as to how to improve the effectiveness of governing bodies in performing their key role—setting the direction of the organization rather than acting as a rubber stamp for management's plans or, as Myles Mace once famously put it, as "ornaments on a corporate Christmas tree" (1971). It is here that higher education has, perhaps, the most to learn.

Again, let me caution that there are fundamental differences between the private sector and higher education. If nothing else, the existence in the private sector of a single objective function with a reasonably accurate measure—shareholder value creation—makes the translation of recommendations from one sphere to the other uncertain. Nevertheless, let me proceed to do exactly that under three headings.

Minimize Agency Problems. The first set of suggestions that might be transferred over to higher education are those designed to reduce the agency problems that result from the divergence of interests between shareholders and executives. An obvious way to achieve this is by having representatives of shareholders dominate governing bodies. Indeed, a common thread through all private-sector initiatives has been to increase the number of independent or outside board directors.[19] This is already more or less universally the case in higher education, where trustees are mainly outsiders. However, an extension of the argument does have implications for governance in higher education.

The Carnegie Commission strongly suggested that faculty and students not serve as representatives on boards of their own institutions (Carnegie Commission 1973, pp. 33–35). This recommendation is in line both with agency theory and with the theory of not-for-profits. Glaeser, for example, demonstrates that not-for-profits have a tendency to migrate toward "worker cooperatives" that operate in the interests of elite workers, and directly attributes the growth of faculty power in the latter half of the nineteenth century to this dynamic (Glaeser 2002). It is also supported by the experience that German firms have had in dealing with codetermination—the right of employees in firms with more than 2,000 people to choose half the members of the supervisory board. Obviously, such an observation is at odds with Neil Hamilton's discussion in chapter 3. Yet if one purpose of this book is to provide a healthy debate, then we need to consider competing points of view on this very important issue.

If the concern is that agents of the institution are able to operate it to further their own interests, it does appear counterproductive to allow them direct representation on the board. If not, we might expect to see institutions liberally increasing faculty pay and reducing student tuition. In practice, this means that membership by faculty and students on boards of trustees should be severely limited (even though as stakeholders in the institution they do possess a right to represent their interests in the governing body), and the relative authority of the board and internal management bodies should favor the board. Faculty powers, for example, should be limited and under the ultimate prerogative of the board.

Supporting the intent to limit agency problems are proposals in the private sector, such as in the Cadbury Report, to separate the roles of chairman of the board and CEO. Again, the argument is to rein in the freedom of action of the CEO and make him or her answerable to the board. In higher education this is, I believe, already typically the case. The president is always hired by the board and nowhere functions as chairman of the board of trustees.[20] In this regard, private industry has much to learn from academia.

Finally, as part of the attempt to minimize the divergence of interests between shareholders and managers, much attention has been paid in the private sector to aligning the compensation of managers with share price performance (Murphy and Jensen 1990). It is this argument that has led to the widespread use of stock options and incentive compensation tied to share price performance.[21]

Unfortunately, this notion is hard to apply to higher education where we lack both a single measure of performance and accurate metrics for the vector of outputs we might wish to reward. If the intent is to focus administrators' attention on the numbers by which they are measured and rewarded, we must be very careful what we wish for (recall the earlier mention of the administration at Boston College monitoring the time faculty spend in their offices).

Improve Board Effectiveness. If the application of agency theory to governance in higher education offers little in the way of improvement, I think there is more potential in changes that the private sector is introducing to improve the effectiveness of boards of directors. One obvious suggestion is to cut down the size of boards (Useem 2002, p. A15). It is already recognized among the educational community that boards with thirty-plus trustees are simply unmanageable (Lazerson 1997). In the private sector, boards of closer to a dozen involved members are seen to be most effective.

Another suggestion is to have relevant outsiders sit on the governing bodies of universities and colleges. To some extent this already happens. Members of the business community, alumni, and others are chosen for their familiarity with the institution. However, there is one glaring difference with the private sector. Executives that sit on boards are chosen for their managerial experience in the business or related businesses of that company. Yet in the governance of our universities and colleges, few educators sit on boards of trustees. In Florida, for example, less than a dozen of 132 recent appointees to the state's boards were educators (Schmidt 2002).

In higher education, the analogue would be to have the president or provost of another educational institution sit on the board. The benefit of this would be substantial. Presidents alone deal with presidential issues. The ability to learn from and share the experience of another president would be extremely valuable to any board. Moreover, the experience of sitting on another institution's board would contribute useful lessons to the other institution. A president would be able to see directly how certain approaches or issues were addressed in the less threatening and more objective context of another university.

A related suggestion that also arises from the value of assistance to the president is to end the heroic presidency and foster a top management *team* rather than an individual to lead an institution. Kerr, for example, argues for "pluralistic leadership" of the university (Kerr 2001, p. 190), and it is true that academia has always relied on a more collegial and inclusive management style. In particular, the role of the provost has always been as critical to the internal administration of a university as that of the president has been to the management of external relationships. Indeed, in the era of "the executive as celebrity," perhaps this is an area where the private sector can learn more from higher education than the other way around. George Keller (chap. 6) disagrees in so far as he puts forth a model of strong administrative leadership.

Last among suggestions to improve the efficiency of existing governance structures is to allow the board to set its own agenda and budget and to be solely responsible for managing the process by which new board members are elected.[22] The ability to decide what should be discussed at board meetings, what information should be presented to the board, and who gets nominated to stand for election, are seen as crucial to effective governance in the private sector. Indeed, the complete independence of the audit, compensation, and governance committees of the board is demanded today by many outside directors as a condition for accepting a board seat. If the board is to act as the guardian of the institution and to fulfill its obligation to oversee the actions of the president and the administration, it must be allowed these functions (Lazerson 1997).

In practice, this means that public universities and colleges should be given the freedom to manage their budgets as they see fit, and not subject to the direct mandate of legislatures at the level of line-item approval. If the board is to have responsibility for governing the institution, it needs to be given the authority to do so.

In particular, only if the board has this freedom does it have a chance to play a critical role in determining a company's strategy. If all it can do is pass judgment on what is presented by management or allocated to it by the legislature, then it cannot fulfill that function. If universities and colleges are looking to their governing bodies to define strategic direction, they must be able to ask for whatever information, analysis, and resources they need to make that decision.

Address Strategy and Structure. However, the most important suggestion that I can make to improve governance in higher education has less to do with governance itself, and everything to do with institutional strategy. If governance is the bottleneck in determining the strategic direction for an institution, then rather than changing the governance structure itself, I would suggest directly changing the strategy. If the blurring of institutional boundaries as the core contracts and the periphery expands is a cause of the inability to develop strategy, short-circuit the problem by clearly articulating a boundary for the institution.

There are two ways to achieve this simple goal. One possible solution in the public sector is to privatize its institutions. Rare though this may have been in the past, it has happened recently to the Oregon Institute of Technology (Public college considers going private 2002), and is increasingly being discussed as a way to curtail governance problems in public education. Rather than have to deal with the complicated expectations and interests of the state and federal governments, just take them out of the picture! Although private institutions also have their own governance issues, at least privatization substantially reduces complexity. As David Kirp has documented, even an institution as visible and viable as the Darden School of Business at the University of Virginia has seriously considered this option (Kirp 2002). If rich benefactors are able to privatize an erstwhile public institution, governance, even with the exact same structure as before, becomes simpler.[23]

The less radical suggestion is for universities and colleges to directly address the cause of their difficulties in governance by decreasing the scope of their institutions. This is a plea for the end of the "multiversity" and the continuing homogenization of higher education and its replacement by a more differentiated and specialized set of institutions, each of which could then adopt a governance structure more carefully tailored to its particular mission (Clark 1993).

One of the consequences of the paradox of scope is that institutions are increasingly overlapping with each other's missions and markets. Lacking a governance structure and a clear strategy, well-intentioned faculty at every institution have taken advantage of the lack of veto power and institutional direction to pursue their own agendas. The result has been the expansion of the periphery. Community colleges have aggressively pursued distance education and honors programs in order to expand beyond their traditional markets. Every institution worth its salt has raised funds for a business school to capitalize on the revenue opportunity. Even research universities are looking to leverage their intellectual content by selling basic freshman courses online. Entrepreneurial faculty bring new research money into departments and establish centers that overlap with other centers, often at the same university. The clarity of mission for all institutions has been lost as they increasingly seek to resemble each other by copying what looks like a good idea elsewhere.

Yet effective strategy requires a clear mission and domain (Porter 1996). California's success in higher education came from "structural differentiation" (Clark 1993). We are all better served if each institution carves out a distinctive position in the market and refrains from unthinking expansion into any and every new activity (Collis 1999). There is in fact a negative competitive externality created by the operation of the paradox of scope within higher education, which results in all institutions converging on the same ground. Rather than the clear separation of the missions of universities and colleges, their domains are increasingly and unproductively overlapping. This is bad both from the perspective of societal welfare—there is a real loss of variety and consumer choice—and for individual institutions as they have to compete more directly and aggressively with each other.

The ideal structure for higher education in the future is not the homogenization of offerings but the differentiation and specialization of those offerings by institutions that distinguish their strategies and satisfy only some subset of customers' needs. In such a future, consumers would be offered real choice, and institutions would face less overt competition as each targeted different segments. Currently the tiering of higher education reflects vertical differentiation around the quality of the educational experience provided. What is lacking is horizontal differentiation in which, at the extreme, Yale specializes in history, Princeton in economics, and Harvard in French.

What this outcome requires is a clarification of the mission and domain of higher education institutions. Tier 1 research institutions might concentrate on educating graduates, stressing the combination of research and apprenticeship that crafts the next generation of academic researchers. No more would they pretend to offer a superior undergraduate education, when it is in fact provided by graduate student TAs. Rather than developing distance education to create a national or even international market presence, community colleges would recommit to their local market, utilizing the best distance education curriculum developed elsewhere to take advantage, at minimal cost, of the undoubted ability of the new technologies to meet their goal of community access. Liberal arts colleges would retreat to the core of residential undergraduate education of the traditional eighteen-year-old student, abandoning attempts to proliferate research institutes or build a nationally recognized sports team. Large state universities would be best placed to develop educational content for the new technologies, since they have a need for "hybrid" classes on campus, and have the scale to fund the investment necessary to develop state-of-the-art courses that truly capitalize on the potential of the new technologies and pedagogies. Following this mandate, societal welfare would increase as higher education offered a wide variety of high-quality options, rather than the bland provision of mediocre similarity.

The implication of this suggestion is for each institution to rein in the paradox of scope by clearly delineating boundaries that define both the domain in which the institution will operate and, more importantly, what it won't do. This means that some activities in the institution will have to be stopped. Yet saying *no* in universities and colleges is always the hardest decision, particularly with the governance structures in place today. We can always gain support for an initiative from multiple constituencies by promising to do something for them at a later date. It is much harder to get consensus around stopping an activity and absolutely harming someone.

The next generation of academic leaders must establish a clear and unique strategy for their institutions. If this sets clear bounds, it will limit the extent to which the paradox of scope leads to an ever-expanding set of unrelated activities, and it will facilitate the design of an appropriate governance structure. With a clear strategy, the appropriate personnel could be chosen for governing boards, and relevant structures and processes put in place. The result would be more differentiated governance that reflects and supports the underlying differences in strategy.

Conclusion

I have laid out the challenge to governance in higher education as the inability of governing bodies to make crucial strategic choices in an era of dramatic change that has blurred institutional boundaries. I have also made some perhaps naïve suggestions for improvements to governance. These lead to a conclusion that, since structure follows strategy (Chandler 1962), before wrestling with governance, every institution needs to determine its strategy.

The real dilemma this conclusion highlights, is that we are stuck in a Catch-22 situation. The current governance structure prevents us choosing the clear strategy that would enable us to improve the governance structure, that would in turn make choosing the strategy easy. How the leaders of our universities and colleges can break out of this paradox is, perhaps, the ultimate challenge to the governance of higher education today.

APPENDIX: THE PARADOX OF SCOPE IN THE
PRIVATE SECTOR

It is useful to recognize that some of the same forces that are driving change within higher education are also leading to the paradox of scope in the private sector.

First, technological innovation is rapidly driving down computer and communications costs. Moore's Law has long demonstrated that computing costs halve every eighteen months as processing speed doubles in that time period. Something even more dramatic is happening to communication costs. Fiber-optic cable essentially reduces communication costs to zero by providing unlimited bandwidth at zero marginal cost. The combination of these reduced information processing costs has facilitated organizational arrangements that lie outside traditional firm boundaries. No longer does a worker have to be physically located in a company's offices to be a functioning member of the team. Instead, remote working from a virtual office becomes feasible. The freedom from the physical need to be collocated with other workers ends one of the main rationales for the firm in its traditional hierarchical form.

Second, increasing competitive rivalry has demonstrated that even small firms can overthrow entrenched incumbents (Yoffie and Kwak 2001). No longer is a huge installed base and accumulated production expertise the only source of sustainable competitive advantage. Instead, the ability to exploit disruptive technologies (Christensen 1997) allows the outsider or the entrepreneurial upstart to capture market leadership. In this state of hypercompetition (D'Aveni 1994), large firms have to learn to match the flexibility and speed of their smaller rivals or else risk being overthrown. This desire to combine the advantages of scale and speed has led to the search for the "boundaryless organization" and the importance of leveraging a web of external relations while at the same time shrinking the bureaucratic and inflexible core of the firm (Welch and Byrne 2001).

Third, globalization allows companies to access factors of production everywhere and anywhere around the world and to create competitive advantages by instantaneously arbitraging those differences (Kogut 1985). To be able to access innovations and low factor costs wherever they arise and for however a short a time they exist, requires a nimbleness that cannot be achieved inside the corporation. Firms must be able to instantly switch sourcing locations or adopt new product or process ideas, and can only achieve this through alliances and other external linkages.

Finally, the redefinition of the implicit contract between employer and employee is revolutionizing the corporation (Ghoshal et al. 2001). Workplace relations have recently seen the demise of the guarantee of lifetime employment that previously characterized the informal contract between large companies and their workers. In its place is the emergence of "free agency," in which all workers are paid their current value by the highest bidder. Employee loyalty, in turn, has seen a corresponding decline since in this environment, "loyalty is a misguided virtue."

A simultaneous shift in workplace demographics—the growth of two-worker families and part-time jobs—and the technical feasibility of working in a home office has reinforced this trend by producing a dramatic growth in the self-employed, who are the archetypal "free agents." Indeed, the full-time employee is already a decreasing part of the employment picture in the United States. Contractors and the self-employed now make up 16 percent of the workforce, while part-time or on-call workers constitute an additional 15 percent (Nardone, Veum, and Yates 1997). This implies that the traditional worker who is clearly identified with a single firm now makes up just two-thirds of the total workforce.

These forces combine to produce pressures on companies to become more flexible and adaptable, that is, smaller, and yet develop more network linkages to maintain access to a much larger set of skills and capabilities. The result has been the paradox of scope—the shrinking of the core activities of the firm as the boundary of the firm simultaneously has expanded through external nonhierarchical relationships such as alliances, joint ventures, and other contractual relationships.

NOTES

1. Kerr himself observes that seventy of eighty-five institutions that have survived nearly 500 years are universities (2001, p. 175).

2. Governance in the private sector is also under criticism with the investigation of Enron and other large corporate collapses.

3. As the scandals surrounding Arthur Andersen reveal, even in the private sector there is no absolute definition of basic accounting measures such as profit and revenue.

4. States differ in whether or not there is a unified governing body for all state institutions (Richardson et al. 1999) and whether such bodies act as a coordinating board or as a planning agency (see Levine 1993, p. 14).

5. When the telegraph and electricity were being introduced in the late nineteenth and early twentieth centuries, contemporary observers used many phrases similar to those employed by excited futurists during the Internet bubble.

6. Since Ronald Coase asked the question that won him the Nobel Prize for Economics, "What determines the limit of the firm?" (Coase 1937), economists have been examining the transactions costs (Williamson 1975) and scope economies (Baumol, Panzar, and Willig 1982) that determine that boundary. Yet it was always clear to the man in the street what was done inside the firm and outside the firm.

7. Strictly, the resource is heterogeneous and in fixed supply so that the firm earns a rent.

8. I accept that this description is a stylized sketch of reality.

9. Many of these changes began in the 1970s and have continued at a slower pace since that date.

10. While the core, broadly defined as full-time students under the age of twenty-four, has risen in absolute terms since 1970, the rate of growth of that core has been less than 1 percent per year.

11. The highest-paid individuals at Harvard University are always the investment managers, some of whom are paid over $10 million per year (Leonard 2002).

12. Salaries in the periphery, of course, can be much higher. Investment managers can earn tens of millions each year. Publishing presidents can earn close to $1 million per year. And medical faculty regularly earn several hundred thousand dollars.

13. It is no surprise, therefore, that Clark Kerr originally introduced the notion of the multiversity in lectures at Harvard in 1963.

14. It is for this reason that I disagree with Bowen, who states, "At its core, the American University is very much the same institution that it has been for some time. In no way is it endangered" (1997, p. 18).

15. As Balderston states, "The proliferation of entities and the widening of institutional boundaries mock any effort at simplification" (1995, p. 72).

16. As Zemsky and Massy observed, "The growth of the periphery lies in the very nature of the entrepreneurial enterprises it spawned" (1995, p. 42).

17. The empirical literature on agency theory is replete with examples of self-serving executive behavior (see Milgrom and Roberts [1992] for a good summary).

18. Unfortunately, abuse of fiscal responsibility does occur within academia, as shown by the recent example of a Yale dean who used institutional funds to pay for his daughter's Harvard tuition.

19. It is still by no means the rule that boards of directors consist of a majority of outsiders.

20. Unfortunately, the average tenure of presidents has fallen below the six years it was already down to in the 1970s.

21. Note that the use of such incentive compensation says nothing about the appropriate level of that compensation. Most of the most flagrant abuses of stock options have concerned the level, not the principle of the compensation system.

22. In the recent controversial election to the board of trustees at Yale, for which a representative of the local community actively campaigned against the architect of the Vietnam Memorial, colleagues were intrigued to see that votes had to be returned to the

administration's offices. Several joked ironically about the dampening effect this would have on their voting!

23. Note that the privatization of public institutions is in line with a more general shift in perspective in the United States over the past thirty years from seeing higher education as the "public provision of a public good, to the private provision of a private good."

REFERENCES

Adelman, C. 2000. *A parallel universe expanded: Certification in the Information Technology Guild.* Washington, DC: U.S. Department of Education.

American Council on Education. 2002. *Crucial choices: How students' financial decisions affect their academic success.* Washington, DC: American Council on Education.

Association of University Technology Managers Inc. (AUTM). 1999. *Licensing survey: 1999.* Northbrook, IL: AUTM.

Balderston, F. 1995. *Managing today's university.* 2d ed. San Francisco: Jossey-Bass.

Barney, J. 1991. Firm resources and sustained competitive advantage. *Journal of Management* 17 (1): 99–120.

Baumol, W., J. Panzar, and R. Willig. 1982. *Contestable markets and the theory of industry structure.* New York: Harcourt Brace Jovanovich.

Bowen, W. G. 1997. No limits. In *The American university: National treasure or endangered species?* ed. R. Ehrenberg. Ithaca, NY: Cornell University Press.

Brint, S. 1994. *In an age of experts: The changing role of professionals in politics and public life.* Princeton: Princeton University Press.

———. 2002. The rise of the practical arts: The development of education for upper-white-collar occupations in American colleges and universities, 1970–1995. In *The future of the city of intellect: The changing American university.* Palo Alto, CA: Stanford University Press.

Buhner, R. 2000. Governance costs, determinants and size of corporate headquarters. *Schmalenbach Business Review* 52:160–81.

Byrne, J. 2002. But changes in the boardroom could rebuild trust. *Business Week* 3787 (June 17): 29.

Campus Computing. 2001. *2001 Campus Computing Report.* Encino, CA: Kenneth Green.

Carnegie Commission. 1973. *Governance of higher education: Six priority problems.* New York: McGrawHill.

Chandler, A. 1962. *Strategy and structure.* Cambridge, MA: MIT Press.

———. 1990. *Scale and scope.* Cambridge, MA: Harvard University Press.

Christensen, C. 1997. *The innovator's dilemma.* Boston: Harvard Business School Press.

Christianson, J., and A. Fajen. 1999. *Computer and network professionals certification guide.* San Francisco: Network Press.

Clark, B. 1993. The problem of complexity in modern higher education. In *The European and American university since 1800,* ed. S. Rothblatt and B. Wittrock. Cambridge: Cambridge University Press.

Cleman, J. 1973. The university and society's new demands upon it. In *Content and context,* ed. L. Kaysen. New York: McGraw Hill.

Coase, R. 1937. The nature of the firm. *Economica* 4:386–405.

Collis, D. 1999. When industries change: Scenarios for higher education. In *Exploring the future of higher education,* ed. J. Meyerson and M. Devlin. New York: Forum Publishing.

———. 2001. When industries change: The future of higher education. *Continuing Higher Education Review* 65:7–24.

———. 2002. New business models for higher education. In *The future of the city of intellect: The changing American university,* ed. S. Brint. Palo Alto, CA: Stanford University Press.

Collis, D., and C. Montgomery. 1997. *Corporate strategy: Resources and the scope of the corporation.* Chicago: Irwin McGraw Hill.

Corbett, M. F., and Associates. 2001. *Why Companies Outsource.* LaGrangeville, NY: Corbett and Associates, Ltd.

D'Aveni, R. 1994. *Hypercompetition.* New York: Free Press.

Digest of Education Statistics, 2001. 2001. Washington, DC: National Center for Education Statistics.

Donaldson, L. 1995. *American anti-management theories of organization.* Cambridge: Cambridge University Press.

Doz, Y., and G. Hamel. 1997. *Winning alliances.* Boston: Harvard Business School Press.

Dun and Bradstreet. 2001. *Barometer of global outsourcing.* Waltham, MA: Dun and Bradstreet.

Ehrle, E., and J. Bennett. 1988. *Managing the academic enterprise.* American Council on Education. New York: Macmillan.

Fisher, J. 1991. *The board and the president.* American Council of Education. New York: Macmillan.

Frank, R., and P. Cook. 1995. *The winner-take-all society.* New York: Free Press.

Geiger, R. 1993. Research universities in a new era: From the 1980s to the 1990s. In *Higher learning in America 1980-2000,* ed. A. Levine. Baltimore: Johns Hopkins University Press.

Ghoshal, S., P. Moran, and C. Bartlett. 2001. Employment security, employability and sustainable competitive advantage. In *Strategy organisation and the changing nature of work,* ed. J. Gual and J. Ricart. London: Elgar Publishing.

Gilmer, S. 1997. *The winds of privatization.* Paper presented at the meeting of the Association for the Study of Higher Education, Albuquerque, N.M.

Glaeser, E. 2002. *The governance of not for profit firms* (Working Paper #8921). National Bureau of Economic Research. Cambridge, MA: NBER.

The GM board guidelines. 1994. *Directors and boards* 19:5–9.

Goold, M., and A. Campbell. 2002. *Designing effective organizations.* San Francisco: Jossey Bass.

Grossman, S., and O. Hart. 1986. The costs and benefits of ownership: A theory of vertical and lateral integration. *Journal of Political Economy* 94:691–719.

Gulati, R., S. Huffman, and G. Neilson. 2002. Managing the multiple facets of relational capital: The case of Starbucks. *Strategy and Business* (August). Available at www.strategy-business.com.

Gumport, P., and B. Pusser. 1997. *Restructuring the academic environment.* Stanford University School of Education. Stanford: National Center for Postsecondary Improvement.

Hannan, M., and J. Freeman. 1977. The population ecology of organizations. *American Journal of Sociology* 82:929–64.

Hot growth companies 2002. 2002. *Business Week* 3786 (June 10): 106–12.

International Data Corporation (IDC). 2001. *Higher education IT spending and the eLearning effect: 2000-2005.* Framingham, MA: International Data Corporation.

Jencks, C., and D. Reisman. 2002. *The academic revolution.* New Brunswick: Transaction Publishers.

Jensen, M. 1989. Eclipse of the public corporation. *Harvard Business Review* 67:61–75.

Jensen, M., and W. Meckling. 1976. Theory of the firm. *Journal of Financial Economics* 3:305–60.

Kauffman, J. 1993. Governing boards. In *Higher learning in America 1980-2000,* ed. A. Levine. Baltimore: Johns Hopkins University Press.

Kerr, C. 2001. *Uses of the university.* Cambridge, MA: Harvard University Press.

Kirp, D. 2002. Higher ed inc: Avoiding the perils of outsourcing. *Chronicle of Higher Education,* March 15, pp. B13–14.

Kogut, B. 1985. Designing global strategies: Comparative and competitive value chains. *Sloan Management Review* (Summer): 15–28.

Lang, L., and R. Stulz. 1994. Tobin's Q, corporate diversification and firm performance. *The Journal of Political Economy* 12:1248–80.

Lazerson, M. 1997. Who owns higher education: The changing face of governance. *Change* 29:10–15.

Leonard, M. 2002. College endowments lose billions in market squeeze. *Boston Globe,* October 13, p. A1.

Levine, A., ed. 1993. *Higher learning in America 1980-2000.* Baltimore: Johns Hopkins University Press.

Lovett, C. 2002. The dumbing down of college presidents. *Chronicle of Higher Education,* April 5, p. B20.

Mace, M. 1971. *Directors: Myth and reality.* Boston: Harvard Business School Press.

Massy, W., ed. 1996. *Resource allocation in higher education.* Ann Arbor: University of Michigan Press.

Meister, J. 1998. *Corporate universities: Lessons in building a world-class workforce.* New York: McGraw-Hill.

Milgrom, P., and J. Roberts. 1992. *Economics, organization, and management.* Englewood Cliffs, NJ: Prentice Hall.

Moe, M., and H. Blodget. 2000. *The knowledge web.* San Francisco: Merrill Lynch & Co.

Murphy, K., and M. Jensen. 1990. Performance pay and top management incentives. *Journal of Political Economy* 98 (2): 225–64.

Nardone, T., J. Veum, and J. Yates. 1997. Measuring job security. *Monthly Labor Review* 120 (6): 26–33.

Nason, J. 1982. *The nature of trusteeship: The role and responsibilities of college and university boards.* Washington, DC: Association of Governing Boards of Universities and Colleges.

Newman, F., and L. Couturier. 2001. The new competitive arena. *Change,* September-October, pp. 11–17.

Peterson's contract services for higher education. 1995. Lawrenceville, NJ: Peterson's Guides.

Pisano, G., and K. Slack. 2001. *Discovering the future: R&D Strategy at Merck.* Boston: Harvard Business School.

Porter, M. 1980. *Competitive strategy.* New York: Free Press.

———. 1996. What is strategy?. *Harvard Business Review* 74:61–78.

Prahalad, C. K., and R. Bettis. 1986. The dominant logic: A new linkage between diversity and performance. *Strategic Management Journal* 7:495–511.

Prahalad, C. K., and G. Hamel. 1990. The core competence of the corporation. *Harvard Business Review,* May-June, pp. 79–91.

Public college considers going private. 2002. *Boston Globe,* February 16, p. 26.

Richardson, R., K. Reeves Braco, P. Callan, and J. Finney. 1999. *Designing state higher education systems for a new century.* Phoenix: Oryx Press.

Richman, B., and A. Farmer. 1976. *Leadership, goals and power in higher education.* San Francisco: Jossey Bass.

Ross, C., T. Pohlmann, and E. Boynton. 2001. Business Process Outsourcing Gains Momentum. November 30 TechStrategy Brief. Cambridge, MA: Forrester Research.

Rothblatt, S., and B. Wittrock, eds. 2002. *The European and American university since 1800.* Cambridge: Cambridge University Press.

Sausner, R. 2002. Building out of the crunch. *University Business,* February, pp. 35–38

Sawhney, M. 2002. The 21st century firm. A presentation at II International E-business Meeting, September, Zaragoza, Spain.

Schmidt, P. 2002. Revamping of higher education governance in Florida. *Chronicle of Higher Education,* May 17, p. A32.

Simons, R. 1995. *Levers of control.* Boston, MA: Harvard Business School.

Simpson, R., and S. Frost. 1993. *Inside college.* New York: Insight Books.

Slaughter, S., and L. Leslie. 1997. *Academic capitalism: Politics, policies and the entrepreneurial university.* Baltimore: Johns Hopkins University Press.

Smallwood, S. 2002. 2 Unions fight to represent 4,000 adjuncts at NYU. *Chronicle of Higher Education,* June 7, p. A14.

ThinkEquity. 2002. *Two years to life: Investment themes in for-profit, post-secondary education.* San Francisco: ThinkEquity.

Thompson, J. 1967. *Organisations in action.* Boston, MA: McGraw Hill.

Thomson Financial Securities Data. 2001. *Joint ventures and strategic alliances.* On-line database retrieved from www.tfsd.com/products/financial/access.asp.

U.S. Census Bureau Current Population Survey Table P-16. 2001. *Educational attainment.* Washington, DC: U.S. Department of Commerce.

U.S. Department of Education. 1996. *Survey of earned doctorates.* Washington DC: National Research Council.

Useem, M. 2002. What Tyco tells us. *The Wall Street Journal,* June 5, p. A15.

Van der Werf, M. 2000. How the University of Pennsylvania learned that outsourcing is no panacea. *Chronicle of Higher Education,* April 7, pp. A38–40.

Welch, J., and J. Byrne. 2001. *Jack: Straight from the gut.* New York: Warner Books.

Wernerfelt, B. 1984. A resource-based view of the firm. *Strategic Management Journal* 5:171–80.

Wertz, R. 2000. *Issues and concerns in the privatization and outsourcing of campus services in higher education* (Occasional Paper #10). New York: Columbia University, Teachers College, National Center for the Study of Privatization in Education.

Willard, D., and K. Byard. 2002. Proposal to sell college dorms needs research. *Beacon Journal,* May 16, p. A6.

Williamson, O. 1975. *Markets and hierarchies: Analysis and antitrust implications.* New York: Free Press.

Winston, G. 2001. Is Princeton acting like a church or a car dealer? *Chronicle of Higher Education,* February 23, p. B24.

Wood, P. 2000. *Outsourcing in higher education* (Eric-HE Digest Series Edo-he-2000-8). Washington, DC: George Washington University Graduate School of Education and Human Development.

World Bank. 2000. *Higher education in developing countries: Peril and promise.* Washington, DC: Task Force on Higher Education and Society.

Yoffie, D., and M. Kwak. 2001. *Judo competition.* Boston, MA: Harvard Business School Press.

Zemsky, R., and W. Massy. 1995. Towards an understanding of our current predicament. *Change* 27:40–49.

CHAPTER THREE

Faculty Involvement in System-wide Governance

Neil W. Hamilton

As other chapters in this volume make clear, scholars have historically neglected to examine shared governance at an institutional level. The scholarship that does exist on institutional-level governance has at least two weaknesses: it tends to be anecdotal and based on one institution, and it tends to lack any underlying theory of shared governance, so it drifts toward the general management literature regarding strategic planning and employee empowerment in non-profit, for-profit, and government enterprises.

We know even less about faculty involvement in system-wide governance. This lack of knowledge is odd because "65% of the students in American public postsecondary education attend institutions whose governing boards cover multiple campuses" (McGuiness 2001). The Kellogg Commission on the Future of State and Land-Grant Universities notes that "Universities, at the cutting edge when it comes to encouraging excellence defined by the intellectual achievement of individuals, are reluctant to think very much about how to achieve organizational excellence" (2000, p. 8). The failure of academics to provide useful research and education on institutional and system-wide governance leaves the field by default to governing boards and senior administrators and the management consultants they employ. As public system institutional governing boards become increasingly politicized and oriented toward business models, the negative consequences of the professoriat's inattentiveness to research and education on these issues become more acute.

This chapter is a first step in understanding how shared governance operates at the system level in four states—California, Georgia, Minnesota, and North Carolina—each having adopted different statewide system structures to organize their institutions of higher education. While these states show remarkable diversity, twenty-five other states have adopted system structures significantly similar to the four studied here.

Based on interviews with faculty and administrative decision makers in each of the four state systems, this chapter outlines how faculty are involved in system-level governance. After summarizing the common themes in the case studies, the chapter then proposes an underlying framework to guide how shared governance should work at the system level.

Selection of the Four States

There exists no typical or standard model among the states to structure higher education systems; the states have chosen a wide spectrum of approaches. In March 2002, Aims McGuiness, writing for the Education Commission of the States, found that among the fifty states, there are nineteen different structures for higher education systems (see Figures 3.1–3.4). The states also lack a typical or standard model of faculty involvement in system-level decision making. For example, there is no consensus on whether there should be a system-wide faculty senate or assembly. Professor Gabriel Kaplan, based on a 2001 survey on higher education governance, found that of the responding institutions that were part of a larger system, 29 percent had a system-wide senate composed of faculty representatives, 3 percent had a system-wide senate composed of representatives from faculty, students, and staff, and 68 percent had no system-wide senate (2002, p. 10). The 1994 *State Postsecondary Education Structures Handbook* indicates that while almost every state includes a student member(s) on its system coordinating and governing boards, only seven states included a nonvoting faculty member and only three states included a voting faculty member on one or more of the system-level boards (Education Commission of the States, 1994, pp. 136–49).

I selected California, Georgia, Minnesota, and North Carolina for interviews because, based on Aims McGuiness's taxonomy of system governance models, each offered a fundamentally different approach to system organization that might influence faculty involvement in system governance. Based on academic tradition concerning shared governance, I hypothesized that the degree of faculty involvement would vary depending on the degree to which the institutions in the system had a research mission. The greatest faculty involvement in system-level decision making therefore should be in systems dominated by re-

Table 3.1. Four Models of System Governance

Model A:	The state has three separate systems to organize its institutions of higher education. One system is for research universities, a second is for master's universities and baccalaureate colleges, and a third is for community colleges. The state also has a state-level higher-education coordinating board.
Model B:	The state combines all research universities, master's universities, baccalaureate colleges, and community colleges into one statewide system.
Model C:	The state separates the flagship research university into one system that the research university dominates and combines the master's universities, baccalaureate colleges, and community colleges into the other system.
Model D:	The state separates the research universities, the master's universities, and the baccalaureate colleges into one system and the community colleges into the other.

search universities. At the time of selection, I did not know whether or not the systems within a state had a system-wide faculty senate or assembly, nor did I know whether or not the systems had a faculty union.

Table 3.1 summarizes the four models of system governance analyzed in this chapter.

A few states each have a separate system for research universities, master's universities and baccalaureate colleges, and community colleges. California's structure for higher education (Figure 3.1) includes a state-level coordinating board. Public institutions are organized under three state-level governing boards: one for research universities, one for other state universities, and one that sets the policy for locally governed community colleges. Connecticut, Louisiana, and Nebraska have similar structures.

Several states combine all the research universities, master's universities, baccalaureate colleges, and community colleges into one statewide system. In Georgia (Figure 3.2), two separate boards govern public institutions: one combines the research universities, other university campuses, and two-year community colleges, and the other governs technical colleges. Wisconsin is similar. Eleven other states have a similar state-level board governing a combination of two or more universities as well as community colleges.

Some states allow the flagship research university to dominate one system, and they combine the master's universities, baccalaureate colleges, and community colleges into another system. Minnesota's (Figure 3.3) two separate state-level boards are responsible for all public institutions. The planning/

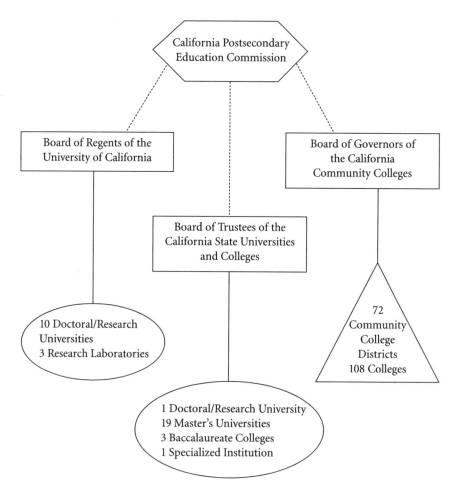

Figure 3.1. California. In figures 3.1–3.4, the dotted line indicates a coordinating relationship and the solid line indicates a governing relationship. All classifications are based on the Carnegie classification system in 2000. See McGuiness, *Models,* p. 8.

service agency has no coordinating authority related to the governing boards. Vermont is similar. Tennessee has a state-level coordinating board but is otherwise similar.

A number of states separate the research universities, the master's universities, and baccalaureate colleges into one system and the community colleges into the other. In North Carolina (Figure 3.4), the state-level board is responsible for all public universities and colleges, and a second board is responsible

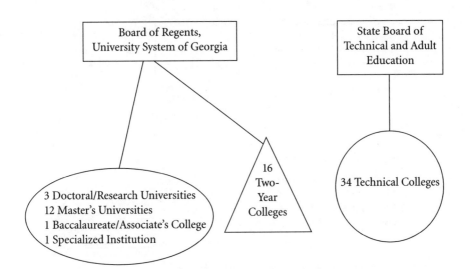

Figure 3.2. Georgia. McGuiness, *Models,* p. 3.

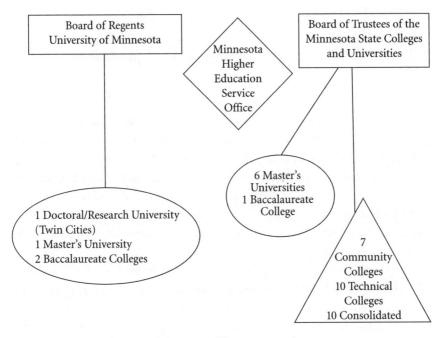

Figure 3.3. Minnesota. McGuiness, *Models,* pp. 2, 6, and 11.

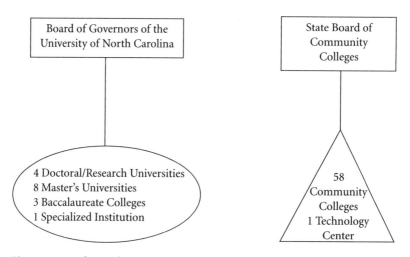

Figure 3.4. North Carolina. McGuiness, *Models,* p. 4.

for all community and technical colleges. Maine and New Hampshire are similar. Six other states also have a state-level governing board over all universities, but in those states, the state-level board for community colleges is only a coordinating board.

Faculty Involvement in System-level Decision Making

California

1. California Postsecondary Education Commission. The commission is not a governing board. It is a sixteen-member advisory group to the governor and the legislature. The commission's most significant responsibilities are comprehensive statewide planning for postsecondary education and advice to the governor and legislature on policies and budget priorities (California Postsecondary Education System 2002). No faculty members sit on the commission. The faculty senates for two of the three California systems send observers to the commission meetings.

Recommendation 38 of the Joint Legislative Committee's 2002 California Master Plan for Education points out that the commission is impeded by a plethora of statutory and legislative directives regarding its work that are beyond its capacity to fulfill. The Joint Legislative Committee also finds that the commission has not been assigned sufficient authority to *require* coordinated efforts on the part of postsecondary segments. The recommendation of the committee is that the legislature should review the commission's founding statutes to ensure that it has the capacity and the authority both to carry out its mission as the coordinating entity for postsecondary education and to serve as the chief objective adviser to the governor and the legislature regarding continuing improvement of California postsecondary education (California 2002 master plan for education 2002a).

2. *Board of Regents of the University of California.* The board of regents governs ten doctoral/research universities and three research laboratories.[1] California's individual universities do not have separate boards. The mission of the system is to provide public undergraduate and graduate instruction in the liberal arts and sciences and in the professions. It has sole authority among public systems to award the doctoral degree in all fields of learning and has exclusive jurisdiction over graduate public education in the professions of law, medicine, dentistry, and veterinary medicine. The system is the primary state-supported academic agency for research (California master plan for education 2003).

The system has an academic senate consisting of almost all full-time faculty members in the system as well as the system president and senior administrators down to the level of dean (Standing order 105.1 of the Regents of California 2002). The academic senate has an elected representative body, the academic assembly, consisting of the system president, forty faculty representatives elected by faculties at the individual institutions, the chair and vice chair of the assembly (members of the senate elected by the assembly to these posts), and sixteen ex officio members, including the chairs of each individual institution's senate and the chairs of the standing academic senate committees. The assembly meets three or four times a year. The assembly or an individual institution's senate may initiate a "memorial," which is a mail ballot of all members of the academic senate on an issue. The academic senate reserves the power of referendum concerning decisions of the academic assembly.

The academic council is the assembly's executive committee, consisting of the chair and vice chair of the assembly, the chairs of each individual institution's senate, and the chairs of the six standing academic senate committees. The academic council meets monthly and acts on all matters except legislation. The academic senate has seventeen committees (including the six standing committees referenced above) and several task forces in which approximately

250 senate members assist in the work of the assembly and the academic council. There is no system faculty union.

Two faculty members—the chair and the vice chair of the academic assembly—sit on the board of regents as non-voting members participating fully in discussion. They also attend and participate in board committee meetings. If an issue before a board committee affects the faculty, the chair of the board committee may work with the chair of the relevant senate committee.

The board of regents, by standing order, has provided that "(a) The Academic Senate, subject to the approval of the Board, shall determine the conditions for admission . . . and for degrees . . . ; (b) The Academic Senate shall authorize and supervise all courses and curricula offered under the sole or joint jurisdiction of the departments, colleges, schools, graduate divisions, or other University academic agencies . . . ; . . . (d) The Academic Senate is authorized . . . to select a committee to advise the President concerning the budget; and (e) The Academic Senate shall have the right to lay before the Board, but only through the President, its views on any matter pertaining to the conduct and welfare of the University" (Standing order 105.1 of the Regents of California 2002).

The system president and senior administrators attend the first two hours of all academic council meetings. While the academic council and senate committees have a significant consulting relationship with the president and senior administrative staff, a 1998 academic senate task force report notes that "[A] truncated involvement of the Senate in policy formation has also arisen on occasion in areas where the Senate has direct purview, such as admissions" (University of California Academic Senate Task Force report on governance 1998). "In policy areas in which the Academic Senate is advisory, such as University budget, administrations have often viewed the Senate role as limited. The process of shared governance in these circumstances tends to be cursory, with the Senate often only informed of policy changes" (University of California Academic Senate Task Force report on governance 1998, p. 6).

The next five years should see increased faculty involvement in shared governance because the front-burner issues of admissions and affirmative action in admissions are in the areas of responsibility specifically delegated to the academic senate. Moreover, the wave of retirements among tenured professors over the next ten years will create an enormous surge in hiring, which again is the faculty's primary responsibility.

3. *Board of Trustees of the California State Universities and Colleges.* The Board of Trustees governs one doctoral/research university, nineteen master's universities, three baccalaureate colleges, and one specialized institution.[2] There are also individual boards at each institution. The primary mission of the system is instruction in the liberal arts and sciences through the master's degree, in the professions and applied fields that require more than two years of postsecondary education, and in teacher education. The system engages in faculty research consistent with the primary mission of instruction (California 2002 master plan for education 2002c).

The system has an academic senate consisting only of faculty members (the vice chancellor is an ex officio, nonvoting member). The senate meets every other month with committees meeting in the alternate months. There is one faculty union for the system; the union's scope of representation is limited by statute to issues of wages, hours of employment, and other terms and conditions of employment.[3] The academic senate and the union cooperate on key issues of mutual interest. For example, they have formed a joint task force on raising the proportion of tenure-track faculty in the system and a joint task force on faculty workload.

One faculty member serves as a voting member of the board of trustees. The executive committee of the academic senate attends board meetings and has the right to speak and make presentations. Executive committee members may also attend the board's committee meetings.

The senate's executive committee also meets with the system chancellor on the day before the board meetings. The system chancellor and the board chair often attend the academic senate's plenary sessions. The executive committee of the senate also works very closely with the vice chancellor of academic affairs. The relationships among the senate, the chancellor, and the board are consultative, so when the senate ultimately recommends a policy to the chancellor and board, they adopt the recommendation in most cases.

In 2000, the senate undertook a study of system-wide shared governance, receiving back 135 surveys out of 224 distributed. Although not disputing the adequacy of the shared governance processes in place, the faculty respondents expressed a view "that administrators have taken the initiative in the area of academic policy and that faculty members have been relegated to a reactive or defensive mode. Thus the faculty job has become to stop bad things from happening rather than promulgating good academic policy" (The California State University 2001, p. 5).

With respect to the relationship of collective bargaining to shared governance, the report noted that

> administrators were more critical of the impact of the union on shared governance than were the faculty. Administrators most often noted that having a union creates a confusing and adversarial situation that leads to a non-professional environment . . . Faculty members are divided on the impact of union representation on shared governance. Many see it as positive. Some believe the union's impact is mixed or nonexistent. Still others feel that the union has a negative influence on shared governance.
>
> Those making positive comments most often suggested that the union is willing to be more outspoken than the Senate in dealing with the administration . . . Those who take a negative view of the effect of collective bargaining on shared governance say that it removes issues from collegial discussion, divides the faculty, makes communication more difficult with faculty, makes senators more timid about taking up issues that may be in bargaining, makes the administration more hostile, and creates an "us" versus "them" environment, exactly the opposite of shared decision-making. (The California State University 2001, p. 7)

The survey asked what might be done to encourage active participation in shared governance by new faculty. Most administrators and faculty agreed that the changing demands of the workplace have resulted in new faculty being less likely to participate in governance activities than earlier generations of faculty had been (The California State University 2001, p. 29).

4. Board of Governors of the California Community Colleges. The Board of Governors sets policy and provides guidance for seventy-two community college districts that include a total of 108 community colleges.[4] The primary mission of the system is both "to offer academic and vocational instruction at the lower division level for both younger and older students, including those persons returning to school" and "to advance California's economic growth . . . through education, training and services that contribute to continuous work force improvement" (California Community Colleges 2002).

Each of the seventy-two community college districts in the state has a locally elected board of trustees responsive to local community needs and charged with the operation of the local college. Recommendation 34 of the 2002 California Master Plan for Education points out that "the California Community College

System has suffered from fragmentation for decades stemming from governance responsibilities having been assigned by statute to local boards of trustees . . . The Community College System, to be effective, needs a clear statement of functions and authority for the Board of Governors and the local boards of trustees." The recommendation proposes that the board of governors has responsibility for overall governance, the determination of system policy priorities, budget advocacy, and accountability for the multicampus system (California 2002 master plan for education 2002b).

There is a system-wide academic senate consisting solely of faculty members. The senate meets twice a year and elects an executive committee to conduct ongoing activities of the senate. There are also three major faculty unions and a number of independent unions. The unions focus on the terms and conditions of employment like compensation and benefits. The senate and the unions work together on the community college council of faculty organizations.

Two faculty representatives serve as voting members of the board of governors. Other faculty regularly attend board meetings. Two academic senate and four faculty union officials also serve on the nineteen-member consultation council. The board created the consultation council in response to a California education code mandate to establish a consultation process at the state level. The chancellor or any member of the consultation council may bring a matter for discussion. The chancellor gives substantial deference to jointly developed recommendations but reserves the right to make a different recommendation to the board. In the event that the chancellor takes a different recommendation to the board, the chancellor will discuss with the council his or her reasons for recommending a different action (Executive orders of the chancellor on consultation 2002).

The board itself reserves the right to reject the recommendations of the chancellor or to adopt different recommendations. When rejecting or adopting a recommendation different from that of the consultation council, the board will provide a clear and substantive rationale. Throughout the consultation process, "the advice and judgment of the Academic Senate will be primarily relied upon whenever the policy involves an academic or professional matter."[5]

The 2002 California Education Master Plan does not water down the faculty role in the consultation process.

Georgia

1. Georgia Education Coordinating Council. Georgia has a statewide Education Coordinating Council (ECC) consisting of the governor and the senior officials of the state agencies responsible for kindergarten through graduate education. The ECC includes both the chancellor and the chair of the board for the University System of Georgia. The ECC is principally a forum for interagency communication regarding education policy and programs. While the ECC is advisory to the governor, it has substantial power with respect to policy recommendations. No faculty sit on the ECC, although individual faculty members occasionally speak at the ECC's quarterly open meetings. Faculty involvement takes place at the level of subcommittee input on design, development, and implementation of specific initiatives.

2. Board of Regents, University System of Georgia. The board of regents governs three doctoral/research universities, twelve master's universities, one baccalaureate/associate's college, two specialized institutions, and sixteen two-year institutions.[6] The vision of the system is to provide excellent education at all levels, to pursue "leading-edge basic and applied research, scholarly inquiry and creative endeavors," and to bring these intellectual resources "to bear on the economic development of the State and the continuing education of its citizens" (University System of Georgia vision statement 2002).

Georgia has no institutional-level boards. There is no system-wide faculty senate or assembly, and there is no union.

There are no faculty members on the system board. Because board meetings are public, faculty are free to attend. Faculty are involved on board committees when they are the authors of new academic program proposals or serve on special projects or task forces.

The faculty influence system decision making through a system-wide advisory council composed of the chancellor, senior vice chancellors, and the presidents of the institutions in the university system. There are also twenty-three academic and fifteen administrative committees that are part of the advisory council. Faculty members constitute the majority of the membership of the academic committees. The membership of each committee consists of one voting member appointed by the president or head of each institution offering work in the field with which the committee is concerned, such as biological sciences, for example. The term for membership is one year. The duty of each member is to represent the position of the appointing institution. The representative is expected to confer with colleagues and appropriate officials at their home institution on issues to be brought before the committee. A dean or department chair may occasionally be selected as a representative. All reports, recommendations, and studies from academic committees requiring the ultimate consideration of the advisory council are submitted first to the administrative committee on academic affairs, which is composed of the chief academic officers of the institutions in the system.

Looking at where system-shared governance is headed over the next five years, Associate Vice Chancellor Wolfe believes that "There may potentially be some weakening of the faculty involvement over the next five years as business and industry exert greater influence on the content, design, development, and implementation of academic programs, particularly in science, mathematics, engineering, and technology. Boards and administrations are listening more and more to business and industry."[7]

3. State Board of Technical and Adult Education. The Georgia State Board of Technical and Adult Education govern thirty-four technical colleges.[8] The mission of the system is workforce development and career preparation. The state board delegates some power to the local board of directors at each technical college. Only the local board can initiate new programs for a technical college. The local board conducts searches for the college's president and recommends three candidates to the state board.

There is no system-wide faculty senate, and although the governor could appoint a faculty member, no faculty members have yet served on the state board. State board meetings are open and held in locations throughout the state; occasionally a faculty member speaks at an open meeting of the board. There is no faculty union.

The principal involvement of faculty at the state level is their responsibility for the curriculum and standards in the programs that the local boards decide to initiate and the state board approves. The technical colleges are divided into six consortia; faculty members from the five to six colleges in a particular consortium elect one faculty member in each program area to represent that consortium. The six elected faculty members (one from each consortium) for each program area meet to set statewide program design and standards. The state board defers substantially to these faculty recommendations.

The system works well to provide job preparation attuned to local conditions for the Georgia workforce. There are no significant changes in shared governance anticipated.

Minnesota

1. The Board of Regents of the University of Minnesota. For historical reasons the University of Minnesota combines a large, nationally ranked research university in the Twin Cities with a master's degree institution in Duluth and two baccalaureate colleges.[9] The mission of the Twin Cities campus emphasizes research. The institutions do not have individual boards. The top administrators for the Twin Cities campus also serve as the top administrators for the system—so the chancellor and provost for the Twin Cities campus are, respectively, the president and executive vice president of the University of Minnesota system.

A system-wide university senate consisting of faculty members is dominated by faculty from the Twin Cities campus. The senate meets three times per semester. There is no faculty union.

While no faculty member sits as a member of the board of regents, the chairs of the senate committees attend meetings of the board of regents committee having a similar jurisdiction. The university senate is a policy-influencing body with more than twenty standing committees that work closely with the appropriate university administrators. Decision making is highly consultative, and occasions are rare when the president does not follow the faculty recommendation.

Because of the increasing complexity of governance issues, over the past several years, the major senate committees have met more frequently; the committees are more involved in consultation with the administration. There also has been a significant increase in administrator/faculty working groups and task forces to address specific institutional problems. This trend should continue.

2. Board of Trustees of the Minnesota State Colleges and Universities (MnSCU). The Board of Trustees governs six master's universities, one baccalaureate college, and twenty-seven community and technical colleges.[10] The system mission and vision emphasize teaching and economic development. Research is mentioned but receives no emphasis (Minnesota State Colleges and Universities strategic plan 2002, p. 1). There are no governing boards at the institutional level.

There are no faculty members on the board of trustees, no system-wide faculty senate, and only two institutional faculty senates. The system has two unions, one for the master's universities and one for the community and technical colleges.

Faculty involvement at the system level comes through the unions. The system chancellor and senior staff meet monthly with the presidents of the unions. The recent advisory commission on strategic direction for the system had thirty-one members including both union presidents but no faculty members. The commission's recommendations focused on access, workforce development, and on-line learning. There was no mention of research (MnSCU Citizen's Advisory Commission 2002, p. 2). The unions tend to focus on the economic and job security aspects of the employment relationship.

The MnSCU system is the result of a merger of three systems that occurred in 1995. Each former system had a different set of expectations and governance structures, and the differences are still being worked out. The merged system has experienced frequent changes of board membership and administrative leadership. The system has yet to formalize shared governance except through the unions.

North Carolina

1. Board of Governors of the University of North Carolina. The board of governors of the University of North Carolina system governs four doctoral/research universities, eight master's universities, three baccalaureate colleges, and one specialized institution.[11] The system mission addresses teaching as "the primary service that the university renders to society . . . The relative importance of research and public service, which enhance teaching and learning, varies among the constituent institutions, depending on their overall missions" (The University of North Carolina mission statement 2002, p. 2). There are institutional boards of trustees to which the board of governors has delegated some powers, including the power to recommend names of candidates for the institution's chancellor to the president of the system, who then recommends a final candidate to the board of governors.

There is a system-wide faculty assembly that meets four times a year. There is no union. The faculty assembly chair attends board meetings and several of the committee meetings at each board meeting. The chair has no vote and is not included in the social gathering that precedes each board meeting. Overall informal contacts between the assembly chair, other faculty, and the board are limited.

The faculty assembly principally serves an advisory role to the board and the administration, but it is not without influence. Current assembly chair Professor Richard Veit notes, "We have the ear of the administration and the opportunity to make suggestions, engage in dialogue, and receive a response, but we are rarely consulted per se. Members of the administration are very cooperative as far as attending assembly meetings and committee meetings upon request and reporting to us, and the assembly has had influence through these channels. On the other hand, initiative is almost exclusively from us; I cannot recall an instance in my term as chair where I was contacted by any of the administrative staff seeking faculty opinions/suggestions on substantive policy decisions."[12]

Over the past ten years, there have been no formal changes in faculty involvement in system governance. However, the current system president is more likely than her immediate predecessor to respond to faculty input.

2. North Carolina State Board of Community Colleges. The State Board of Community Colleges governs fifty-eight community colleges and one technology center.[13] The mission of the system is to provide workforce education, support for economic development, and services to communities in the state. There are institutional-level boards of trustees that have substantial power, including the selection of the president of the institution and the initial determination of the programs that the institution will offer.

There is no system faculty senate, although the North Carolina Community College Faculty Association was formed in 1998. Less than half of the faculty belong to the association. There is no faculty union.

No faculty member serves on the state board of community colleges, but the faculty association sends a representative both to board meetings and to each board committee meeting. The board does the most important work in committees, and faculty members speak regularly at committee meetings.

The system president seeks to build consensus with the faculty on strategic objectives and legislative objectives because the legislature responds favorably to joint efforts of the board, administration, and faculty. The president cannot recall any recent issue where there has not been consensus.

The faculty's greatest frustration is legislative inaction on faculty pay issues. If the legislature continues its inaction on this issue, the faculty's strong support for joint initiatives will be difficult to maintain.

Summary of the Case Studies

Based on academic tradition concerning shared governance, I hypothesized that the degree of faculty involvement in shared governance would vary depending upon the extent to which the system had a research mission. This sample of nine systems in four states is not sufficient to provide any valid test of the hypothesis, but the data do provide some support for it.

A system emphasis on research is indicated by the extent to which the system mission emphasizes research and the extent to which the mix of institutions in the system tilts toward the research university(ies). Based on these indicators, my hypothesis would have predicted that faculty involvement in system decision making would fall roughly on the following spectrum from most to least: University of California, University of Minnesota, University of North Carolina, University of Georgia, California State University, Minnesota State Colleges and Universities, California Community and North Carolina Community Colleges, and the Georgia Technical Colleges.

There is more faculty involvement in system-shared governance at the California State University system than in either the University of Georgia or the University of North Carolina systems. There is as much faculty involvement in governance at the California Community College system as at the two systems dominated by research universities—the University of California and the University of Minnesota. Academics in California have succeeded in creating a culture amenable to shared governance.

The faculty and faculty unions in the California Community College system are the only ones with sufficient political power to obtain state-level education code regulations requiring a consultation process at the system level. At the institutional level, the regulations require primary reliance on the advice and judgment of the local academic senate whenever a policy involves academic or professional matters. Further research on community and technical college systems would indicate the degree to which faculty involvement in decision making in the California Community College system is an anomaly.

Historically, academic tradition and the relationship among the mission of knowledge creation, academic freedom, peer review, and shared governance have been hostile to the involvement of state legislatures and executive branch agencies in dictating shared governance relationships. Legislative and executive branch involvement in the university is a double-edged sword. The academic profession has not wanted to risk opening the door to legislative and executive branch intervention in internal governance because those branches of government are vulnerable to the influence of the zealotry that infects the voting public from time to time.

With the exception of the California Community College system, the general principle on shared governance at the system level seems to be that the stronger the research focus of the system, the stronger the faculty's consulting role with the system board and administration. Faculty do not have ultimate decision-making power in any system.

In the systems in the study that had unions—California State University (CalState), California Community Colleges, and MnSCU—the union principally focuses on terms and conditions of employment (such as compensation, benefits, and job security). In California, the unions work with the senates on issues of common interest.

Looking back ten years and forward five years, the respondents in this survey voice a general concern that the faculty role in shared governance is increasingly passive and reactive rather than proactive. There is, in general, an increase in governing board and administrative use of business models of management. The University of Minnesota system is an exception to this trend, but that system, several years ago, struggled through a major crisis regarding proposed tenure code changes by the regents that almost led to a faculty union. The regents, under intense media, legislative, and public pressure, backed down. There also seems to be a slow trend toward more state-level coordination of all systems.

Framework to Guide System-level Shared Governance

What principles should guide faculty involvement in system-level decision making? It is important to distinguish good management practice from the shared governance tradition in colleges and universities. The latter long predates the former. In the last several decades, the trend in good management practice has emphasized employee participation in decision making. The apparent success of participative Japanese management models in the 1980s and the need to motivate creativity in a high-tech workforce and to respond quickly to changing markets in the 1990s have favored participative decision making in corporate organizations.

The shared governance tradition in the United States (predating current participative management practices by sixty years) flows from the unique mission of the university: to create knowledge and to develop in students the skills of critical inquiry (the discipline of dissent). Ironically, managers in high-tech businesses where knowledge creation is critical can learn a great deal from the much older participative decision process found in the universities. U.S. universities have been the most successful competitors in the world for intellectual talent. They have also been the most successful global competitors in motivating that talent to create knowledge. Once creative and intelligent people have achieved some threshold of material benefit, many are motivated principally by the respect and support of their peer communities to serve a high purpose rather than by the goal of making absentee owners wealthier. The markets for students, professors, grants, and endowments are increasingly highly competitive on a global scale. Nearly all of the world-class universities are in the United States. These competitive results lend support to the effectiveness of the governance structures that produce them.

Understanding shared governance requires an understanding of the relationships among the mission of the university, academic freedom (the conditions of employment necessary for faculty to achieve the mission), peer review (as the linchpin of academic freedom), and shared governance (as the negotiated mechanics of peer review).

As will become clear by a perusal of George Keller's chapter on the need for stronger administrative voice and Robert O'Neil's chapter on academic freedom, my thoughts are closer to O'Neil's than Keller's. At the same time, we all seem to accept the conditions that Marginson and Collis have laid out. Ours is not so much a difference in interpretation, then, but in what to do if we accept the interpretation. The mission of higher education is to create and disseminate knowledge. Knowledge creation includes the scholarship of discovery, integration, application, and teaching. Dissemination of knowledge in higher education involves a unique kind of teaching that is closely related to knowledge creation but that is different from teaching in secondary education: the teaching of the discipline of dissent. The discipline of dissent requires that the student become familiar with what is already known about a subject as well as learn how to question that orthodoxy. Teaching at this level develops in the student an understanding of first principles in a discipline(s), a critical analytical ability, and an understanding of the methods for resolving disputes within and among the disciplines (Hamilton 2000, pp. 15–16; Ashby 1968–69, p. 64).

It is higher education's unique mission of knowledge creation and the teaching of the discipline of dissent that justifies our tradition of academic freedom, peer review, and shared governance. In this tradition, knowledge is the evolving critical consensus of a decentralized community of "checkers," who adhere to the principle that knowledge claims must be capable of being checked and withstand checking, regardless of the source of the claim or the identity of the checker. The academic profession constitutes a significant proportion of the decentralized community of checkers on which knowledge creation depends.

In virtue of the academic profession's special competence in the community of checkers—including knowledge of the existing scholarship and mastery of the techniques of investigation and validation in the disciplines—the profession has sought unique conditions of employment that protect a professor's right to offend employers (and other powerful interests who influence employers) in the pursuit of knowledge. Challenging existing orthodoxy has always posed risks in employment settings. Academic freedom describes these conditions of employment, whereby college and university employers, acknowledging higher education's unique mission of creating knowledge and teaching the discipline of dissent, have granted exceptional vocational freedom of speech to professors in research, teaching, and extramural utterance without lay interference. This freedom is granted on the condition that individual professors meet correlative duties of professional competence and ethical conduct. The faculty as a peer collegium also has correlative duties of peer review, both to monitor and maintain minimum standards for each professor and to create a culture of high aspiration with respect to professional ideals (Hamilton 2000, pp. 15–16).

It is this tradition of faculty self-governance in peer review of professional competence and ethical conduct that makes academic freedom unique, not the tenure system that has many parallels in other employment settings. Peer review is the linchpin of academic freedom.

The tradition of shared governance is a corollary of, and necessary condition for, the concepts of academic freedom and peer review. What do rights of freedom to research and freedom to teach mean where peer review in the context of a discipline (not the governing board or the CEO) determines competence and ethical conduct? The peer-review paradigm means that peers define both the minimum standards and professional ideals that define competence and ethical conduct in the discipline for both professors and students.

The mechanics of shared governance have been subject to negotiation over the past century. There is a wide consensus that the faculty peer collegium, exercising its peer-review responsibility, should have primary authority over core academic issues including standards for admitting students; curriculum; procedures of student instruction; standards of student competence and ethical conduct; maintenance of a suitable environment for learning; the standards of faculty competence and ethical conduct; and the application of those standards in faculty appointments, promotions, tenure, and discipline.

The faculty's efforts to secure a consulting role on other decisions have been more controversial, as Keller notes in chapter 6, and more often resisted by governing boards and senior administrators. The American Association of University Professors (AAUP) has acknowledged in its statements that the governing board and its administrative agents have primary authority over decisions on mission, strategic planning, fiscal and physical resources, budgeting, decisions to create new departments, schools, or universities, and the selection and assessment of deans and presidents. Yet the AAUP also has argued that these decisions should be informed by consultation with the faculty (AAUP 2000, p. 217). Consultation in this tradition includes allowing sufficient information and time so the faculty can understand and consider the issues, confer with the administration and governing board, and present faculty recommendations.

Boards and administrations do not always agree. For example, the 1998 Association of Governing Board's Statement on Institutional Governance defines the faculty as just one stakeholder to be considered in decisions and provides for consultation with stakeholders only on some of the decisions on which the AAUP has argued faculty should be consulted (Hamilton 1999, p. 24).

The most critical lesson for governing boards and administrators to learn is that the mission of higher education and of the academic profession is creating knowledge and teaching the discipline of dissent. The faculty's areas of primary authority in shared governance and its claims for a consulting role on other decisions follow directly from this mission. Faculty members want governance ideas relating to the mission to be subjected to the same type of informed public criticism and the give-and-take of reasoned argument that are foundational for research and critical inquiry. Both teaching and research take place on timetables, and shared governance also should be subject to time constraints as called for by the circumstances.

The shared-governance tradition has developed in the context of an individual institution, but its rationale applies also to state-level systems. The system governing board and administrators should grant the faculty primary authority over the core academic issues listed above. Many of the decisions at the state-system level presumably involve policy, strategic planning, and budget issues in which faculty have had only a consulting role under the shared governance tradition. Such decisions at the system level also can benefit from faculty input.

System board members and administrators must remember that knowledge creation occurs from the bottom up, not from the top down, and knowledge creation infuses teaching from the bottom up. The board and the administration create no knowledge. Although Terence MacTaggart takes issue with this point in the next chapter, I suggest that the faculty are in the best position to advise on the movement of knowledge in the disciplines and on how the board and administration should create optimal conditions to foster the creation of knowledge and the teaching of critical inquiry.

Burton Clark, in his 1983 book, *The Higher Education System,* captured how change occurs in a bottom-heavy knowledge creation organization.

> Despite the belief of many observers that academic systems change significantly only when pressured by external forces, such systems increasingly exhibit innovation and adaptation among their bottom units. Invention and diffusion are institutionalized in the work of the departments and counterpart units that embody the disciplines and professions. Universities . . . move ahead in a somewhat self-propelled fashion in those areas of new thought that are perceived by academics as acceptable within general paradigms of academic knowledge. Such change is widely overlooked since it is not announced in master plans or ministerial bulletins and is not introduced on a global scale. It occurs in segments of the operating level that exchange with one another and is not characteristic of the larger entities. In a bottom-heavy knowledge institution, grass-roots innovation is a crucial form of change.
>
> . . . The leading false expectation in academic reform is that major results can be obtained by top-down manipulation. Such reforms are occasionally initiated and implemented, but more commonly small results follow from multiple efforts at the top, in the middle, or at the bottom that entail wrong experiments, false starts, and zigzag adjustments, a mélange of actions out of which precipitate some flows of change. Dramatic examples of such flows are found in the evolutionary buildup of knowledge in first the physical sciences and then the biological sciences in the twentieth century, accompanied by an increasing dominance of these fields in resources and power within universities and national systems. (Clark 1983, pp. 234–35)

Academic tradition ties the shared governance tradition directly to peer review, academic freedom, and the mission of the university to create knowledge and teach critical inquiry. To the degree that the mission of a state system is workforce and economic development, the system mission does not fit within this model; it is far more closely aligned with the teaching mission of secondary education. Similarly, faculty involvement in decision making in those systems would look more like that in secondary education.

The data on allocation of faculty time support the conclusion that faculty at two-year institutions have little interest in and spend very little time on research. The percentage of faculty interested primarily in research varies from 79 percent at a doctoral/research university to 25 percent at a master's university to 7 percent at community colleges (Blackburn and Lawrence 1995, pp. 234–35). For these same institutional types, the amount of time faculty wish to devote to research varies from 42 percent, to 19 percent, to 4 percent, respectively (Blackburn and Lawrence 1995, p. 85). The majority of faculty at public universities spend nine or more hours a week on research and scholarly writing, whereas 60 percent of public community college faculty spend no time on research (Higher Education Research Institute, UCLA 1999, p. 30).

To determine the degree of faculty involvement in decision making at the system level, the shared governance tradition asks first what is the mission or core identity of the system. If the system mission emphasizes knowledge creation, then the faculty's consulting role is critical to realize the mission. If the system mission does not include knowledge creation, or does so only marginally, the question of faculty involvement in decision making is best resolved by reference to good administrative practice in secondary schools.

Mission clarity is important in determining optimal faculty involvement in system governance. If there is a broad spectrum of institutions in a system with respect to the importance of the research mission, then there will be less clarity with respect to both system mission and optimal shared governance. In this study, the Georgia university system combines the greatest range of institutional types, followed by the MnSCU system. The three California systems are examples of how to combine institutions with a similar mission into one system. For populous states that can afford three systems, California's division makes sense. For less populous states, North Carolina's division into two systems in which the two-year institutions are in a system separate from the graduate and four-year institutions makes the most sense.

Only three systems in this study had faculty unions: the CalState system, the California Community College system, and the MnSCU system. The 2001 CalState system Academic Senate Report on Shared Governance noted a division in the faculty—with some positive and some negative views—on the impact of union representation on shared governance. In the MnSCU system, the union representation is the faculty's sole voice; there is no tradition of shared governance at the state level in this system.

The unions, pursuant to the law governing collective bargaining, focus on the terms and conditions of employment, particularly job security, salary, and benefits. These mandatory bargaining subjects exclude issues of critical importance to the shared governance tradition, such as curriculum and policies on admissions and grading. Unions have almost no interest in the peer collegium's correlative duty to enforce standards of competence and ethics on individual professors. That is management's job. We need research exploring the impact of unions on shared governance at the system level.

Conclusion

The faculty's role in system-level shared governance flows from the mission of the system. University of California president emeritus Clark Kerr observed in 1994 that national systems of higher education in developed countries were converging on a model of higher education with three differentiated levels: research universities with a knowledge creation and dissemination mission conducted on a national and international plane, comprehensive universities conducted on a regional plane, and community colleges and technical schools focused on the local labor market (Kerr 1994, pp. 91–93, 98). Differentiated missions call for differentiated governance structures.

The single most important system governing board function is mission clarity. If the legislature has created a system with a mission that is too diffused or broad, the system governing board should press for reconsideration. The most sensible structure to maintain mission coherence and clarity is to follow the California model. If a three-system structure is too expensive, the North Carolina model is less desirable but workable.

If knowledge creation is one principal focus of the system mission, then the faculty should play an informed consultative role in system-level policy decisions. Rather than get bogged down trying to decide which specific decisions merit consultation with the faculty, the system governing board should invite the chairs of each faculty senate committee corresponding to a board committee to attend the board committee meetings. The system administrators should meet regularly with the faculty senate committee chairs to seek faculty input on significant decisions or policies. The University of Minnesota and the University of California academic senates achieve this goal with different structures.

The governing board and the administration can place appropriate time constraints on the faculty consultative process in light of the urgency of the issue at hand.

MacTaggart emphasizes that *both* responsible trusteeship *and* shared governance define the uniquely American equilibrium of authority in higher education. To reach the university's mission, this balance is preferable to rule entirely by the guild model of some earlier European universities, the corporate model of the marketplace, or the administrative model of government (MacTaggart 2002, p. 7). The balance model has served to make U.S. higher education the strongest system in the world in terms of world-class contributions to the creation of knowledge.

The balance model must be renewed in each generation of board members, administrators, and faculty. The faculty, through their research and teaching, have the principal responsibility to ensure that this renewal occurs. If the faculty do not undertake this leadership, the trends toward politicized boards and administrators drawn to business models and management consultants will continue at both the institutional and system levels.

NOTES

1. Information given in a phone interview with M. Bertero-Barcelo, Executive Director of the Academic Council, University of California, October 10, 2002.

2. J. A. Kegley, Chair of the Academic Senate, California State University, personal communication, September 23, 2002.

3. J. A. Kegley, personal communication, September 29, 2002.

4. K. Clark, Vice President of the Academic Senate for the California Community Colleges, phone interview, September 23, 2002.

5. Standing orders of the chancellor on consultation. Retrieved November 12, 2002 from www.cccco.edu/executive/consultation/standing_orders.htm. The California Education Code provides even more specific direction for shared governance at the local community college district level. The code requires that the governing board of a community college will consult collegially with the academic senate of the institution, meaning either rely primarily on the advice of the academic senate or commit to reaching mutual agreement with the academic senate, on a list of ten specific matters including curriculum, grading policies, shared governance structures, and processes for program review and institutional planning and budget development.

6. J. Wolfe, Associate Vice Chancellor for Academic Affairs, University System of Georgia, phone interview, September 23, 2002.

7. Ibid.

8. K. Breeden, Commissioner of the Georgia Department of Technical and Adult Education, phone interview, September 26, 2002.

9. G. Engstrand, Coordinator of the University Senate, University of Minnesota, phone interview, September 18, 2002.

10. L. Baer, Minnesota State Colleges and Universities Vice Chancellor, personal communication, September 23, 2002; M. Murphy, Associate Vice Chancellor, interview, June 18, 2002.

11. R. Veit, Chairperson, University of North Carolina Faculty Assembly, personal communication, September 17, 2002; B. Brown, Associate Vice President of the UNC Office of the President, personal communication, September 26, 2002.

12. Veit, personal communication.

13. H. M. Lancaster, President of the North Carolina Community College System, phone interview, September 30, 2002.

REFERENCES

Ashby, E. 1968–69. A Hippocratic oath for the academic profession. *Minerva* 7 (Autumn/Winter): 64.

American Association of University Professors (AAUP). 2000. Statement on government of colleges and universities. *Policy documents and reports.* 9th ed. Washington, DC: AAUP, p. 217.

Blackburn, R., and J. Lawrence. 1995. *Faculty at work.* Baltimore: Johns Hopkins University Press.

California 2002 master plan for education. 2002a. Retrieved November 12 from www.sen.ca.gov/masterplan/0207302NDDRAFTMASTERPLAN.PDF.

———. 2002b. Retrieved November 12 from www.sen.ca.gov/masterplan/020909THE MASTERPLANLINKS.HTML (Section 11—Appendices—Summary Recommendations). Recommendation 34.

———. 2002c. Retrieved November 12 from www.sen.ca.gov/masterplan/020909THE MASTERPLANLINKS.HTML (Section 11—Appendices—Summary Recommendations). Recommendation 35.

California Community Colleges mission. 2002. Retrieved November 12 from www.ucop.edu/acadinit/mastplan/cccmission.htm.

California master plan for higher education. 2003. Retrieved January 5 from www.univerisityofcalifornia.edu/aboutuc/masterplan.html.

California Postsecondary Education System. 2002. About the commission. Retrieved November 12 from www.cpec.ca.gov/SecondPages/Commissionhistory.asp.

The California State University. 2001. Shared governance reconsidered: Improving decision-making in the California State University. March 29. Retrieved November 12, 2002, from www.calstate.edu/acadsen/SharedGovReport.pdf.

Clark, B. 1983. *The higher education system: Academic organization in cross-national perspective.* Berkeley: University of California Press, pp. 234–35.

Education Commission of the States. 1994. *State Postsecondary Education Structures Handbook.* Denver, CO: Education Commission of the States, pp. 136–49.

Executive orders of the chancellor on consultation. 2002. Retrieved November 12 from www.cccco.edu/executive/consultation/excecutiveorders.htm.

Hamilton, N. W. 1999. Are we speaking the same language? Comparing AAUP and AGB. *Liberal Education* 85 (Fall): 24.

———. 2000. The academic profession's leadership role in shared governance. *Liberal Education* 86 (Summer): 15–16.

Higher Education Research Institute, UCLA. 1999. The American college teacher: 1998–1999 HERI faculty survey report. Los Angeles: Higher Education Research Institute.

Kaplan, G. 2002. Results from the 2001 survey on higher education governance. February. Retrieved November 12 from www.ksg.harvard.edu/2001survey/2001%20Governance%20Survey%20Results.pdf.

Kellogg Commission on the Future of State and Land-Grant Universities. 2000. Returning to our roots: Toward a coherent campus culture. Retrieved November 12, 2002, from www.nasulgc.org/Kellogg/kellogg.htm.

Kerr, C. 1994. *Higher education cannot escape history.* Buffalo: State University of New York Press.

MacTaggart, T. 2002. Paper on governance standards. January 19. Unpublished paper.

McGuiness, A. 2001. Governance and coordination: Definitions and distinctions. December. Retrieved November 12, 2002, from www.ecs.org/clearinghouse/31/62/3162.htm.

———. 2002. Models of postsecondary education coordination and governance. March. Retrieved November 12 from www.ecs.org/clearinghouse/34/23/3423.htm. Pp. 2–11.

Minnesota State Colleges and Universities strategic plan—2002–2005. 2002. Designing the future: A plan for serving students and communities. Draft version 7.0, June 13. Unpublished document.

MnSCU Citizen's Advisory Commission. 2002. Access to success (2). St. Paul: Minnesota State Colleges and Universities.

Standing order 105.1 of the Regents of California. 2002. Retrieved November 12 from www.ucop.edu/regents/bylaws/so105.html.

Standing orders of the chancellor on consultation. 2002. Retrieved November 12 from www.cccco.edu/executive/consultation/standing_orders.htm.

University of California Academic Senate Task Force report on governance. 1998. Findings of the Panel of Corporate Governance. April 4. Retrieved November 12, 2002, from www.ucop.edu/senate/p2final.html.

The University of North Carolina mission statement. 2002. September 28. Retrieved November 12 from www.northcarolina.edu/mission.cfm.

University System of Georgia vision statement. 2002. Retrieved November 12 from www.usg.edu/admin/regents/statements.html.

CHAPTER FOUR

The Ambiguous Future of Public Higher Education Systems

Terrence J. MacTaggart

It is increasingly difficult to talk about "public systems of higher education" as if they shared common structures, purposes, or even a future as bodies that govern or coordinate colleges and universities in the United States. To be sure, relations among governing and coordinating boards and the states have resisted equilibrium from the start (Berdahl 1971, p. 269). Yet instability is more profound and widespread now than in the past. In recent years several governing systems have disappeared completely, replaced by local campus governing boards and, sometimes, statewide coordinating agencies. Statewide coordinating boards have seen their budgets slashed well in excess of the cuts bestowed on higher education as a whole (Schmidt 2002, pp. A26–A27). Some systems are evolving into amorphous entities whose purposes seem to be dictated by political expediency rather than a durable concept of the public good.

This breakdown in the way most states have administered their higher education services for forty years raises important questions for educational leaders and policy makers, as well as students of governance. Do these changes herald a new era in which institutional ambitions combine with local political interests to trump a broad, statewide public agenda for higher education? Does the more competitive market that David Collis has outlined in chapter 2 inevitably provide a better substitute than bureaucracies, plans, and rules for assuring that public needs are met? In cases where both the market and old-style bureaucracies are found wanting, what effective alternatives exist? It is clear that in many states, confidence in systems of higher education has been shattered, but as yet there is little consensus on how it can be restored.

After discussing the fragmentation of system and coordinating board authority, I follow the lead established by Neil Hamilton in chapter 3 and offer case studies of individual states. I present the cases of Maryland and Florida as illustrations of many of the complexities surrounding the devolution of control from systems to campuses. Both states have restructured their higher education systems twice in recent years. Maryland represents a relatively thoughtful and politically mature approach to restructuring, although the effectiveness of the final product has yet to be tested. In Florida, political leaders have campaigned for grass-roots support in citizen referenda first to eliminate a system board, then to restore one. I describe some of the causes of these changes and comment on the consequences for the capacity of states to envision and carry out a higher education agenda that addresses public needs. Finally, I suggest some areas of study where new thinking and analysis might help policy makers come to better decisions about governance in the public interest.

Governing and Coordinating Structures

Roughly half of the states have chosen to congregate some or all of their public institutions under one or a few system governing boards. While no two states manage statewide governance in precisely the same way, still some generalities describing state structures are helpful. Clark Kerr and Marian Gade provide this widely accepted taxonomy of *governing* boards:

> *Consolidated governance systems:* One board covers all two-year and four-year campuses ("fully consolidated") or one board covers all four-year public campuses, including research universities and other four-year institutions ("partially consolidated"), with separate arrangements for two-year institutions. These systems "govern" because they appoint chief executive officers for the campuses as well as for the system. These are often referred to as "superboards."
>
> *Segmental systems:* Separate boards cover separate types of campuses, such as research universities, comprehensive colleges and universities, and community colleges.
>
> *Campus-level boards:* These boards are "autonomous" where they have full authority over a single campus and are not covered by a system board . . . They exercise "delegated authority," where they exist within a system but can make some decisions on their own . . . They are "advisory" where they exist within a system but can only give advice, not make binding decisions. (1989, pp. 116–17)

Although states oscillate between governing and coordinating structures, at any time about half of the states look to coordinating boards to regulate budget and program requests of their public institutions. Most states have employed relatively "strong" boards with significant control of the budget and programs, while other coordinating boards play largely advisory roles. And a handful of states, some with governing boards, host planning or service agencies without budget or academic program approval portfolios (McGuinness 1997, p. 58).

Kerr and Gade characterize *coordinating* boards this way:

> *Budgetary coordination:* The state's coordinating council prepares a single budget for all public institutions for submission to state authorities.
>
> *Advisory coordination:* A state advisory council advises on the budgets prepared by the individual segments and/or individual campuses.
>
> *Voluntary coordination:* Any coordination that exists is provided by the institutions on their own initiative, or by some "planning" agency outside the budget process. (p. 117)

Governing and Coordinating Roles Obscured

The once fairly consistent distinctions between system governing boards and statewide coordinating boards have blurred and are becoming more obscure as local campus boards assume more governing authority. System governing boards oversee multiple institutions, which themselves lack individual boards of trustees. Historically, governing board responsibilities have included hiring (and firing) campus presidents, approving (or denying) institutional budget requests, and program review and approval, as well as personnel matters such as union contract negotiations. It is for these reasons, I submit, that one does not see much faculty involvement on such boards. As Hamilton notes in the previous chapter, faculty are generally involved in issues of knowledge creation, and boards generally do not deal explicitly or extensively with such matters. Finally, the system executive, variously called either a president or a chancellor, serves as the direct supervisor of campus executives, represents the system in the legislature, and manages central administrative functions.

Coordinating boards, by contrast, regulate institutions or systems that in turn are overseen directly by their own governing boards. While they vary in authority, as Kerr and Gade point out, coordinating boards might comment upon or approve institutional or system board operating budget requests as well as evaluate programs and performance (p. 117).

Both governing and coordinating boards serve with different degrees of success as buffers between the institutions and political intrusion. However, system governing boards tend to advocate for the interests of the institutions they oversee. Coordinating boards often share closer relations with the governor's office, and it is increasingly common for governors to appoint coordinating executives directly from their own staffs.

These broad distinctions between governing and coordinating authority are breaking down as local institutional boards capture many of the responsibilities formerly held by these overarching entities. Partly in response to this diminished role, as well as in recognition of their reduced political status, several legislatures have dramatically downsized their coordinating entities (Schmidt 2002, pp. A26–A27). When individual colleges and universities assume greater responsibility for managing their own affairs, for example, for budget requests to the legislature, for renovation and new construction, for their own legal matters and internal auditing, for hiring and firing their presidents, then system boards come to look more like coordinating agencies. As the market replaces bureaucracy and rule for distributing resources and managing institutional boundaries, many system governing boards as well as coordinating boards feel themselves left without a familiar purpose.

Instability Becomes Normal

The most obvious feature of current academic governance is instability as states eliminate, consolidate, restructure, and often recreate in different forms their various governing and coordinating entities. In 1994 New Jersey replaced one of the strongest coordinating boards in the country with campus governing boards and a statewide agency with planning but not budget authority. Now New Jersey's current governor has taken on restructuring public higher education as a major priority for his administration. In addition to a proposed reconfiguration of the state's medical and research institutions, Governor Jim McGreevey has called for a summit to discuss reestablishing some central authority for the remaining public universities. West Virginia replaced its two governing boards with a new coordinating agency. The Florida Board of Education, a K–20 "super board" intended to oversee all public education in the state including elementary and secondary education, the community colleges, and eleven universities, replaced the Florida State University System as well as the community college board on July 1, 2001. Fifteen months later, following a hotly contested referendum, Florida's voters chose to restore some level of statewide governance for its comprehensive institutions through a new board of governors. The Sunshine State, however, will maintain its local campus boards and the K–20 "super board" as well.

In the early 1990s, Illinois eliminated two of its multicampus governing boards in favor of local campus boards, while retaining the strong statewide coordinating organization, the Illinois Board of Higher Education. In 1991 the Minnesota legislature passed a bill collapsing the three systems that governed its community colleges, technical colleges, and state universities into one larger system and marginalized its coordinating board. The merger itself took effect four years later. Maryland in 1988 and Colorado over several years liberated individual institutions to become independent public entities with their own boards of trustees no longer subject to system authority. At least ten other states are actively discussing governance change. As state leaders scramble for some way out of their continuing budget crises, conversations about restructuring have become more frequent and more serious if we agree with the conclusions drawn by Marginson and Collis in chapters 1 and 2.

Responsibility Shifts from Systems to Campuses

Many system governing boards and coordinating boards have been hollowed out as their authority over budgets, programs, and personnel matters shifts to constituent campuses.

As recently as 1992, D. Bruce Johnstone, the former chancellor of the State University of New York and a thoughtful commentator on the role of multicampus systems, could offer this confident summary of the responsibilities of system boards and their executives. His commentary is worth mentioning here in order to illustrate how far many states have moved in shifting authority from system to campus leaders. In addition to performing administrative services such as providing legal counsel and human resource policies, Johnstone describes key system functions as:

- Leadership to the system, to public higher education, and to higher education generally, including the establishment of a system-wide mission, the approval of constituent campus missions, and advocacy for the needs of the state and its students and its citizens;
- The appointment, compensation, periodic evaluation, occasional

removal, and constant support of campus or institutional chief operating officers;
- The allocation of resources among the institutions comprising the system;
- The assessment, approval, initiation, and rescission of academic programs and research endeavors;
- Policies and programs to ensure student access to the system as a whole;
- The oversight of board and system-wide policies dealing with the needs, interests, and behavior of students. (pp. 4–5)

What is striking about this list is the degree to which many states have devolved these responsibilities from systems to campuses. To be sure, "classic" governing systems with many of the features Johnstone describes continue in such states as California, the Dakotas, Georgia, North Carolina, and Wisconsin. Illinois, Kentucky, and Texas, among others, maintain strong and effective coordinating boards.

Yet in many other states the locus for the responsibilities Johnstone describes has shifted to the campuses. Prominent university presidents and political leaders have taken up the mantle of leadership, especially for aligning academic assets with economic development. Increasingly, local campus boards, rather than the system, dominate in selecting, and removing, presidents. In Maryland and Florida, state law and political leaders play a major role in deciding where the money goes, and in these states and elsewhere, approval authority for undergraduate programs remains at the campus. (However, the new board of governors in Florida may assert its right to program approval.)

Administrative functions have been decentralized as well. In Oregon, for example, the system achieved substantial administrative independence from the state during the early 1990s. More recently, campus presidents made a concerted effort to shift that authority to their institutions and to become much more independent of the Oregon University System. Partly in response to the presidents' initiative as well as in recognition of the bleak economic outlook for the state, Chancellor Richard Jarvis has proposed a creative new "deal" between the system and the state. In exchange for guaranteed funding, the system promises to limit tuition increases, balance such increases with financial aid, and grant greater operating autonomy to the campuses (OUS 2002, p. 2).

Most system and coordinating board executives report that their authority over constituent campuses has diminished in favor of a more laissez-faire, market-oriented approach (Epper 1999, p. 3; McGuinness 1997, p. 9).

Accelerants to Change

Why has the pace of restructuring accelerated over the past dozen years? Aims McGuinness identifies "perennial issues" (1997, p. 31) that lead these agencies and their executives to feel caught between the "dog and the fireplug" (Ashworth 2001). Frustration with program duplication, especially at the graduate level, conflict among aspiring institutions, legislative reaction to lobbying by competing institutions and systems, unjustifiable barriers to articulation and transfer, and concerns over the effectiveness of boards and their executives are among the chronic pressures that incite debate over restructuring (McGuinness 1997, pp. 31–32).

McGuinness also identifies several more contemporary reasons why the pace of governance change has quickened. He sees changes in government leadership, a declining consensus over the public purposes of higher education, and greater political involvement from legislators and their staffs as contributing to restructuring. He also notes that gaps between what the public expects from colleges and universities and the expectations of academics, as well as the pervasive influence of market-based views of how government should operate, are characteristic of the current environment (1997, pp. 34–39).

The closer one looks at the interplay of politics, personality, and policy in states where radical change has occurred or seems imminent, the more certain critical factors emerge. I characterize these as the failure of boards and executives to bridge the gulf between academic and political culture, rigidities within systems that prevent them from transcending their organizational boundaries, the determination and power of individual political leaders, the influence of reinventing government ideas championing decentralized authority and free market competition, and the lack of a clear role for systems in serving the public's legitimate expectations.

A Culture Gap

System leaders who have developed traits congenial to success in the academy often find themselves lacking the skills needed to make their case to the public and to compete with other agencies and interests in the statehouse. Systems may blame ambitious campuses and their leaders for fomenting discord, but this ignores the reality that successful systems incorporate campus goals into statewide initiatives as part of the process of assembling a political base. Successful system chancellors match a feel for sound educational policy with a flair for how to sell good ideas and gain support in the state capital.

Political savvy has always been a desirable trait in public educational leaders. However, in the current environment, with its interest group politics, term limits encouraging legislators to get action more quickly, and more intense competition for state dollars, stronger political skills have become essential. System leaders, who exhibit "the common touch," who communicate easily with politicians of all stripes, and who maintain their credibility with lawmakers inevitably will perform better than those who define themselves primarily as academic administrators.

New Political Strategies

As important as these skills may be, it is equally necessary to develop effective political strategies. Strategies that work include casting the system's budget request as a response to well-recognized state needs rather than the academy's priorities, exploiting a statewide system's potential for garnering grass-roots support from local communities, and recognizing that a skillfully designed agenda lends itself to coalition politics. Advocates for women's and minority rights, for the disabled, for business groups and organized labor can and have been outspoken supporters of the higher education agenda. Systems with personable leaders and broad-based political support tend not to be the objects of restructuring and can resist such attempts more easily than those perceived as isolated from the political and economic life of the state.

New Leadership Styles

In the face of this dissolution of authority, some individual system leaders have carved out new, activist roles for their organizations centered on influencing public opinion and political action. These entrepreneurial leaders seek greater support for their priorities by identifying their work with popular issues, especially work-force training and economic development. Many of these new-style leaders demonstrate an unprecedented presence in the halls of the capitol and wage sophisticated public campaigns to gain support. Internally, the most successful of these new leaders recognize that they must display collaborative leadership styles as well as the political acumen of majority leaders plagued with fractious members. If some leaders have adapted well to the new environment, it must be said that others seem adrift without the familiar scaffolding of bureaucratic authority.

Rigid Boundaries

However able leaders may be, there are also instances where it seems no amount of political savvy on the part of educators will avert restructuring. One of these situations occurs when existing governance structures are poorly designed to address "important cross-cutting issues" (McGuinness 1997, p. 38). For example, legislators in Minnesota had grown increasingly frustrated with the inability of three of its four higher education systems—one each for the state's community colleges, technical colleges, and state universities—to cooperate on a single agenda and to resolve problems of articulation and transfer. As proficient as the three system heads were in making the case for their organizations, some legislators were distressed by their inability to cooperate. This frustration enabled one strong political leader, state senate leader Roger Moe, to force an otherwise unpopular merger of these three systems. Structures designed to ensure the orderly development of their segment of higher education are often ill equipped to meet current demands for stronger ties with K–12 education or work-force development across two- and four-year institutions.

Activist Political Leaders

Political leaders determined to bring about change tip the governance debate from rhetoric to action. In 1991, Moe would not allow the Minnesota legislature to adjourn until they had passed *his* merger bill. He possessed the will and the power to turn back repeated efforts over the next four years to repeal the merger legislation. Certainly the changes in Maryland, New Jersey, and Florida would not have occurred were it not for the priority given restructuring by Governors Schaeffer, Whitman, and Bush. Moreover, the most recent restructuring in Florida would not have occurred without the initiative of the popular former governor, now senator, Bob Graham. If New Jersey returns to some form of centralized coordination of its comprehensive universities, it will be because Governor McGreevey leads the charge. With tight budgets preventing most governors from proposing high-cost initiatives, we can be assured that some activist governors will turn to restructuring proposals as a way to make their marks.

Reinventing Higher Education

A preference for market-oriented practices for delivering public services remains strong among politicians who believe that less government is better government. Studies arguing that privatization is not inevitably superior to public management (Donahue 1989, p. 13) and the political clout of public employee unions resistant to privatization and decentralization will likely have limited effect. Republican governors, who continue at this writing to rule in a majority of the states, generally prefer options of less government oversight and fewer regulations. Thus, it is not surprising that two Republican governors, Christine Todd Whitman in 1994 and Jeb Bush in 2001, reduced statewide coordination. However, Democratic governors also have supported vesting more authority in individual institutions; Parris Glendenning of Maryland approved, though he did not actively lead, the most recent restructuring in that state. The continuing widespread influence of the reinventing government movement among leaders in both major parties will contribute to continuing interest in governance restructuring.

Unconnected to the Public Agenda

Finally, there is a growing awareness of the need for public higher education to tie into a compelling "public agenda" that transcends traditional academic and institutional self-interest. Thus far, definitions of the agenda focus on educating the new work force in states with growing populations, preparing more students for knowledge-intensive industries, developing the current work force so as to improve a state's ability to compete for jobs, and conducting research that can be commercialized in the short term. Some reform-minded researchers have argued that higher education should adopt a broader social agenda including initiatives like civic engagement and adult literacy (The National Center 2002, pp. 5A–6A). However, efforts to embrace this more liberal and far-reaching agenda have been spotty.

While some coordinating-board states, notably Illinois, Kentucky, Texas, and a few others, are successfully identifying their raison d'être with a public agenda, many coordinating boards and systems are not. Instead, individual institutions, including some of the land grants and many urban comprehensives, have identified themselves with this popular political property. In some instances, systems are viewed as stultifying university efforts to respond to public needs. Systems and statewide agencies that do not associate themselves with a compelling public agenda or are unable to redefine the agenda so they have a crucial role in delivering it face an uncertain future.

Governance Change in Maryland

Maryland has substantially restructured system-level governance twice in the past fifteen years. In 1988, the state combined the state college system and the universities comprising the University of Maryland to create the University System of Maryland (originally named the University of Maryland System) as a unified organization with one executive, the chancellor. Ten years later, another governor established a task force, popularly dubbed the Larson Commission after the able retired navy admiral who chaired it, to examine governance and finance in higher education. Acting on the recommendations of the Larson Commission, the legislature shifted much of the system's authority to the constituent universities, substituting a more competitive market for central coordination and leadership. Pierce and Hagstrom (1983) subtitle their analysis of Maryland as "the Superimposed Civilizations." They go on to describe the unstable political substrate of the state:

> Maryland fits only reluctantly into a single portrait. What, after all, does the blue-collar port city of Baltimore, 55 percent black, have in common with the Washington, D.C., suburb of Montgomery County, which has among the highest family incomes in the nation? What do the watermen of the somnolent Eastern Shore have in common with the residents of mountain-locked Cumberland? What do people who live in the almost continuous string of middle-class suburbs from Washington to Baltimore, in Prince Georges and Anne Arundel and Baltimore Counties, have in common with the others? Not very much, except that they all live within Maryland's convoluted boundaries. (p. 126)

Against this background, in 1988 activist governor William Schaefer set out in the second year of his first term to unite the fragmented collections of institutions in Maryland. Influenced in part by the Hobitzell Commission, which recommended, among other things, a marked strengthening of the State Board of Higher Education (Berdahl and Schmidtlein 1996, pp. 165–66), Governor Schaefer intended to create a strong centralized governing board that could harness the state's diverse institutions in service of public needs. Governor Schaefer reportedly wanted to "push one button" (Berdahl and Schmidtlein 1996, p. 165) in bringing about change. He felt that a united higher education system under one executive and single board of trustees would give him one number to call.

Schaefer inherited the five campuses of the University of Maryland system under President John Toll and a board of trustees; the six campuses of the baccalaureate regional institutions with a system executive and system trustees; two public campuses with their own boards—Morgan State and St. Mary's College; a state board for the seventeen community colleges; and a coordinating board to oversee all this, the State Board for Higher Education.

What actually resulted from a sinuous debate in the legislature that involved nearly every faction within high education differed radically from the governor's original design.

Expectations Thwarted

In their incisive study of the prism of political forces that distorted the governor's proposal on its path to becoming law, Berdahl and Schmidtlein understate that "the results from the reformed structure were very mixed" (1996, p. 189). A partial list of their thoughts on the gaps between expectations of major players and the actual consequences follows:

- The flagship campus at College Park and its advocates expected budget increases and special recognition as the state's leading research institution. However, following two years of increases, the flagship experienced the same level of reductions as the rest of the institutions in the recession of the early 1990s. Although the new chancellor, Don Langenberg, appeared sympathetic to College Park's requests for special treatment, the flagship campus and its advocates felt strongly that it would never reach its potential so long as it remained shackled by regulations of a system that included smaller and less prestigious institutions.

- "The mess in Baltimore" (p. 190), referring to the separate institutions in the Baltimore area which the *Baltimore Sun* felt should be merged or better coordinated to yield one preeminent research university, remained largely unchanged following merger. As Berdahl and Schmidtlein point out, "even the Joint Graduate School of UMB [University of Maryland Baltimore] and UMBC [University of Maryland Baltimore County] has not opened its ranks to qualified faculty from other institutions in the area" (p. 190). Thus, another major expectation, one especially important to the editors of the region's largest newspaper, remained unsatisfied.

- The two public institutions with their own boards preserved their autonomy from the system and in so doing not only strengthened the case for a stronger coordinating board but also served as a constant reminder to others that schools outside the system could do better than those within. Morgan State, one of the four predominantly black institutions in the state and the only one outside the system, received better funding than the others in part because its leaders enjoyed "direct access to the governor's office in ways not usually encouraged from within the UM system" (p. 190). St. Mary's College, the other public institution outside the system, in return for agreeing to limits on its state funding, got its own governing board and substantial operational freedom from state control. Under the leadership of an entrepreneurial president, it experienced great success in private fund-raising and attracted national recognition as a public liberal arts college.

- Instead of a strong *governing* board uniting all of the baccalaureate and graduate institutions that Governor Schaeffer sought, Maryland received a system board with somewhat compromised authority for those institutions along with a much stronger *coordinating* board— the Maryland Higher Education Commission(MHEC). Since the governor appointed this board's executive from a list of three and that executive occupied a seat on his cabinet, MHEC was better positioned than the system to capture gubernatorial support. Its first secretary, Shaila Aery, proved especially adept at using this advantage to enhance the credibility of MHEC, often at the expense of the system. Although relations between MHEC and the system improved in later years, political leaders remained skeptical of the system's effectiveness. The responsibilities of both boards overlapped and were confusing to educators and legislators alike. The institutions in particular felt overly constrained by these two layers of bureaucratic authority (pp. 190–91).

Donald Langenberg, the first executive of the new system, a distinguished physicist and for several years head of the National Association of System Heads, is justly credited with some important achievements. He pushed through improvements in the use of technology, student transfer, and administrative efficiencies including capital planning and procurement (p. 191). Langenberg also championed closer ties between higher education and K–12. Yet rivalries among institutions and competing demands from regions in this state of "superimposed civilizations," along with a chronic dissatisfaction with the system in the legislature, continued and led in 1998 and 1999 to another major overhaul of governance in Maryland.

A Second Restructuring in Maryland

A decade after the creation of the system, a different governor, Parris Glendenning, along with the legislature, created a twenty-three-member commission to study governance and finance of the University System of Maryland. Whatever the official mandate for the review, it was in fact driven by the ambitions of the College Park campus for greater freedom to seek resources from the state, the aspirations of Towson University for resources and greater autonomy in initiating new programs, the perennial concerns of advocates of Baltimore and the historically African-American institutions, and the continuing dissatisfaction of the legislature with the system. Thus the sources of discontent that drove the 1988 restructuring remained to animate the new one ten years later. As part of a team from the Association of Governing Boards (AGB) retained by the commission to make recommendations on governance change, I had the opportunity in 1998 and 1999 to interview educational and political leaders.

Senate Bill 682

With several university presidents, as well as influential legislators, sitting on the task force, it is not surprising that, as translated into Senate Bill 682 and passed into law in the spring of 1999, the AGB's recommendations combined to reduce system authority and endow the presidents and their local boards of trustees with greater independence. Bill 682 recognized College Park's desire for greater eminence by guaranteeing it special financial support and the opportunity, in statute, of meeting with the governor to make its case for resources beyond the system recommendation. Towson and the other institutions were empowered to offer new academic programs without system or coordinating board approval for a period of three years. Other provisions in the lengthy sixty-five-page bill combined to reduce the authority of Maryland's coordinating board for budget and program oversight as well.

Although the system and the board of regents remain, they hold less authority than before the passage of Senate Bill 682. They retained responsibility for the selection and evaluation of presidents, for initial budget planning, and for setting expectations for institutional performance. The system also became a public corporation with greater independence from several state regulatory agencies.

Following this restructuring, an editorial in the *Baltimore Sun* on the search for a chancellor to replace Langenberg calls attention to the challenge facing his successor: "It's critical that the next chancellor understand the secondary role he or she will play in unifying higher-education personalities and building support for the university. This isn't a power post in the traditional sense" (Picking a chancellor 2001, p. 1).

In 2002, the regents persuaded William Kirwin, a former president of the University of Maryland at College Park, to leave Ohio State and return to Maryland to assume the role of chancellor. It is ironic that while president at College Park, Kirwin argued that the system stymied the development of the flagship campus's drive to reach the top tier of research institutions. Many observers agree that a major challenge now facing this experienced and personable leader will be to unite the highly autonomous campuses, and especially College Park, in a common agenda.

Governance Change in Florida

A "perfect storm" is the metaphor one seasoned Florida observer used to describe the deluge of political forces that led to the fall of the board of regents of the Florida State University System (Trombley 2001, p.7). Beginning with a citizens' referendum endorsing a "system of free public education" in 1988, by July 1, 2001, the old regime had been supplanted by a combination of a new statewide board of education whose control spanned all primary, secondary, and higher education in the Sunshine State and local university boards for each of the state's eleven public universities (p. 4). Just fifteen months later, Florida voters chose to restructure higher education again by endorsing a new board of governors to oversee the public universities, while retaining the local campus trustees. Florida eclipses most other states in the neon intensity of its political life, yet it represents only an extreme example of the forces that are disrupting contemporary higher education governance.

Florida created a statewide board of regents for the State University System of Florida in 1965 (a less imposing board had actually existed since 1905) in large part to shield academia from one of the most egregious examples of political interference in the nation's history. A legislative committee, known after its chair as the Johns Committee, investigated suspected communism and homosexuality in Florida's universities over a nine-year period beginning in the 1950s. At least thirty-nine professors and deans at three universities were fired as a consequence of this legislative commission (Trombley 2001, p. 3). Another consequence was the creation in 1965 of the Florida board of regents to oversee its growing universities and, importantly, to buffer them from the kind of political interference represented by the Johns Committee.

The storm that tore apart the state's thirty-four-year-old system of higher education and replaced it with one more responsive to political influence may have gathered force with the refusal of the regents, under then chancellor Adam Herbert, to bow to legislative demands to create new professional programs in their districts. By spurning legislative ambitions to initiate a new medical school at Florida State University and new law schools at Florida International University and Florida A&M on the grounds of cost, the regents alienated powerful legislators. Among the most influential of these was John Thrasher, a former speaker of the Florida House of Representatives and a graduate of Florida State. The legislature overrode the regents and created the new schools anyway (Trombley 2001, p. 6).

Herbert angered the St. Petersburg delegation by refusing to consider a local citizen as a candidate for the University of South Florida on the basis of relevant qualifications (Trombley 2001, p. 6). It is ironic that by exercising their classic responsibility as a buffer between the universities and ambitious politicians, the regents and the chancellor contributed to the demise of the system.

While key legislators sought the overthrow of the system for political reasons, the popular governor, Jeb Bush, favored it on the grounds that less government represented better government. He also reportedly believed that a "seamless system that is more student oriented" could be achieved with one "super board" overseeing education at all levels in the state (Trombley 2001, p. 5). Bush has consistently pursued devolutionary policies, but it must also be said that the chance to name over a hundred new trustees to prestigious positions on eleven local campus boards is an attractive opportunity any politician would relish. Bush's initial selections for trustee positions came largely from his majority party (Klein 2001, p. 1B).

There is some disagreement surrounding the voters' intentions in the 1988 referendum. The citizens approved a "system of free public education" (Trombley 2001, p. 4), yet many in the state argue that this did not imply uniting governance of K–12 with higher education. Whatever changes the voters thought they had approved, they intended it to take place in January 2003. The legislature accelerated the process so that the new regime came into being eighteen months sooner on July 1, 2001.

The legislature retained its prerogatives in other areas of local concern as well. For example, thanks to the initiative of a powerful local legislator, New College, formerly a 650-student unit of the University of South Florida, became the eleventh state university. Another powerful legislator, state senator Don Sullivan, assured that two branches of the University of South Florida in St. Petersburg and Sarasota got greater independence, including separate budget authority and the right to seek separate accreditation (Klein and Rado 2001, p. 1B). The legislature also granted the state's community colleges the authority to seek approval to grant bachelor's degrees in some fields.

A Second Restructuring in Florida

Criticizing the new structure for reopening public higher education to "political meddling" (Trombley 2001, p. 3), the well-regarded former governor and now senator Bob Graham led a vigorous and well-financed campaign to restore a statewide governing board. To lend more stability to his proposed new board, he cast the proposition (Amendment 11 on the ballot) as a constitutional change that could be revised again only through a popular vote. His plan was to create a board of governors to restore a buffer between the campuses and the politicians. Sixty percent of the voters agreed with Graham. On Election Day in November 2002, they approved a compromise structure that includes a statewide board of governors intended to oversee the public universities and insulate them to a degree from political intrusion.

The new board shares authority with campus trustees. The board of governors will hold approval authority for new programs and facilities, negotiate contracts with faculty and other unions, determine the powers of local trustees, and appoint nearly half of the local board members. The campus boards retain the right to set tuition and hire and fire presidents (Peltz 2002, p. 7B).

The battle over governance issues was hotly contested, with faculty unions, several major editorial writers, some businesses, and the Democratic gubernatorial candidate supporting Graham's initiative. Governor Bush, the higher education executive, Jim Horne, his board chair, and the local campus boards and their presidents opposed the constitutional amendment.

In the course of the debate, Graham argued that constitutional status would restore some stability to the system and bring "cost-savings to Florida taxpayers from looking at higher education as a system, as opposed to warring parties" (Peltz 2002, p. 7B). Consistent with his preferences for local control, in defending his "reform," Governor Bush contended that his approach would serve better by joining authority and responsibility at the university level (p. 7B).

Faculty Unions Engage

Union support consisted of voter turnout drives and financial contributions. The faculty lined up with the Graham initiative for several reasons. Faculty unions generally feel that they will experience more consistent and professional contract administration when the employer of record is a large system rather than an individual campus. It is also true that in a system the compensation levels of the highest paid faculty, typically those at the most prestigious research institutions and professional schools, are thought to act as leavening for higher pay levels across the board. In this case, faculty were also concerned with what they regarded as the politicization of the local boards and perceived threats to academic freedom. The chief of the professors union contended that under the decentralized approach, "political appointees control everything about academic freedom and legislators have the power to dry up any university's money if they don't like what is going on." He expressed the hope that the new system would provide a "buffer that insulates higher education institutions against politicians" (Peltz 2002, p. 7B).

Consequences Uncertain

It is too soon to say if the board of governors will be effective in at least impeding the penchant of Florida's legislators to call the shots at its universities. The new seventeen-member board includes fourteen members appointed by the governor who opposed its creation, plus the commissioner of education, the chair of the advisory council of the faculty senates, and the president of the Florida Student Association. The majority of members of the local campus boards will also be the governor's appointees. The chairman of the Florida Board of Education, Jim Handy, reportedly assured the university presidents that Bush's appointments to the new board of governors would share the governor's views and that they, in turn, would simply reappoint members to the campus boards (Universities to keep Bush plan 2002, p. B5). At this time, the legislature has not enacted enabling legislation, nor has there been a determination of the power relationships among the board of governors, the campus boards, and the existing board of education.

In the power vacuum left by the departure of the board of regents, the presidents of Florida's eleven universities have formed an advocacy group entitled the State University Presidents Association. Two presidents, Gordon Michaelson of New College of Florida and Sandy D'Alemberte of Florida State, opposed making the consortium formal on the grounds that it might create conflict with the board of education (Powers 2002, p. B2). The group's initial actions were to speak out against two items on the November 2002 ballot: a proposal to reduce class size in K–12 and the Senator Bob Graham initiative to eliminate the statewide board (Brewer 2002, p. 1B). Following the election, which endorsed a return to some statewide governance, the presidents have pledged to cooperate with the new model.

Comparisons and Contrasts

From a distance, there are similarities between the restructuring in Maryland and Florida. Following widespread but not universal dissatisfaction with the first attempts, both set about governance change a second time. Currently, both have a system governing board—Maryland retained its existing board, Florida recreated one—that shares substantial authority with numerous local governing boards. While the Florida board of governors, as defined in the 2002 referendum that gave it life, is supposed to "be responsible for the coordinated and accountable operation of the whole university system" (Florida Department of State 2002, p. 1), still local campus boards select their own presidents. It appears that the Florida Board of Education will retain some as yet undefined authority over the new system board. Maryland's board of regents selects campus presidents, but it shares power with the coordinating board and with local campus boards. In sum, trustees on both boards, including those to be named in Florida and those sitting in Maryland, wield substantially less authority than their predecessors.

Process Differences

If the outcome of restructuring in both states is roughly similar, there are striking differences in the *process* in each case. From its initiation in 1988 when Governor Schaeffer announced that he wanted to "push one button" (Berdahl and Schmidtlein 1996, p. 165) to get results in higher education, the restructuring package followed a tortuous path through the political process and resulted in legislation that perpetuated frustrations among universities and interest groups. A decade later, Maryland adopted a more deliberative approach. The

1999 change legislation in Maryland followed closely the recommendations of the Larson Commission, which spent months hearing testimony and deliberating over options and alternatives. In addition to college presidents, the Larson Commission included key legislators thus helping to ensure broad-based support for its recommendations.

Governor Bush and one of his key advisors, it has been reliably reported, sketched out the new system in Florida on a napkin one evening in a restaurant (Trombley 2001, p. 5). To be sure, task forces played a role in the Florida transition, but political will and political action clearly dominated the process. As we have seen, the second governance change in Florida came about after a battle pitting an incumbent governor against a former one, a Democratic gubernatorial candidate against a Republican one, and faculty unions against campus presidents and trustees.

Policy Differences

The issues highlighted in the policy debates differed in both states as well. If the change process in Florida was largely political, political intrusion also represented a key policy difference. In the ramp up to the plebiscite in Florida, an editorial writer for the *St. Petersburg Times* wrote that by replacing the board of regents, "Florida has replaced any semblance of independence with pure politics" (Traxler 2002, p. 1B). In championing the cause for restoration of a system board, Senator Graham emphasized the buffering role that the board of governors would play in partially separating the universities from activist politicians. For his part, Governor Bush emphasized the virtues of local control and responsibility in making the case for largely independent local governing boards.

Certainly Maryland's legislative leaders worked to insure that institutions in their regions were treated fairly in the change process. Yet in Maryland the issues driving change had little to do with the legitimacy of legislative involvement. Instead, the debate focused on ensuring that campuses received enough independence and access to resources to fulfill their missions. After discussion of the merits of retaining the board of regents and the role of that group and the coordinating board, the Larson Commission and ultimately the legislature chose to retain these comprehensive boards but to grant more independence to the constituent institutions and special status to the flagship campus at College Park. Thus, the debate in Maryland addressed the governance complexities of enabling regional institutions to respond to community interests, encouraging presidents to be more entrepreneurial, and recognizing the distinct needs and potential contributions of the preeminent research university, all the while creating a workable balance of power and function among campuses, regional interests, and the state as a whole.

Change as Parable

The changes in Maryland and Florida offer insights for other states contemplating governance reform and to educational leaders and others seeking to understand the current restlessness. Given the idiosyncrasies of political history and culture in each state, it is difficult to hold up one or the other as a model other than to underline the obvious point that using a broadly representative commission with a widely respected chair makes great sense. Instead, it is probably more helpful to attempt to understand what actions (and inactions), pressures, ideas, and interests, contributed to the drama of restructuring as these deeper elements will be present in other states as well.

The accelerants to change listed earlier offer a useful entrée to the broader relevance of these two cases. I earlier identified five factors that contribute to the current dizzying pace of governance change. These include the failure of higher education leaders to bridge the culture gap between academic administration and the statehouse, rigidities in systems that preclude them from resolving problems that cut across educational sectors, the determination of individual political leaders, the reinventing government movement, and the gap between the behaviors of systems and the most widespread and deeply felt needs of society.

Cultural Conflicts

The culture of academic administrators reflects a preference for rational decision making, for evaluating options in light of academic values such as quality and reputation, for lengthy discussion of options, and a vocabulary more Latinate than vernacular, to name just a few features. By contrast, the statehouse culture is built on compromise and quid pro quos, trade-offs among interests, the chronic need to establish a majority within a committee and on the floor, and a preference for the language of the people. While acknowledging that the chancellors in Florida and Maryland held strong academic values and were men of great integrity, observers in both states concur that they were less comfortable engaging the politicians in Tallahassee (Trombley 2001, p. 7) and Annapolis.

In addition to possessing the common touch, educational leaders are more effective if they exercise the skills of communicating easily with legislators, realize that political coalitions are essential, and orchestrate their own formal or informal caucuses to support higher education. Systems and public institutions whose spokespersons don't speak the language of the legislature will not represent their interests well. Partly because they cannot find candidates from academia with these attributes, boards of trustees nationally turn more frequently to former legislators and political leaders to head up their systems and institutions. At this writing, three Florida politicians are active or likely candidates for presidential vacancies in their home state (James 2002, p. B1).

Rigid or Ambiguous Boundaries

Insofar as systems allow their natural organizational boundaries to prevent them from addressing what McGuinness calls "cross-cutting issues" (1997, p. 38), they increase the likelihood that political leaders will seek restructuring as a way to get these problems solved. The shift to a K–12 model in Florida in 2001 illustrates this point. The abrasion between structures designed to manage a segment of education and the needs of the state that cut across those structures will likely intensify as states emphasize improving K–12 education and workforce training. In Kentucky, this led to a much stronger coordinating board committed to reform across all educational sectors. Higher education leaders who are unable to transcend their conventional borders may find those borders erased along with their offices.

Confusion over responsibilities creates pressure for change. Ambiguous boundaries between the Maryland Higher Education Commission and the board of regents frustrated colleges and universities, confused legislators, and became a major topic of the Larson Commission. Retained in part to accommodate the needs of the powerful independent sector as well as the two independent public institutions in Maryland, MHEC continues in Maryland with a diminished role.

Activist Leaders

Enough has been said about the role of political leaders in galvanizing the various interests and pressures to bring about change. Suffice it to say that with depleted treasuries forestalling initiatives with real price tags, governors and powerful legislators wishing to make their mark will be tempted to turn to governance reforms whose costs are less apparent.

The Entrepreneurial Ideology

Since the publication of Osborne and Gaebler's book, which gave a name to the reinventing government movement in 1992, finding market-based ways to deliver public services has been a goal of politicians in both major parties. In contrast to the centralizing intentions of the 1988 restructuring in Maryland, Senate Bill 682, which incorporates the recommendations of the Larson Commission, makes the point that "the presidents of University institutions must have significant autonomy to manage their institutions" (1999, p. 5). That bill goes on to remove program approval and other "barriers to the ability of University institutions to respond quickly to public demands and needs" (p. 5). In the past, systems and coordinating agencies were expected to restrain university ambitions for growth in programs and funding. Now they are criticized for hampering responsiveness to local needs and markets. Institutions aspiring to manage with fewer constraints will abet preferences for decentralized organizations, nimble and responsive institutions, and degrees of privatization. Both pressures suggest that devolution will continue for the foreseeable future.

Lost Rationale

From the 1960s through the early 1990s, statewide governing bodies endured because they were thought to be preferable to unbridled competition or direct control from the governor's office. Further, these agencies were thought to add value by restraining institutional ambitions, adjudicating disputes and rivalries among institutions and regions, offering one voice in the legislature, and bringing some rationality to planning and distributing resources. Now that the benefits of the marketplace have eclipsed the virtues of centralized management and discipline, systems need to find a different raison d'être.

A recent report of the National Center for Public Policy and Higher Education states the problem clearly: "In the absence of deliberate policy, discretionary choice and individual pursuit of opportunity—often described as the workings of markets—become increasingly powerful forces determining the shape and direction of a state's higher education institutions. One expression of this phenomenon is the declining power of many state systems of higher education to oversee or contain the growth and ambitions of individual institutions within a state" (2002, p. 3A).

Without effective statewide governance, the report goes on to argue, the market alone will not meet even a basic public agenda calling for "broad access, economic development, a publicly engaged citizenry, a skilled work force, and research that promotes improved standards of living" (p. 5A).

Systems that exert focused statewide leadership on this public agenda and maintain as much institutional independence as possible represent an effective paradigm. To the extent they actually deliver measurable improvements in participation, the economy, and so on, they will also perform an important public service.

Choices for Policy Leaders

The changes in Maryland, Florida, and across the country raise a number of questions affecting the possibilities for statewide governance in the contemporary political environment in many states. These questions include: What processes seem to work best in engineering durable new structures? What structural models are emerging to reflect the changing demographic and political landscape? And where should the balance between free-market competition among institutions and state oversight of them be struck?

Change Processes

Since systems and coordinating boards are typically the creation of state legislatures, it remains the prerogative of governors and legislators to eliminate, change, and recreate governing structures when in their minds circumstances demand change. While it is certain that policy makers will increasingly look to structural change, what remains open for debate is the means they will employ. Typical processes include a "blue-ribbon" commission, submitting a bill through the legislature, citizen referenda, the efforts of a single strong political leader, trustee-led change within a large system, and summits bringing together civic, business, political, and educational leaders. Most often several of these processes will be combined. For example, the work of the Larson Commission in Maryland laid the policy and political groundwork that led to passage of Senate Bill 682.

The Maryland approach has much to offer as a model, with its broadly representative commission, testimony from campus leaders and presumably unbiased outside experts, and a carefully crafted final report that largely defined the legislation. A political consensus formed during the commission hearings and debates, and thus the legislative process proceeded smoothly and the new structure has been widely accepted. States that rely largely on political processes alone, either the legislative process or citizen referenda, often find this consensus lacking. In these cases, the change faces strong resistance, as in a 1991 restructuring in Minnesota, or outright attempts to overturn it, as happened in Florida.

Emerging Structures

Changing demographics, the rise of city-states, shifts in the political power of regions, and ethnic and interest-group politics bring pressure to change governance structures that were designed to accommodate different political environments. Colleges and universities, particularly those in urban areas, are becoming too important to their regions and too politically connected to be ruled by a statewide governing entity whose headquarters is located in the capital or a rival region. Governance models are changing to reflect this more complex political and economic landscape.

In the past, larger states with distributed economic and population centers have tended to favor local institutional governing boards coupled with statewide coordinating boards. Illinois and Ohio illustrate this model. Exceptions to this preference, of course, include Georgia, North Carolina, and Wisconsin, all of which host durable statewide governing boards.

Future governing structures will be hybrids of current models, with power more widely distributed among campuses, statewide governing entities, and the executive and legislative branches. State regulatory agencies such as departments of finance will likely play a lesser role than in the past. Although Maryland retained its system governing board and the voters of Florida choose to recreate theirs, both boards have less authority than in the past, and their governing responsibilities are broadly shared with their constituent campuses.

A mismatch between governing structures and expectations for them represents a constant danger during restructuring. New Jersey, at the instigation of Governor McGreevey, is examining a unique new structure for Rutgers, the University of Medicine and Dentistry of New Jersey, and the New Jersey Institute of Technology that would recombine elements of these schools into three institutions located in the north, central, and southern parts of the state. The three, each with their own president, would be affiliated under a system executive designated as the chancellor. The ambiguities are highlighted in the executive summary of the report of the commission proposing the change. On the one hand, each of the new universities "would have significant academic and administrative autonomy" and would be "largely independent" (Commission 2002, p. 2). Yet the chancellor of the new system, to be called the University of New Jersey, would have the powers of "hiring university presidents, writing the budget requests, approving new schools, system-wide planning, and relations with government and other external parties" (p. 2). These apparent conflicts may be resolved as the proposal is further defined.

There remains a tendency in many states to create hybrid agencies with expectations for leadership that conflict with campus expectations for independence. The result is a muddled paradigm for governance that is unlikely to be effective or durable.

Limits to Free-Market Competition

Both the 1999 restructuring in Maryland and 1988 change in Florida were conducted in the name of applying something like free-market principles to higher education. Yet both states ultimately chose to put some constraints on what otherwise would have been almost unfettered competition among rival institutions. To date, only Michigan, with its unique, constitutionally protected, and long-standing model of institutional independence (Peterson and McLendon 1998, p. 158) and New Jersey, which developed a council of presidents to offer a modest degree of coordination (Greer 1998, p. 100), exist without some more or less authoritative restraint on competition. As mentioned earlier, Governor McGreevey is encouraging a discussion of the return to some kind of central authority in New Jersey.

For all the rhetoric extolling the benefits of laissez-faire competition for students and dollars, at the end of the day preferences for some level of control and coordination prevail. The precise structure of these newly recalibrated instruments for governance, their specific responsibilities, and evaluating their effectiveness in managing public higher education to serve public interests should be carefully considered.

Rethinking Governance

This deep uncertainty surrounding governance in many states creates several opportunities to rethink both the role of statewide coordination and how it might best be exercised. With renewed interest in defining and pursuing a public agenda for higher education which transcends institutional advancement, students of governance should focus on what governance structures best support pursuit of fundamental public needs. Assuming that a public agenda is not exclusively the province of public-sector institutions raises the question of appropriate roles for independent and for-profit colleges and universities. For the public sector in particular, we need a deeper understanding of what constitutes an effective balance between institutional autonomy and self-governance on the one hand and state control on the other.

Defining and Implementing a Public Agenda

The public agenda for higher education is an economic one, at least in the minds of most policy makers consulted as part of a study of how several states are deploying their higher education assets to respond to public needs (Mac-Taggart and Mingle 2002, p. 4). Work force development at all levels and applied research that can be fairly quickly commercialized constitute the most compelling rationales for public funding of higher education. However, some of those interviewed as part of the study mentioned a general yearning for a more humanistic role for higher education in their states. Some described this work in terms of creating a stronger public awareness of culture, philosophy, the arts, and the duties of responsible citizenship. Still others cast the argument for public higher education in terms of social justice. Citing John Rawls's *Justice as Fairness* (1971), one commentator envisioned broad access to higher education for all social classes as a fundamental obligation of a just society. Suffice it to say, however, the preponderance of opinion saw the role of higher education as preparing individuals for greater career opportunity and for upgrading the work force. Sandra Ruppert confirms that state legislative leaders share the view that higher education's chief purpose is to support economic opportunity and development (2001, p. 1).

There is little doubt about what the public wants, although there is plenty of comment from would-be reformers from across the intellectual spectrum on what the public needs. The National Center for Public Policy and Higher Education in their 2002 *Policy Perspectives* laments the "deafening silence" (p. 3A) with which most public and independent institutions have met the center's national report cards on state performance. As noted earlier, this essay also finds that the diminution in the power of statewide governing and coordinating agencies makes it even less likely that institutions will make the public's wants their chief priority (p. 3A). The current challenge is to develop new thinking on policies and practices that actually will enable or require institutions to respond to public priorities.

There are several promising avenues for research and reflection on this theme. One is to connect case studies of what seem to be effective state practices with rigorous quantitative analysis of results. Recognizing that it is notoriously difficult to attribute specific causes to, say, increases in participation by low-income persons, research combining quantitative analysis with informed, qualitative judgments on college and university programs still would be a useful contribution to policy making.

It also would be useful to develop alternatives for the functions and authority of system and coordinating boards in better connecting institutions to public priorities. McGuinness's thoughts on a new model for effective governance (1996, pp. 203–29) might serve as a springboard for thinking about policies and structures that give a greater role to market forces. For example, in lieu of management by rule, system and coordinating boards might act as brokers between the state and its institutions. New or modified strategies might include seeking bids from independent and for-profit educational as well as public vendors for well-defined services and negotiating and overseeing charters granted to specific institutions. Detailed models for potentially more effective state governance policies and structures would be very useful for policy makers wishing better alternatives than ad hoc approaches.

Finally, fresh thinking on how the public agenda might be served by public, independent, and for-profit institutions would enliven the debate. Such a discussion might begin by questioning what is distinctively "public" about public colleges and universities beyond state support. Since institutions in the independent sector are in fact reliant on state support—through direct subsidy in a few cases, indirectly through student financial aid in most cases, and through a "tax subsidy" by virtue of their tax-free status—it would be interesting to speculate on what their obligations to support a public agenda might be. The expanding for-profit sector operates largely free of state oversight once approval to offer programs has been granted. These academic endeavors feature highly efficient delivery models, a clear focus on target student populations, and a far greater willingness to evaluate learning results than conventional institutions. Should these institutions be encouraged to participate more fully in the task of meeting broader public needs, and, if so, how would that be accomplished?

Reexamining the Balance between Autonomy and Control

The clear trend of the past several years has been toward granting greater independence to individual institutions and relying less on central authority. This devolutionary process has been driven by a complex amalgam of institutional and regional aspirations, frustration with governing systems, and a widespread belief that decentralization, deregulation, and a free-market approach would be more effective. Now that we have more examples of devolution in practice, we are in a better position to judge its effectiveness. In particular, it will be important to discern if this newfound freedom has resulted in measurable improvements in access for low-income and minority students, in better preparation of a work force, in affordability, in completion rates, and, where appropriate, in research that actually benefits society. In other words, to what extent has the new autonomy contributed to the public agenda as opposed to a more strictly academic agenda of institutional enhancement?

Based on the few examples of Michigan, New Jersey, and the charter college concept at St. Mary's College of Maryland, in 1998 I concluded that experiments in deregulation resulted in no worse outcomes for access and, in some instances, substantially better qualitative results. I did observe that a more competitive environment did not reduce costs to the taxpayer or consumers (MacTaggart 1998, p. 177). Now that we have more examples to study, these conclusions should be reexamined.

Students of higher education governance might focus on questions such as these. Under what conditions do free-market principles work best? Using Berdahl's distinctions between procedural and substantive autonomy (1998, pp. 60–61), what specific powers should devolve to institutions and what authority should remain with the state? It is often asserted that low-income states with small populations benefit from strong statewide control, while a laissez-faire approach is more congenial to larger, affluent states with stronger regional population and economic centers. How well does this generalization hold up in a time of reduced resources and renewed demands for service that put public needs ahead of institutional priorities?

The "federal" pattern well described by Richardson and his associates represents a particular balance between central and campus control. Richardson characterizes this model as "a state agency that is neither state government nor higher education that acts as an interface between state government and institutions" (1999, p. 172). While intellectually appealing, it would be interesting to know what it would take to replicate this model beyond large, complex states like Texas and Illinois.

The Charter College Model

The idea of charter colleges in which public institutions are overseen by their individual boards and receive substantial amounts of procedural autonomy in return for an agreement or charter to achieve certain standards of access and quality offers another model of balancing autonomy and control. In his study of St. Mary's College of Maryland, Robert Berdahl evaluated the experiment of "giving a state institution a hybrid public-private status by state law, to see whether privatizing some of its functions would allow it to become so efficient and effective that it could increase quality, maintain access, and raise increasing amounts of funds from nonstate sources" (1998, p. 59). Subsequently, he and I expanded the concept of charter colleges in a monograph published by the Pioneer Institute for Public Policy in Massachusetts (Berdahl and MacTaggart 1999, p. 1).

Both studies championed the idea of bestowing more procedural or administrative responsibility upon institutions that appeared to have the leadership capacity to use it well, while reserving state control of mission. Several more institutions have sought charter status in their states, although some of these attempts amount to marketing strategies to reposition former teacher institutions as distinctive public liberal arts colleges.

Colorado recently granted Metropolitan State College of Denver and Fort Lewis College their own boards of trustees, as it had in 1991 for the Colorado School of Mines. How are the experiments in Colorado and elsewhere in local campus autonomy working in terms of their stated purposes? Does the charter college notion seem to work best at institutions with especially focused missions such as public liberal arts colleges, or does it lend itself to universities with multiple degree levels and locations? Could the model work on a broad scale involving virtually all of the public institutions in a state, and, if so, how would the compact or charter be designed and monitored? What is the role of the state in defining the charter and ensuring that its requirements are met?

Summary

The traditional consensus over the ultimately stabilizing role of systems is breaking down, and a new synthesis has yet to emerge. No new standard of statewide governance will develop for the foreseeable future, but instead we are apt to see multiple hybrid models emerge from political and policy debates within each state.

Following the dissipation of authority from systems and coordinating boards to individual colleges and universities, statewide educational and political leaders find it increasingly difficult to achieve public goals. Thoughtful analyses of governance stand to make a substantial contribution if they help policy makers understand, in a practical way and in their respective states, the kinds of governance structures (as well as policies and leadership styles) that are likely to deliver the best results to the public. No one should be seduced by unqualified generalizations on either side of the autonomy-control debate, least of all political and educational leaders who are charged with harnessing the potential of their higher education systems to better serve the needs of the people.

REFERENCES

Ashworth, K. 2001. *Caught between the dog and the fireplug, or how to survive public service.* Washington, DC: Georgetown University Press.

Berdahl, R. 1971. *Statewide coordination of higher education.* Washington, DC: American Council on Education.

———. 1998. Balancing self-interest and accountability: St. Mary's College of Maryland. In *Seeking excellence through independence: Liberating colleges and universities from excessive regulation,* ed. T. MacTaggart & Associates. San Francisco: Jossey-Bass.

Berdahl, R., and T. MacTaggart. 1999. *Charter colleges: Balancing freedom and accountability.* Boston: Pioneer Institute for Public Policy Research.

Berdahl, R., and F. Schmidtlein. 1996. Restructuring and its aftermath: Maryland. In *Restructuring higher education: What works and what doesn't in reorganizing governing systems,* ed. T. MacTaggart & Associates. San Francisco: Jossey-Bass.

Brewer, B. 2002. University Leaders Balk at Ballot Proposals. *St. Petersburg Times,* August 16, p. 1B.

Commission on Health Science, Education and Training. 2002. *Report of the commission on health science, education and training.* Trenton, NJ: Governor's Office.

Donahue, J. D. 1989. *The privatization decision: Public ends, private means.* New York: Basic Books.

Epper, R. 1999. *Deregulation of state-level academic program policies.* January. Denver: State Higher Education Executive Officers.

Florida Department of State. 2002. Text of Amendment 11. Retrieved December 16 from http://election.dos.state.fl.us/initiatives/initdetail/asp?account=34498@segnum=1.

Greer, D. 1998. Defining the scope and limits of autonomy: New Jersey. In *Seeking excellence through independence: Liberating colleges and universities from excessive regulation,* ed. T. MacTaggart and Associates. San Francisco: Jossey-Bass.

James, J. 2002. Politics a key to university vacancies, 3 state schools seek presidents. *The Miami Herald,* December 10, 1B. Retrieved December 13 from LexisNexis (1822:0:74364650).

Johnstone, B. 1992. *Central administration of multi-campus college and university systems: Core functions and cost pressures, with reference to the central administration of the state of New York.* Studies in Public Higher Education, no. 1. Albany: State University of New York.

Kerr, C., and M. Gade. 1989. *The guardians: Boards of trustees of American colleges and universities, what they do and how well they do it.* Washington, DC: The Association of Governing Boards of Colleges and Universities.

Klein, B. 2001. Bush's trustees mostly in GOP. *St. Petersburg Times,* May 8, p. 1B.

Klein, B., and D. Rado. 2001. SPJC gets special status. *St. Petersburg Times,* May 6, p. 1B.

MacTaggart, T. 1998. Implementing independence. In *Seeking excellence through independence: Liberating colleges and universities from excessive regulation,* ed. T. MacTaggart & Associates. San Francisco: Jossey-Bass.

MacTaggart, T., and J. Mingle. 2002. *Pursuing the public's agenda: Trustees in partnership with state leaders.* Washington, DC: Association of Governing Boards, Center for Public Higher Education Trusteeship and Governance.

McGuinness, A. 1996. A model for successful restructuring. In *Restructuring higher education: What works and what doesn't in reorganizing governing systems,* ed. T. MacTaggart & Associates. San Francisco: Jossey-Bass.

———. 1997. The functions and evolution of state coordination and governance in postsecondary education. In *1997 state postsecondary education structures sourcebook.* Denver: Education Commission of the States.

The National Center for Public Policy and Higher Education. 2002. Of precept, policy and practice. In *Policy perspectives: A special supplement to national crosstalk.* San Jose, CA: The National Center for Public Policy in Higher Education.

The Oregon University System (OUS). 2002. The "Deal." Retrieved December 15 from www.ous.edu/thedeal.

Osborne, D., and T. Gaebler. 1992. *Reinventing government: How the entrepreneurial spirit is transforming the public sector.* Reading, MA: Addison-Wesley.

Peltz, J. 2002. University question splits top politicians. *The Sun-Sentinel,* October 24, p. 23. Retrieved October 26 from LexisNexis (1822:0:69118944).

Peterson, M., and M. McLendon. 1998. Achieving independence through conflict and compromise: Michigan. In *Seeking excellence through independence: Liberating colleges and universities from excessive regulation,* ed. T. MacTaggart & Associates. San Francisco: Jossey-Bass.

Picking a chancellor. 2001. *The Baltimore Sun,* May 21, p. 1. Retrieved May 21 from www.sunspot.net/news.

Pierce, N., and J. Hagstrom. 1983. *The book of America: Inside 50 states today.* New York: W.W. Norton and Company.

Powers, S. 2002. Universities' presidents bond together; to increase their influence over policy. *The Orlando Sentinel,* August 16, p. B2.

Rawls, J. 1971. *Justice as fairness.* Cambridge, MA: Harvard University.

A report of a taskforce to study the governance, coordination and financing of the University System of Maryland. 1999. Annapolis, MD: Department of Legislative Services.

Richardson, R., K. Bracco, P. Callan, and J. Finney. 1999. *Designing state higher education systems for a new century.* Phoenix, AZ: American Council on Education, The Oryx Press.

Ruppert, S. 2001. *Where do we go from here? State legislative views on higher education in the new millennium: Results of the 2001 higher education issues survey.* Washington, DC: National Education Association.

Schmidt, P. 2002. Budget ax falls hard on state higher education agencies. *The Chronicle of Higher Education,* September 13, pp. A26–A27.

Senate Bill 682. 1999. Higher education–University System of Maryland—Coordination, governance, funding. Annapolis: State of Maryland.

Traxler, H. 2002. New system has higher education in Florida taking a lower road. *St. Petersburg Times,* October 2, p. 1B.

Trombley, W. 2001. Florida's new K–20 model. *National Crosstalk* 9 (2): 1–11. Retrieved May 24 from www.highereducation.org/crosstalk/ct0401/news0401-florida.shtml.

Universities to keep Bush plan. 2002. *The Orlando Sentinel,* December 12, p. B5. Retrieved December 13 from LexisNexis (1822:0:74364650).

CHAPTER FIVE

Governing the Twenty-first-Century University

A View from the Bridge

James J. Duderstadt

> In the 1850s, when the current forms of lay board governance were established, the average American college had fewer than one hundred students and less than 1% of white males attended college. Over the past century, universities have evolved from a trustees-plus-president "imperium" to a more faculty-based hegemony to a somewhat more broadly based sovereignty that includes government (state and federal) and students.
>
> HAROLD T. SHAPIRO

> In reality, the practice of shared governance—however promising its original intent—often threatens gridlock. Whether the problem is with presidents who lack the courage to lead an agenda for change, trustees who ignore the institutional goals in favor of the football team, or faculty members who are loath to surrender the status quo, the fact is that each is an obstacle to progress. If higher education is to respond effectively to the demands being placed upon it, the culture of shared governance must be reshaped.
>
> NATIONAL COMMISSION ON THE ACADEMIC PRESIDENCY

Despite dramatic changes in the nature of scholarship, pedagogy, and service to society, U.S. universities today are organized, managed, and governed in a manner little different from the far simpler colleges of a century ago. We continue to embrace, indeed, enshrine, the concept of shared governance involving public oversight and trusteeship by governing boards of lay citizens, elected faculty governance, and experienced but generally short-term and usually amateur administrative leadership. Today, however, the pace of change in our society is exposing the flaws in this traditional approach to university governance.

University governing boards comprised of lay citizens face a serious challenge in their ability to understand and govern the increasingly complex university and its relationships to broader society. This task is made even more difficult by the politics swirling about and within many governing boards—particularly those of public universities—that not only distract boards from their important responsibilities and stewardship but also discourage many of our most experienced, talented, and dedicated citizens from serving on these bodies.

While faculty governance continues to be effective and essential for academic matters such as curriculum development, faculty hiring, and tenure evaluation, it is increasingly difficult to achieve true faculty participation in broader university matters such as finance, capital facilities, and external relations. When faculty members do become involved in university-wide governance and decision making, all too often they tend to become preoccupied with peripheral matters such as pay, parking, and the plant department rather than strategic issues such as the protection of academic values or the proper balance among undergraduate, graduate, and professional education. The faculty traditions of debate and consensus building, the highly fragmented and compartmentalized organization of academic departments, and the faculty's primary loyalty to their academic discipline and the marketplace rather than to their institution seem increasingly incompatible with the breadth and rapid pace required to keep up with today's high-momentum, high-risk, university-wide decision environment.

University presidents and other academic administrators are frequently caught between these opposing forces, between external pressures and internal campus politics, between governing boards and faculty governance. Moreover, the imbalance between responsibility (considerable) and authority (modest) characterizing the contemporary university presidency inhibits strong, visionary leadership in higher education at a time when it is desperately needed. Little wonder that most university administrators keep their heads low, avoid making waves, and polish their resumes for their next career steps.

Today it is appropriate to question whether the key participants in shared governance—the lay governing board, elected faculty governance, and academic administrators—have the expertise, discipline, authority, and accountability necessary to cope with the powerful social, economic, and technological forces driving change in our society and its institutions. More specifically, is it realistic to expect that the shared governance mechanisms developed decades ago can serve well the contemporary university or the rapidly changing society dependent upon its activities? Can boards comprised of lay citizens with little knowledge of academic matters or the complex financial, management, and legal affairs of the university be expected to provide competent oversight for the large, complex institutions characterizing U.S. higher education? What is the appropriate role for the faculty in university governance, and is this adequately addressed by the current determination and conduct of faculty governing bodies? Can academics with limited experience in management serve as competent administrators (i.e., as deans, provosts, and presidents)? And, finally (and most speculatively), what works, what does not, and what can we do about it? As will become clear, my answers to these questions vary somewhat from the chapters by Neil Hamilton (chap. 3) and Terrence MacTaggart (chap. 4). Hamilton and I differ philosophically with regard to the role of the faculty, and MacTaggart works at the system level, whereas I am more concerned with the individual board.

I must stress an important caveat before examining these issues. There is remarkable diversity in the forms of governance used by U.S. colleges and universities because these have evolved from the history and traditions of a highly diverse collection of institutions. Beyond the obvious differences between public and private universities, liberal arts colleges and research universities, and those with organized (unionized) faculties and those with traditional faculty anarchies, there are other strong differences even among institutions with similar academic characteristics. As Hamilton notes, institutions such as the University of California have long traditions of strong faculty governance at the campus-wide or system-wide level. Others, such as the University of Michigan, stress this role at the level of the academic unit through faculty executive committees, relying upon deans to address academic concerns at the university level. States such as Ohio and North Carolina have statewide governing boards determining educational policy and funding priorities; others, like California, rely on governing boards at the university system level working within the framework of carefully negotiated master plans; and some, including Michigan, recognize through state constitution the autonomy of a unique governing board for each college and university. Although this chapter attempts to identify and address issues common to most colleges and universities, it is clearly influenced by my experience with large, public research universities such as the University of Michigan.

The Way Things Are Supposed to Work

Perhaps the most authoritative description of how the shared governance model of the university is supposed to work was articulated in 1967 in a joint statement formulated by the American Association of University Professors (AAUP), the American Council on Education (ACE), and the Association of Governing Boards of Universities and Colleges (AGB). In theory, shared governance delegates academic decisions (criteria for student admissions, faculty hiring and promotion, curriculum development, and awarding degrees) to the faculty and administrative decisions (acquiring resources and planning expenditures, and designing, building, and operating facilities) to the administration, leaving the governing board to focus on public policy and accountability (compliance with federal, state, and local laws; fiduciary responsibilities; and selecting key leadership such as the president). In other words, shared governance allocates public accountability and stewardship to the governing board, academic matters to the faculty, and the tasks of leading and managing the institution to the administration.

Of course, from a legal perspective, *shared governance* is a misnomer. By law or by charter, essentially all of the legal powers of the university are held by its governing board, although generally delegated to and exercised by the administration and the faculty, particularly in academic matters. The function of the lay board in U.S. higher education is simple, at least in theory: the governing board has final authority for key policy decisions and accepts fiduciary and legal responsibility for the welfare of the institution. Because of its very limited expertise, however, it is expected to delegate the responsibility for policy development, academic programs, and administration to the faculty and other professionals with the necessary training and experience. In the case of private institutions, governing boards are typically elected by alumni of the institution or self-perpetuated by the board. In public institutions, board members are determined by political mechanisms, either governor appointments or popular election.

There are actually two levels of faculty governance. The key to the effective governance of the academic mission of the university—that is, who gets hired, who gets promoted, what gets taught, and how funds are allocated and spent—involves an array of faculty committees (promotion, curriculum, and executive committees), typically at the department, school, or college level. Although a department chair or dean, may have considerable authority, he or she is generally tolerated and sustained only with the support of the faculty leaders within the academic unit.

The second form of faculty governance occurs at the university level and usually involves an elected body of faculty representatives, such as an academic senate, that serves to debate institution-wide issues and advise the university administration. In sharp contrast to faculty governance at the unit level, which has considerable power and influence, the university-wide faculty governance bodies are generally advisory. Although they may be consulted by the administration or the governing board on important university matters, they rarely have any executive authority.

Actually, there is a third level of informal faculty power and control in the contemporary research university because an increasing share of institutional resources flow directly to faculty entrepreneurs as research grants and contracts from the federal government, corporations, and private foundations. These research programs act as quasi-independent revenue centers with considerable influence, frequently at odds with more formal faculty governance structures.

Like other complex organizations in business or government, the university requires competent management and administration. While long ago universities perhaps were treated by our society—and its various government bodies—as well intentioned and benign stewards of truth, justice, and the American way, today we find that the university must contend with the same pressures, standards, and demands for accountability that any other public corporation faces. Of course, the term *university administration* sometimes conveys a sinister connotation (akin to that of *federal government, bureaucracy,* or *corporate organization*) to faculty and governing boards alike. In reality, however, the university administration is simply a leadership network that extends throughout the institution. As a general practice, those administrative officers responsible for academic programs (department chairs, dean, provosts) are selected from among the faculty and continue to have academic rank. Those responsible for various administrative, support, and business functions of the university, such as finance, physical plant, and government relations, generally have experience and training in these areas.

At the helm of the U.S. university is the president (or chancellor). University presidents are expected to develop, articulate, and implement visions for their institutions that sustain and enhance their quality. Through their roles as the CEOs of their institutions, they also have significant management responsibilities for a diverse collection of activities, ranging from education to health care to public entertainment (e.g., intercollegiate athletics). Since these generally require the expertise of talented specialists, the president is the university's leading recruiter, identifying talented people, hiring them to fill key university positions, and directing and supporting their activities. Unlike most corporate CEOs, the president is expected to play an active role in generating necessary resources, whether by lobbying state and federal governments, seeking gifts and bequests from alumni and friends, or making clever entrepreneurial efforts. There is an implicit expectation on most campuses that the president's job is to raise money for the provost and deans to spend, while the chief financial officer and administrative staff watch over their shoulders to make certain they all do it wisely.

The presidency of a U.S. college or university is an unusual leadership position from another interesting perspective. Although the responsibility for everything involving the university usually floats up to the president's desk, direct authority almost invariably rests elsewhere. There is a mismatch between responsibility and authority that is unparalleled in other social institutions. As a result, many, including many university presidents, have become quite convinced that the contemporary university is basically unmanageable and unleadable, at least from the office of the president.

The Challenges to Effective University Governance

The modern university comprises many activities, some nonprofit, some publicly regulated, and some operating in intensely competitive marketplaces. It teaches students, conducts research for various clients, provides health care, engages in economic development, stimulates social change, and provides mass entertainment, such as through college sports. The organization of the contemporary university compares in scale and complexity with many major global corporations. The very complexity of the university has made substantive involvement in the broader governance of the university problematic for all participants.

The increased complexity, financial pressures, and accountability of universities demanded by the government, the media, and the public at large require stronger management than in the past (Balderston 1995). Yet as universities have developed the administrative staffs, policies, and procedures to handle such issues, they also have created a thicket of paperwork, regulations, and bureaucracy that has weakened the authority and attractiveness of academic leadership.

Broad participation in university governance is hampered by bureaucratic policies, procedures, and practices, as well as by the anarchy of committee and consensus decision making.

As Simon Marginson (chap. 1) and David Collis (chap. 2) point out, the pace and nature of the changes occurring in our world today also pose formidable challenges to tradition-bound institutions such as the university. In business, management approaches change in a highly strategic fashion, launching a comprehensive process of planning and transformation. In political circles, sometimes a strong leader with a big idea can captivate the electorate, building momentum for change. The creative anarchy arising from a faculty culture that prizes individual freedom and consensual decision making poses quite a different challenge. Most big ideas from top administrators are treated with either disdain ("this too shall pass") or ridicule. Formal strategic-planning efforts often meet with the same reaction, unless, of course, they are attached to clearly perceived budget consequences or faculty rewards. The academic tradition of extensive consultation, debate, and consensus building before any substantive decision is made or action taken poses a particular challenge in this regard because this process is frequently incapable of keeping pace with the profound changes occurring higher education.

The character of the participants in shared university governance seems increasingly incompatible with the challenges the university faces in serving a rapidly changing society. Many university presidents believe—although they are understandably discreet in stating—that one of their greatest challenges is protecting their institutions from the deteriorating quality of their governing boards. In theory, members of governing boards are expected to serve as stewards for their institutions, advocates for higher education, and defenders of academic values. In practice there has been a pronounced shift in recent years toward a greater emphasis on oversight and public accountability. This is particularly the case with the governing boards of public universities. As the politics of board selection have become more contentious, board members have increasingly advocated strong political agendas, for example, to restructure the curriculum to stress a specific ideology or eliminate social commitments such as affirmative action. Instead of buffering the university from various political forces, some boards have become conduits for political issues beyond the campus (National Commission on the Academic Presidency 1996).

A recent study commissioned by the AGB (Ingram 1998) concluded that many university trustees lack both a basic understanding of higher education and a significant commitment to it. Too much time is spent concentrating on administrative matters rather than the urgent questions of educational policy. Inexperienced boards all too often become captivated by the illusion of the quick fix, believing that if only the right strategic plan is developed or the right personnel change is made, then everything will be fine, their responsibilities will be met, and their personal influence over the university will be visible (Ingram 1998).

There is little doubt that the deterioration in the quality of governing boards and the confusion concerning their roles and the increasingly political nature of their activities has damaged many public universities and threatens many others. There is an old saying that no institution can be better than its governing board. Today, however, the counterpoint seems to apply to many universities: A governing board is rarely as good as the institution it serves.

Although faculty involvement in academic matters is essential for program quality and integrity, faculty participation in university-wide governance and leadership is problematic. As we have noted, the complexity of the contemporary university hinders substantive faculty involvement in its broader governance. On most campuses, faculty suffer from a chronic shortage of information—and hence understanding—about how the university really works. In part, this lack arises because university administrations have attempted to shield the faculty and the academic programs from the forces of economic, social, and technology change raging beyond the campus. However, there are deeper issues.

The faculty culture typically holds values that are not necessarily well aligned with those required to manage a complex institution. For example, the faculty values academic freedom and independence, whereas the management of the institution requires responsibility and accountability. Faculty members tend to be individualistic, highly entrepreneurial lone rangers rather than the team players required for management. They tend to resist strong, visionary leadership and firmly defend their personal status quo. It is frequently difficult to get faculty commitment to—or even interest in—broad institutional goals that are not congruent with personal goals.

Beyond the difficulty of getting faculty involved in broad institutional goals, there is an even more important condition that prevents true faculty governance at the institution level. Responsibility and accountability should always accompany authority. Deans and presidents can be fired. Trustees can be sued or forced off governing boards (at least in private universities). Yet the faculty, through important traditions such as academic freedom and tenure, are largely insulated from the consequences of their debates and recommendations. It would be difficult, if not impossible, either legally or operationally, to ascribe to faculty bodies the requisite level of accountability that would necessarily accompany executive authority.

Of course, many of the most outspoken critics of faculty governance come from within the faculty itself. They note with dismay that those elected to faculty governance often seem interested in asserting power and influence only on matters of personal interest such as compensation and staff benefits. I agree with Hamilton in chapter 3 when he says that faculty should have a substantive and sustained voice in matters pertaining to knowledge production. Tragically, however, it has been difficult to get faculty governance to focus on those areas clearly within their unique competence such as curriculum development, student learning, academic values, and ethics. Little wonder that many of the most active faculty members are reluctant to become involved in the tedious committees and commissions generated by shared governance.

The contemporary university is buffeted by powerful and frequently opposing forces. The marketplace demands cost-effective services. Governments and the public demand accountability for the expenditure of public funds. The faculty demands (or at least should demand) adherence to long-standing academic values and traditions such as academic freedom and rigorous inquiry. Power in a university is broadly dispersed and in many cases difficult to perceive. Although the views and roles of each of the players in shared university governance are highly diverse, most groups do share one perspective: They all believe they need and deserve more power than they currently have. The long-standing tradition of shared governance, in which power is shared more or less equally among all potential decision makers, is cumbersome and awkward at best.

Part of the difficulty with shared governance is its ambiguity. The lines of authority and responsibility are blurred, sometimes intentionally. Although most members of the university community understand that the fundamental principles of shared governance rest upon the delegation of authority to the faculty in academic matters and to the administration in operational management, the devil in the details can lead to confusion and misunderstanding. Turf problems abound. One of the key challenges to effective university governance is to make certain that all of the constituencies of shared governance—governing boards, administrations, and faculty—understand clearly their roles and responsibilities.

Prescriptions for Change

So, what to do? In the spirit of stimulating debate (and fully aware that this may be simply tilting at windmills), it seems appropriate to offer several suggestions. Here the key theme is the importance of infusing more expertise and accountability into university governance while preserving those important traditions and values critical to the academy.

Fundamental Principles

It is useful to begin with several key principles. University leadership, governance, management, and decision making should always reflect the fundamental values of the academy, that is, freedom of inquiry, openness to new ideas, commitment to rigorous study, and love of learning. Yet, these processes also should be willing to consider and be capable of implementing institutional change when necessary to respond to the changing needs of our society.

Luc Weber, former rector at the University of Geneva, suggests that higher education would do well to draw its practitioners' attention to two concepts from the economic theory of federalism that was developed to address the challenges faced by the European Economic Community (Weber 2001). First, one should stress the importance of *externality* in all decisions, that is, that the benefits or costs of a decision accrue not only to the members of the community making the decision but also to the broader community they serve. The business community would recognize this as a "customer-oriented" strategy, focusing on those whom we serve. Second, a principle of *subsidiarity* should characterize governance in which decisions are made at the lowest possible level consistent with expertise and accountability. Centralization is a very awkward approach to higher education during a time of rapid change.

Restructuring Governing Boards

Nothing is more critical to the future success of higher education than improving the quality and performance of boards of trustees. Today, during an era of rapid change, colleges and universities deserve governing boards comprised of members selected for their expertise and experience who are capable of governing the university in ways that benefit the long-term welfare of the institution as well as the more immediate interests of the various constituencies it serves.

For public boards, the need is particularly urgent. As long as the members of the governing boards of public universities continue to be determined through primarily political mechanisms without careful consideration or independent review of qualifications or institutional commitment, and are allowed to pursue political or personal agendas without concern for the welfare of the institution or its service to broader society, the public university will find itself increasingly unable to adapt to the needs of a rapidly changing society.

As the contemporary university becomes more complex and accountable, it may be time to set aside the quaint U.S. practice of governing universities with boards comprised of lay citizens, with their clearly inadequate expertise and frequently political character, and instead shift to true boards of directors similar to those used in the private sector. Although it may sound strange in these times of scandal and corruption in corporate management, it is nevertheless my belief that university governing boards should function with a structure and a process that reflects the best practices of corporate boards. Corporate board members are selected for their particular expertise in areas such as business practices, finance, or legal matters. They are held accountable to the shareholders for the performance of the corporation. Their performance is reviewed at regular intervals, both within the board itself and through more external measures such as company financial performance. Clearly, directors can be removed either through action of the board or shareholder vote. Furthermore, they can be held legally and financially liable for the quality of their decisions— a far cry from the limited accountability of the members of most governing boards for public universities.

Every effort should be made to convince leaders of state government that politics and patronage have no place in the selection of university governing boards or in attempts to determine their administrative leadership. Quality universities require quality leadership. Even as public university governing boards have become increasingly political and hence sensitive to special interests, they also have become less accountable for their quality and effectiveness. Not only should all university governance be subject to regular and public review, but also the quality and effectiveness of governing boards should be an important aspect of institutional accreditation.

In 1995, the AGB took an important first step toward addressing this issue through a series of recommendations. First, they proposed that the size of public boards be increased to fifteen or more members to minimize the vulnerability of small boards to the behavior of maverick members. The boards should include a majority of carefully selected members who have demonstrated experience with large organizations, their financing, and their complex social and political contexts. Some experience with and interest in higher education was also considered a desirable criterion, of course.

As the AGB demonstrates in its report, there is little positive evidence to support the partisan election of governing boards. Yet, as total reliance on gubernatorial appointment also has problems, the wisest course may be to use a variety of mechanisms to determine the composition of a given board. For example, one might imagine a board comprised of twenty-four members: eight nominated by the governor and approved by the legislature, eight elected at large on a nonpartisan basis, and eight representing certain constituencies such as alumni, students, business, and labor. With overlapping terms, such a board would be highly representative and yet stable against the dominance of any political or special-interest group.

Although it is important to provide board members with sufficient tenure to develop an understanding of the university, it is also a good idea to avoid excessively long tenures. It is probably wise to limit university board service to a single term because this would prevent members from "campaigning" during their tenure for future appointment or election to additional terms.

Again drawing on the experience of corporate boards, let me make the more radical suggestion that university presidents in public universities should have some influence over the selection of board members, as do their colleagues in private universities and CEOs in the corporate sectors. Here I am not proposing that university presidents actually nominate or select board members. Yet consideration should be given to their right to evaluate and possibly veto a proposed board member if the individual is perceived as unduly political, hostile, or simply inexperienced or incompetent.

Proposals for Strengthening Faculty Governance

Perhaps the simplest approach to identifying possible reforms in faculty governance is to examine where it seems to work well and why. From my own experience—as a faculty member, a former member of faculty governance at both the academic unit and university level, and a former university president—faculty governance seems to work best when it focuses upon academic matters such as faculty searches, promotion and tenure decisions, and curriculum decisions. Why? Because the rank-and-file faculty members understand clearly that not only do they have the authority to make these decisions but also that these decisions are important to their academic departments and likely to affect their own teaching and research activities. As a result, the best faculty members, namely those with the strongest reputations and influence, are drawn into the academic governance process, either through formal election or appointment to key committees (hiring, promotion, tenure, curriculum, executive) or at least are consulted for influential opinions in their role as department "mandarins."

In sharp contrast, most active faculty members view university-wide governance bodies such as faculty senates primarily as debating societies, whose opinions are invariably taken as advisory by the administration and the governing board. It is therefore rare that a distinguished faculty member will spare the time from productive scholarship, teaching, or department matters for such university service. Of course, there are exceptions, but more commonly those outspoken faculty members with an ax to grind are drawn to academic politics, frequently distracting faculty governance from substantive issues to focus instead on their pet agendas. Advisory bodies, paid only lip service by the administration or the board of trustees, will rarely attract the attention or engage the participation of those faculty most actively engaged in scholarship and teaching. Hence a key to effective governance is to provide faculty bodies with executive rather than merely advisory authority, thereby attracting the active participation of the university's leading faculty members.

Furthermore, the process of graduate education through which we prepare the next generation of faculty should be restructured to produce not just scholars and, we hope, teachers, but also citizens of the university community who recognize and accept their responsibility to participate in governance activities. We should seek a change in the current faculty culture by reestablishing institutional loyalty and service as valued and rewarded activities.

Balancing Responsibility with Authority

The academic tradition of extensive consultation, debate, and consensus building before any substantive decision can be made or action taken is yet another challenge. To be sure, the voluntary culture (some would say anarchy) of the university responds better to a process of consultation, communication, and collaboration than to the command-control-communication process familiar from business and industry. However, this process is simply incapable of keeping pace with the profound changes facing effective governance of the public university. Not everything is improved by making it more democratic. A quick look at the remarkable pace of change required in the private sector—usually measured in months, not years—suggests that universities must develop more capacity to move rapidly. This will require university leaders to occasionally make difficult decisions and take strong action without the traditional consensus-building process. Universities need to better define those areas in which the special competence of the faculty requires their consent (academic programs and policies), those areas in which faculty advice will be sought and considered but not considered authoritative (funding priorities), and those areas in which faculty need not be consulted at all (parking?).

The leadership of the university, as George Keller discusses in more detail in chapter 6, must be provided with the authority commensurate with its responsibilities. Academic leaders, whether at the level of department chairs, deans, vice-presidents, or even the president, should have the same degree of authority to take actions, to select leadership, and to take risks and move with deliberate speed, that their counterparts in the corporate world and government enjoy. The challenges and pace of change faced by the modern university no longer allow the luxury of consensus leadership, at least to the degree that *building consensus* means seeking the approval of all concerned communities before action is taken. Nor do our times allow the reactive nature of special-interest politics to rigidly moor the university to an obsolete status quo, thwarting efforts to provide strategic leadership and direction.

While academic administrations generally can be drawn as conventional hierarchical trees, in reality the connecting lines of authority are extremely weak. In fact, one of the reasons for cost escalation in higher education is the presence of a deeply ingrained academic culture in which leaders are expected to "purchase the cooperation" of subordinates, to provide them with positive incentives to carry out decisions. For example, deans expect the provost to offer additional resources to gain their cooperation on various institution-wide efforts. Obviously, this bribery culture is quite incompatible with the trend toward increasing decentralization of resources. As the central administration relinquishes greater control of resource and cost accountability to the units, it will lose the pool of resources that in the past was used to provide incentives to deans, directors, and other leaders to cooperate and support university-wide goals.

Hence, it is logical to expect that the leadership and management of universities increasingly will need to rely on lines of true authority just as their corporate counterparts do. That is, presidents, executive officers, and deans almost certainly will have to become comfortable with issuing clear orders or directives from time to time. So, too, throughout the organization, subordinates will need to recognize that failure to execute these directives will likely have significant consequences, including possible removal from their positions. I am not suggesting that universities adopt a top-down corporate model inconsistent with faculty responsibility for academic programs and academic freedom. However, although collegiality will continue to be valued and honored, the modern university simply must accept a more realistic balance between responsibility and authority.

Clearly, leadership strength should be rebuilt at middle levels within the university, both by redesigning such positions to better balance authority and responsibility, and by providing leadership development programs. This may involve some degree of restructuring in the organization of the university to better respond to its responsibilities, challenges, and opportunities. In this regard, there should be more effort made to identify "the administration" as a broader body than simply as the executive officers of the university, including deans, chairs, and directors. It is also critical to get this broader group to be perceived—and to perceive themselves—as spokespersons for university objectives.

Structural Issues

While it is probably impolitic to be so blunt, the simple fact is that the contemporary university is a *public corporation* that must be governed, led, and managed with competence and accountability to benefit its various stakeholders. To be sure, the presence of lay citizens on governing boards is useful in representing the myriad views of the society served by our universities. So too, the complexity and importance of the contemporary university requires capable management and administration provided by trained professionals. Yet I believe it absolutely essential that experience with academic values and the activities of teaching and scholarship must permeate all levels of university governance. Furthermore, this experience can be provided only by those who have toiled in the vineyards of teaching and research as faculty members.

Put another way, the key to achieving adequate competence and accountability in the governance of the contemporary university is to infuse in all of its components the perspectives of practicing faculty members. As we noted earlier, this has long been accomplished at the level of individual academic units through the use of various faculty committees to address crucial issues such as faculty hiring and promotion, student admission and performance, and curriculum and degree program development. It can be achieved in the management of the university by appointing faculty members to leading administrative positions, provided, of course, that they are given the training necessary to manage complex organizations and functions in a competent and accountable fashion.

It is also my belief that all university governing boards, public and private, would benefit greatly from the presence of distinguished faculty members from other institutions and either active or retired university presidents or other senior administrators among their membership. Since the experience of most lay board members is so far removed from the academy, it seems logical to suggest that boards would benefit from the experience such seasoned academicians might bring. After all, most corporate boards find it important to have experienced business leaders, either active or retired, among their membership. University boards should do the same.

An equally controversial variation on this theme would be to provide faculty with a stronger voice in true university governance by appointing faculty representatives as members of the governing board. This would be similar to the practice in many other nations of governing universities with unicameral bodies consisting of a balance of lay citizens, faculty members, administrators, and perhaps even students. It may be time to explore this approach in U.S. colleges and universities.

A Balance of Interests and Influence

Shared governance is, in reality, an ever-changing balance of forces involving faculty, trustees, and administration (Keohane 1998). Yet at a deeper level, it represents the effort to achieve a balance among academic priorities and values, public responsibility and accountability, and financial, management, and political realities. However, different universities achieve this balance in quite different ways. At the University of California, for instance, a strong tradition of campus and system-wide faculty governance is occasionally called upon to counter the political forces characterizing the governing board, examples being the loyalty oath controversy of the 1950s, the Reagan takeover of the UC Board of Regents in the 1960s, and the debates over the use of affirmative action in student admission during the 1990s.

In contrast, at the University of Michigan, campus-wide faculty governance has historically been rather weak, at least compared to faculty influence through executive committee structures at the department, school, and college levels. Hence the tradition has been to develop a strong cadre of deans through aggressive recruiting and the decentralization of considerable authority to the university's schools and colleges, and then to depend upon these academic leaders to counter the inevitable political tendencies of the university's regents from time to time.

Where is the influence of the university administration—and particularly the president—in this balancing act? Usually out of sight or perhaps out of mind. After all, senior administrators, including the president, serve at the pleasure of the governing board and are also mindful of faculty support because they may be only one vote of no confidence away from receiving their walking papers. It always has been necessary for the U.S. university president to champion the needs of the academic community to the board and the broader society while helping to ensure that the academic community is in touch with society's interests and needs. Therefore, it also is not surprising that the administration is usually quite reluctant to be caught publicly in skirmishes between the governing board and the faculty.

The danger of such a bilateral balance of power arises when one party or the other is weakened. When the faculty senate loses the capacity to attract the participation of distinguished faculty members, or when a series of poor appointments at the level of deans or executive officers weakens the administration, a governing board with a strong political agenda can move into the power vacuum. Of course, there also have been numerous examples of the other extreme, in which a weakened governing board caved into unrealistic faculty demands, for example, replacing merit salary programs with cost-of-living adjustments or extending faculty voting privileges to part-time teaching staff in such a way as to threaten faculty quality.

It All Comes Back to Values

The history of the university in the United States is one of a social institution created and shaped by public needs, public policy, and public investment to serve a growing nation. Yet in few places within the academy, either at the level of governing boards or in government higher education policy, does there appear to be a serious and sustained discussion of the fundamental values so necessary to the nature and role of the university at a time when it is so desperately needed (Zemsky and Wegner 1998). Instead, the future of higher education in the United States has increasingly been left to the valueless dynamics of the marketplace.

Perhaps this is not so surprising, as for much of the last century the college curriculum has been largely devoid of any consideration of values. Although some might date this abdication to campus disruptions of the 1960s, in truth it extends over much of the twentieth century. As scholarship became increasing professionalized and specialized, any coherent sense of the purposes and principles of a university became fragmented. Values such as tolerance, civility, and personal and social responsibility have been largely absent from the academic curriculum. Most of our undergraduates experience little discussion of values in their studies. Our graduate schools focus almost entirely on research training, with little attention given to professional ethics or even preparation for teaching careers, for that matter. Our faculties prefer to debate parking over principles just as our governing boards prefer politics over policy. In this climate, our university leaders keep their heads low and their values hidden, and prepare their resumes for their next institutions.

In any consideration of how our universities are governed and led, it is important always to begin with the basics, to reconsider carefully the key roles and values of the university that should be protected and preserved during a period of change. For example, how would an institution prioritize among roles such as educating the young (undergraduate education), preserving and transmitting our culture (libraries, visual and performing arts), basic research and scholarship, and serving as a responsible critic of society? Similarly, what are the most important values to protect? Clearly academic freedom, an openness to new ideas, a commitment to rigorous study, and an aspiration to achieving excellence would be on the list for most institutions. Yet what about values and practices such as shared governance and tenure? Should these be preserved? At what expense? We need to act in such a way as to preserve our core missions, characteristics, and values. Only a concerted effort to understand the important traditions of the past, the challenges of the present, and the possibilities for the future can enable institutions to thrive during a time of such change.

Final Observations

It is my belief that the complexity of the contemporary university and the forces acting upon it have outstripped the ability of the current shared governance system of lay boards, elected faculty bodies, and inexperienced academic administrators to govern, lead, and manage. Today, far too many colleges and universities find that the most formidable forces controlling their destinies are political in nature—from governments, governing boards, public opinion, and, at times, even faculty governance bodies. Many of my university president colleagues—particularly those associated with public universities—believe that the greatest challenge and threat to their institutions arises from the manner in which their institutions are governed, both from within and from without. Universities have a style of governance that is more adept at protecting the past than preparing for the future. All too often, shared governance tends to protect the status quo—or perhaps even a nostalgic view of some idyllic past—thereby preventing a serious consideration of the future.

It seems clear that the university of the twenty-first century will require new forms of governance and leadership capable of responding to the changing needs and emerging challenges of our society and its educational institutions. To be sure, shared governance models still have much to recommend them, at least in theory if not in practice. The contemporary university has many activities, responsibilities, constituencies, and overlapping lines of authority that are well addressed by the tradition of public oversight and trusteeship, shared collegial internal governance of academic matters, and experienced administrative leadership. Yet the increasing politicization of governing boards; the ability of faculty senates to use their powers to promote special interests, delay action, and prevent reforms; and weak, ineffectual, and usually short-term administrative leadership all pose risks to the university. Although shared governance may have much to recommend it, it must be adapted to a new time and new challenges.

Governing board members should be selected for their expertise in areas related to the nature of higher education and the contemporary university and their commitment to the welfare of the institution. Trustees should be challenged to focus on policy development rather than to intrude into management issues. Their role is to provide strategic, supportive, and critical stewardship for their institutions and to be held publicly, legally, and financially accountable for their performance and the welfare of their institutions.

The faculty should become true participants in the academic decision process rather than simply monitors of the administration or defenders of the status quo. Faculty governance should focus on those issues of most direct concern to academic programs, and faculty members should be held accountable for their decisions. Faculties also need to accept and acknowledge that strong leadership, whether from chairs, deans, or presidents, is important if their institutions are to flourish during a time of significant change.

The contemporary U.S. university presidency also merits a candid reappraisal and likely a thorough overhaul. The position of university president may be one of the more anemic in our society because of the imbalance between responsibility and authority, the cumbersome process used to select university leaders, and the increasing isolation of "professional" academic administrators from the core teaching and scholarship activities of the university. Yet it is nevertheless a position of great importance, particularly considering the long-term impact a president can have on an institution.

In conclusion, it is simply unrealistic to expect that the governance mechanisms developed decades or even centuries ago can be adequate either for the contemporary university or the society it serves. To assign the fate of these important institutions to inexperienced and increasingly political lay governing boards isolated from accountability is simply not in the public interest. Furthermore, during such times of dramatic change, we simply must find ways to cut through the Gordian knot of shared governance, of indecision and inaction, to allow our colleges and universities to better serve our society. Our institutions must not only develop a tolerance for strong leadership; they should demand it. To blind ourselves to these realities is to perpetuate a disservice to both present and future generations.

NOTES

Epigraphs: Harold T. Shapiro, "University Presidents—Then and Now," in *Universities and Their Leadership,* edited by William G. Bowen and Harold T. Shapiro (Princeton: Princeton University Press, 1998), pp. 65–99; National Commission on the Academic Presidency, *Renewing the Academic Presidency: Stronger Leadership for Tougher Times* (Washington, D.C.: Association of Governing Boards of Universities and Colleges, 1996).

REFERENCES

Balderston, F. E. 1995. *Managing today's university: Strategies for viability, change, and excellence.* San Francisco, Jossey-Bass, p. 398.

Ingram, R. T. 1998. *Transforming public trusteeship.* Public Policy Paper Series. Washington, DC: Association of Governing Boards.

Keohane, N. O. 1998. More power to the president? In *The presidency.* Washington, DC: American Council on Education.

National Commission on the Academic Presidency. 1996. *Renewing the academic presidency: Stronger leadership for tougher times.* Washington, DC: Association of Governing Boards of Universities and Colleges.

Weber, L. E. 2001. Critical university decisions and their appropriate makers: Some lessons from the economic theory of federalism. In *Governance in higher education: The university in a state of flux,* ed. W. Z. Hirsch and L. E. Weber. London: Economica.

Zemsky, R., and G. Wegner. 1998. A very public agenda. *Policy Perspectives* 8 (2).

A Growing Quaintness

Traditional Governance in the Markedly New Realm of
U.S. Higher Education

George Keller

The way that most colleges and universities are governed has not received much
scholarly attention since the turbulent 1960s and early 1970s. Yet there recently
has been a resurgence of interest in the topic. Why is this so?

The reason is simple. U.S. institutions have been criticized from many
quarters for their sluggishness in making basic operational changes despite profound shifts in the nation's demography, science and technology, and finances;
the new importance of knowledge; and the growing internationalism that
Simon Marginson discusses in chapter 1. When curious souls probe to discover
the factors that obstruct the ability of colleges to make significant, strategic
changes, they usually find that the governance structures are the main obstacle.

For one thing, the United States, as James Duderstadt outlines, is unique
among nations in using outside lay persons—business leaders, lawyers, clergy,
other educators, and government officials—as trustees who have the final governing authority over a college or university. The tradition is rooted in the manner in which colleges were born in the United States (Herbst 1982), based considerably on Reformation ideas about religious and community control over
the way young people are educated. The claim today is that most trustees are
busy outsiders who can devote little more than general and part-time oversight
to the college's increasingly complex operations. They cannot direct change.

However, the more forceful charge is that the inability to make significant,
rapid changes in academe is the result of a newer tradition, often called *shared
governance*. This widely accepted practice requires presidents, provosts, and
deans to consult about alterations and initiatives often and widely with their
faculty members, and even to cede the power to shape the university's cur-

riculum, hire and promote professors, and determine the requirements of all degrees to the teachers themselves. Since most faculty tend to be jealous of their privileges and wary about being managed like workers in a profit-making corporation, critics have begun to focus on the practice of shared governance as a more serious obstacle to educational change than the passivity and inattention of the board of trustees. Campus presidents and deans are hampered, it is said, from managing and leading their institutions and instead must behave more like the chairpersons of U.S. congressional committees.

The question therefore arises: Are the traditional forms of college and university governance still appropriate? Have the conditions inside and outside colleges shifted so profoundly that the old forms are becoming obsolete?

Origins in the Sixties

In 1963, the American Association of University Professors (AAUP) began a major effort to write a joint statement with the American Council on Education (ACE), representing campus presidents, and the Association of Governing Boards (AGB), representing trustees, on the way colleges and universities should be governed. Governance at the institutions at which nearly all professors were employed had previously not been a priority concern of the AAUP. In its early years the organization did form a Committee T on the Place and Function in University Government and Administration, which issued a statement in 1920 urging increased faculty involvement in the determination of educational policies, selection of personnel, and preparation of the budget. However, protection of the academic freedom of professors, chiefly through tenure, was, and still is, the AAUP's dominant concern. That overriding concern reached a high point in 1940 with the now-famous statement of Principles on Academic Freedom and Tenure (Metzger 1993), as Robert O'Neil elaborates in chapter 7.

The time was ripe. Enrollments in the mid-1960s were expanding, new colleges were being established, and government monies were pouring into colleges and universities, especially for research. The academic programs of nearly every U.S. institution were growing in size and scope. Knowledge was emerging as the key to every advanced society's progress. Clark Kerr, the University of California president, said in his April 1963 Godkin lectures at Harvard: "The university today finds itself in a quite novel position in society . . . We are just now perceiving that the university's invisible product, knowledge, may be the most powerful single element in our culture, affecting the rise and fall of professions and even of social classes, of regions and even of nations . . . Intellect has also become an instrument of national purpose, a component part of the military-industrial complex" (1964, pp. v, vi, 124).

College and university professors in the 1960s were being elevated to a role of special importance in society. It seemed appropriate that a growing number of them, along with the AAUP, now desired a greater voice in managing the institutions in which they carried out their work. So in October 1966 the council of the AAUP adopted the Statement of Government of Colleges and Universities, a document designed for a period of extraordinary growth.

The 1966 statement was not a radical declaration. Since the emergence of more professional scholars in the late nineteenth century, professors had been gaining influence over educational policies and personnel appointments. The 1920 Committee T statement from AAUP said, "There should be a recognized mode of procedure for the joint determination, by trustees and faculty, of what is included in the term educational policies" (p. 27). In what is probably the best book ever written about campus governance, sometime-professor and consultant John J. Corson wrote in 1960 of the tradition of "unique dualism" in higher education administration and how the president often "shares with the faculty the opportunity to make decisions about educational program and faculty selections" (pp. 43, 68).

Two things were novel in the 1966 statement. One was the enlarged scope of faculty powers and influence in nearly every area of institutional management. The AAUP in effect suggested that faculty members become co-managers of their institutions, a model that is called "joint effort" in the statement and has come to be called shared governance in academic parlance. Faculty should participate actively in the framing and execution of education policies and long-range plans, "decisions regarding buildings and other facilities," budgeting, selection of the president and deans, and "procedures governing salary increases." In other areas of administration the professors should have virtual autonomy and control. The statement declares that faculty have "primary responsibility" for the overall curriculum, "the subject matter and methods of instruction," research, requirements for the degrees offered, faculty appointments, promotions, and tenure, and "those aspects of student life which relate to the educational process." In these areas the president and trustees should "concur with the faculty judgment except in rare instances and for compelling reasons which should be stated in detail" (AAUP 2001, pp. 218–23).

The other major change was the downgrading of the role of the president, deans, and trustees and of the importance of leadership at the institutions. The AAUP's 1920 Committee T report acutely acknowledged the need for leadership, the burdens of taking on administrative chores by scholars, and the dangers of divided authority: "The lack of concentration of authority and responsibility would conduce to inefficiency; there would be a lack of initiative and leadership; personalities and politics would play too large a part in university government and administration; members of the faculty would spend too much time in the details of administration and executive work, to the neglect of their main duties as teachers and investigators . . . A university needs leadership in its presiding officers" (p. 24).

In advocating enlarged power and controls over university actions for the faculty, the AAUP, with the surprising concurrence of the ACE and the AGB, neglected to appreciate that colleges and universities are organizations that lead precarious lives financially and are in constant need of constructive academic changes and strategic initiatives. The 1966 statement did concede that "the president has a special obligation to innovate and initiate" and "must at times, with or without support, infuse new life into a department." The president also has "ultimate managerial responsibility for a large area of nonacademic activities" and the responsibility for "creation of new resources" (AAUP 2001, p. 221). Nothing was said, however, about the president and deans being fellow intellectuals and educational captains. Nor was anything inserted in the statement, which was sculpted in the financially flush 1960s, about rising campus costs and the possible need for retrenchments or reallocations, though the AAUP did later add terse remarks on budgeting in 1972 and on financial exigency in 1978.

The AAUP's 1966 Statement on Government is to this day—thirty-seven years later—widely regarded as the standard for desirable procedures of campus governance at U.S. colleges and universities.

Growth and Whirlwinds

Since 1966, there has been a torrent of changes and incursions in American higher education. So abundant have they been that the 1966 AAUP statement is coming to seem almost quaint, like the wearing of fedoras by American males. The proper governance of today's colleges and universities increasingly has become an issue rich in confusion, controversy, and consternation (Chait 2002).

The proper governance of tomorrow's academic institutions has become an issue in urgent need of creative constructs and discerning new practices.

To begin with, enrollments in U.S. higher education were 6.39 million students in 1966 and are estimated to be close to 16 million in 2004. The United States is the first country to introduce mass higher education. This development has necessitated the construction of an almost entirely new layer of two-year colleges, the addition of many new graduate schools and programs, the rise of more than 700 new, for-profit, two-year, four-year, and graduate colleges, and an increase in size at most of America's 3,700 accredited colleges and universities. Colleges that used to enroll 800 to 1,100 students in 1966 now enroll 1,800–2,800 students. Numerous universities have more than 20,000 students; a few enroll more than 40,000. Collegiality is increasingly impossible. Several research universities now have annual operating budgets of more than $1 billion, requiring executive management and financing of a kind previously unknown in higher education.

The size, variety, and scale of colleges and universities mean that there are currently many "faculty" who are knowledgeable but not scholarly teachers, and that sharing the governance of a $500 million or $1 billion multifaceted university is far more complex and time-consuming than participating in the quasi-democratic management of a traditional liberal arts college or small university of forty years ago.

The composition of the faculty is different. Roughly half of all faculty at accredited institutions teach only part-time (Gappa and Leslie 1993), and an estimated 16 percent of part-time faculty have taught for ten or more years at their current institution. Professors are on average older, since federal law no longer allows compulsory retirements. Many more instructors come from blue-collar or immigrant families and from minority households; many more are women. More faculty today have second jobs as consultants, real estate agents, start-up entrepreneurs, or practicing artists. A small but growing minority talk about their chief academic task as "social change agents," and fewer seem to pledge themselves to "the search for truth."

The nation's finest professors now can earn nearly a half million dollars or so annually. Columbia recently hired economist Jeffrey Sachs from Harvard at a reported $300,000 a year salary, plus liberal benefits and an institute with an annual operating budget of $10 million or more. Some of these intellectual stars become millionaires, noted authors, and media celebrities and take frequent leaves of absence from their universities (Wilson 2000). Their primary loyalty is increasingly to their academic discipline or to some small international band of scholars that shares their research interests. Except for emergencies or cataclysmic events, faculty senate meetings are widely reported to be sparsely attended, and consultative committee meetings to deal with college financial priorities, educational policies, or realignments are attended begrudgingly (Scott 1997). Acrimony is not unusual at faculty gatherings.

Then there are faculty unions.

U.S. instructors and professors have always regarded themselves as semi-professionals attached to some college or university, not as employees. Most still view themselves as independents, free to lecture or consult elsewhere, own a business, leave their campus to do research or to write, and teach what and how they see fit (Keller 2001). Professors have shunned unions until recently. Yet in the early 1960s, teachers at several two-year community colleges voted to form a faculty union to bargain with their president and trustees over working conditions, pay, faculty privileges, and similar issues. The movement rapidly spread among two-year public colleges and numerous state colleges, even among a few large public universities and private institutions. In the early 1970s the AAUP itself decided to sign up college professors for collective bargaining.

However, in the late 1970s, Yeshiva University in New York City took its opposition to the unionization of its faculty to the U.S. Supreme Court. In 1980 the court ruled that faculty members were actively engaged in the management of Yeshiva University and other private universities through shared governance. Professors, the court decreed, were usually co-administrators who shared in the governance of their institutions, as the AAUP recommended; professors were not merely hired labor or employees. The formation of a faculty union at Yeshiva was denied.

The so-called Yeshiva decision slowed the spread of faculty unions in U.S. higher education, though there were more than 500 unionized colleges and universities (out of 3,700), mostly public ones, by the year 2000. To accommodate faculty unionism, the AAUP has added material welfare and job security to its focus. As of 1995, the AAUP has represented 61,000 faculty at sixty-one bargaining units (Hutcheson 2000, chaps. 5, 6). The emergence of faculty unions has greatly complicated the role of teacher-scholars in the governance of their colleges and universities. Who speaks for the faculty—the faculty union officers and their lawyers or some separate representative group of elected or selected professors?

The faculty union movement of the post-1966 AAUP statement era has revealed a widening split within contemporary U.S. faculty ranks. Many, especially those at the best private colleges and at most research universities, still actively pursue new knowledge, travel, teach from the latest research, and regard themselves as professional scholars. To them tenure is essential as a protection for their freedom to teach controversial findings, advocate unpopular positions, and publish mind-opening books, articles, and reviews. Yet the growth of mass higher education in the United States has brought in its train a large number of post-secondary instructors who pursue relatively little scholarship and seldom publish in peer-review journals, teach mainly from texts and personal experiences or through colloquial student-faculty exchanges, and tend to see themselves as underpaid workers in bureaucratic organizations. To many of them tenure is chiefly protection for job security.

Perceptive observers of higher education such as Donald Light (1974), Edward Shils (1997), and Oliver Fulton (1998) have contended that the vast increase of higher education in recent decades has resulted in the creation of several kinds of "faculty." It may no longer be possible, they contend, to speak of U.S. faculty members as if they constitute a homogeneous group of scholarly professionals deserving of similar privileges and equally capable of sharing in the management of multimillion-dollar academic enterprises.

A Different Edifice

U.S. colleges and universities as institutions have also changed appreciably. Many institutions today run a two-tier operation: a day school mainly for full-time younger students and an evening college mainly for part-time older students. Nearly half of all enrollees currently are twenty-five years of age or older. Many institutions also run a somewhat separate summer school during June, July, and August, using teachers other than regular faculty. Some colleges have established a weekend college; some leading business schools advertise traveling road shows of instruction in central areas such as finance, strategic planning, and the latest forms of management. Growing numbers of U.S. institutions have created academic programs abroad or established branch campuses in other countries.

Naturally, the question arises often about who exactly is the faculty of these new multifaceted colleges and universities. Also, the old-time, nine-to-three o'clock and nine-month daytime college is clearly no longer the sole component of a college or university. The advent of digital technology has enabled many faculty and students to become more connected with colleagues at other universities and with other sources of data and information. The community of scholars is no longer confined to a single campus, and the campus library is often no longer the preponderant source of data, information, and ideas.

The administration of U.S. higher education has been forced to adopt new forms and measures. Admissions offices have been reorganized to deal with a more multiethnic clientele, caused largely by massive immigration to America since 1965, and to handle initiatives for affirmative action and dispense greater financial aid. Enlarged offices for fund-raising have been created to locate and gather new resources for universities, where costs are rising about 40 percent a year faster than the Consumer Price Index (Baumol and Blackman 1995). Numerous state governments have been trimming appropriations to their public colleges and universities, often prompting reductions in staff and programs. As complexities pile up, competition grows fiercer, and aspirations increase, a majority of U.S. institutions have been tugged into strategic planning for their futures, and this more strategic, proactive management has further complicated the shared governance concept (Keller 1983, 1997).

Shared governance also has been damaged by two other developments. One is the growth of oversight, surveillance, and demands by federal and state agencies, by the courts, and, if we accept Marginson's assertions, soon by international associations as well. Government agencies and the courts have shaped women's athletics, minority admissions, faculty hiring, reports on students' academic progress, and private deliberations via "sunshine laws." These pressures have made outside governments and the courts quasi participants in internal decision making (Mortimer and McConnell 1986, chap. 7; Poskanzer 2002). New entities—alumni, business firms, parents, spectators at athletic contests, the media, mayors, and state legislators—desire to share in the way U.S. colleges and universities are run.

The second development has been the eruption of threats to academic freedom and shared governance from inside colleges and universities (Kors and Silvergate 1998; O'Neil 1997). The presumption in the early 1960s was that the menace to faculty freedoms and campus leadership was almost entirely from outside the campus gates. Yet the student uprisings of the late 1960s and then the mounting pressure of what has been dubbed *political correctness* and of ideological assaults by some professors have presented higher education with novel threats from inside universities, almost none of which were envisioned by the AAUP'S 1966 statement. O'Neil expands upon this idea in chapter 7 by outlining how far we have come from the much simpler time when the AAUP statement was written.

The New Segments

In some ways the most significant, if least noticed, change to affect the governance of colleges and universities since 1966 is the gradual separation of the nation's higher education institutions into four functional categories or layers. These layers have evolved because the nation's commitment to mass higher education and the ballooning needs for fresh knowledge and newly educated persons for the economy and polity have pressed U.S. higher education into specialization, much as medicine or law has become more differentiated (Keller 1999–2000). The most prominent of the four layers is that of the one hundred or so major research universities from Yale to Berkeley. These universities have become fecund sources of new ideas, scientific findings, and fresh discoveries— the primary new knowledge generators for society. Teaching undergraduates tends to be an ancillary activity at these institutions, where graduate students, adjuncts, and temporary instructors do almost half the teaching of undergraduates. Research is central, and competition among the leading public and private universities for prestige, grants, and gifts is fierce, as is the recruiting of research staffs. Henry Rosovsky, the former dean and Geyser University Professor at Harvard, has observed that, "Stars bring visibility and luster; they also bring special deals, special—in the sense of privileged—rules of conduct, and discord and jealousy . . . [Competition for prestige] has greatly increased the power of professors and given many of them immunity from institutional control" (Rosovsky and Ameer 1998, pp. 124–25). Research universities tend to be quite large and often resemble industrial conglomerates with semi-independent schools of business, law, medicine, and architecture and with multiple academic communities. Faculty governance at many of these billion-dollar research universities has crumbled, though it often can be lively still in the campus subunits.

The second layer is that of the 120 to 150 better liberal arts colleges, which are small (under 3,000 students) and mostly for undergraduates. At these institutions, which are nearly all private colleges, the old idea of educating young men and women who are historically and culturally aware and broadly knowledgeable and appreciative thrives. These colleges serve society by preparing leaders for business, the professions, and teaching. A community of scholarly teachers, though sometimes ragged, survives at these intimate enclaves. Here is where the AAUP's 1966 model of shared governance is most closely practiced.

The third sector of U.S. higher education is the huge, multifarious array of state colleges and universities, regional private colleges and universities, and colleges of art, technology, and business. This layer of institutions is largely devoted to preparing persons for the nation's workforce needs, from accountants and nurses to engineers and schoolteachers. The institutions carrying out this societal function vary enormously in size, complexity, faculty competencies, and dedication. The governance and management of these colleges and universities also vary greatly.

The fourth category is also diverse, consisting of community colleges, the less well-endowed private colleges, and proprietary schools. They serve the nation by teaching generally underprepared and less intellectually able students and preparing most of them for vocational work, and they usually provide special courses and programs for working adults. This latter task, however, is being taken over increasingly by a new, fast-growing group of for-profit colleges such as the University of Phoenix.

As the Shapiro brothers, both university presidents, have written, "Mass higher education systems are best served when there is differentiation not only among types of institutions as, for example, among polytechnics and universities, institutional and workplace programs, or community colleges and universities, but also among institutions which have the same generic name . . . This kind of stratification is entirely appropriate to a mass and therefore, necessarily heterogeneous system for it allows for an increasing variety of responses that can better match the increasing variety in both the needs and objectives of faculty and students. In addition, such differentiation is economically efficient" (Shapiro and Shapiro 1994).

The functional segmentation of U.S. colleges and universities causes further difficulties, however, for applying a single standard for governance in higher education.

Thinking Anew

If the 1966 statement on shared governance seems quaint and almost archaic because of the radical changes of the intervening years, then how should we think about the governance of colleges and universities in these early decades of the twenty-first century?

To be fair, the AAUP's 1966 Statement on Government perceptively recognized that a few changes were already underway in the mid-1960s. The statement acknowledged that academic institutions were becoming "less autonomous" as legislatures, government agencies, and the courts increasingly "play[ed] a part in the making of important decisions in academic policy." It also granted that, "Joint effort . . . will take a variety of forms appropriate to the kinds of situations encountered" (2001, 20). Moreover, the AAUP never asked to have faculty members on the board of trustees.

It is also necessary to recognize that several particulars of college and university administration have not changed, despite the transformations and novelties of the past decades. The board of trustees is still the ultimate legal authority and arbiter for each institution, and the president is still the chief executive officer of the trustees. While the composition of what is called the faculty in America has metamorphosed, full-time teacher-scholars are still the heart and lungs of every college. Appropriate, responsible freedom for academics is still indispensable.

What is no longer defensible, however, is the underlying supposition that professors form a tidy community of scholars, united in principles and warm-hearted care for their home institutions, and eager and able to share in the administration, financial management, and strategic planning of their colleges or universities. It is also inappropriate to continue to view presidents and deans as administrators mainly of the nonacademic parts of the institution, as fund-raisers principally, and as persons with time for heavy consultations and consensus building to determine what "the community" would like to do. At today's universities, and even more so at tomorrow's institutions, leadership of a high order and management that is responsive to rapid changes is imperative. For both scholars and campus leaders, time is an increasingly scarce resource.

Fresh thinking about the governance of U.S. colleges and universities requires too that both faculty members and campus administrators recognize that there are inevitable tensions, antiquated beliefs, and cascading consequences for actions taken. The reluctance of most faculty bodies to institute changes is famous, while the disposition of many administrators is to pull their institutions in new directions that seem obligatory to meet new conditions and regional or national needs. There is also the tension between devoted scholarship or instruction in a certain field and frequent service to help with local administrative details, tough decisions, and strategic priorities. As the newly founded Association of American Colleges said in 1915 about the fledgling AAUP ambitions, "No way has yet been found to play the cello or the harp and at the same time to direct the orchestra" (Hofstadter and Metzger 1955, p. 483).

A majority of professors cling to medieval privileges while demanding modern trade union benefits, what the late sociologist James S. Coleman called a "structural fault" in academic dogma. The faculty members have the rights of members of a community—control over their own activities and their time—without the normative constraints and demands that such a community provides. They have the rights of employees of a purposive corporation—the security of a salary and other perquisites of such employees—without the obligation to give up control over their time for use toward a corporate goal. The effect of this structural fault is to create a status with special privileges, a status with the autonomy of a community member, the security of a corporate employee, and the obligations of neither (1973, p. 397).

A majority of college and university presidents, vice presidents, and deans cling to either of two extreme views of academic leadership: that of bold, decisive, overriding executive management or that of passive, cautious, highly consultative and consensual administration. Neither is fruitful and conducive to significant gains in quality, financial stability, or stature. Kenneth Mortimer and Thomas McConnell suggest a different path. "The modern president must instead rely heavily on functional authority—that is, authority based on competence, experience, relations incorporating mutual influence and trust, skill in leadership, greater possession of information, and personal persuasiveness . . . The president's task is to win consent, not to command it" (1986, p. 168).

As for cascading consequences, the professorate and university executives need to understand that decisions in the areas for which the 1966 AAUP statement granted each group near-autonomy or strong primary control affect the other party. Faculty want control over the curriculum and courses, the hiring and promotion of faculty, and requirements for the degree. Yet the design of the curriculum is also a matter of the college's educational policy; the faculty's proliferation of boutique courses affects the institution's finances. Many faculty tenure and promotion committees are reluctant to reject relatively weak colleagues during tenure discussions, affecting the quality of teaching for students and the school's reputation. Faculty setting requirements for a degree frequently results in a diminution of general education and a puffing up of departmental majors to capture students.

Administrative decisions about the allocation of monies can shortchange faculty salaries, harm student life, and weaken the admissions office and financial aid. Responsibility for strategic planning and physical plant additions, renewals, and maintenance has consequences for the faculty and the quality of academic activity. The president's management style and public statements influence faculty pride, morale, and productivity. Thus the claim of either the faculty or the administration for virtual self-determination in certain areas is unwarranted and naïve about the intricate ecology of college management.

Clearly, the AAUP's 1966 Statement on Government is no longer adequate, given the numerous changes of the past thirty-seven years. (In a few ways it was not quite adequate even in 1966.) Where does this leave the beau ideal of government for U.S. colleges and universities? How should they be governed in the decades ahead?

What Next?

Sharing David Collis's hesitation (see chap. 2), I add my own considerable trepidation and offer five suggestions that may contribute to the formulation of more contemporary governance observances and practices at U.S. colleges and universities.

First, in a time of fast-paced changes the traditional and absolutely vital commitment to academic freedom for serious, objective teaching scholars should be balanced by an equal appreciation of the need for administrative freedom for sage, dedicated college and university leaders. Unlike physicians or lawyers, professors must work in collective academic organizations; they cannot be solo practitioners. Unless their schools, colleges, and universities are strong, faculty will have difficulty performing well. Strong academic houses require vigorous, visionary, nimble executive leadership (AGB 1996). To keep U.S. colleges and universities strong and among the world's best, the rights of faculty need to be matched with a stronger sense of the imperatives of vigorous, forward-looking management.

Donald Kennedy, biologist and former president of Stanford, has observed that most faculty argue passionately for faculty rights and privileges but tend to neglect the need for beneficial changes and hard decisions. He has called for a "shift in loyalty" with greater concerns for the needs of the institution and its students (1997, pp. 2–3). Henry Rosovsky believes that "most professors have little sense of social contract" (Rosovsky and Ameer 1998, p. 125). The two are thinking of extraordinary self-regarding scholars at elite research universities, so they tend to neglect the allegiances of many of the other four-fifths of

America's faculty. Nevertheless, the accusations have some broad validity. The individual rights of faculty should be balanced better against the corporate rights of institutions to survive, change, serve more effectively, and grow.

With ever-greater financial strains, growing demands for academic renovation, and pleas for increased attention to the needs of students and states, administrative freedom to maneuver and act constructively and more quickly becomes as important as the academic freedom of faculty to control an institution's curriculum, personnel, and promotions. In one of the most vigorous recent essays on campus governance, the former University of Michigan president James Duderstadt (author of chap. 5), writes, "Universities have a style of governance that is more adept at protecting the past than preparing for the future" (2001, p. 48). He adds, "Universities must develop more capacity to move rapidly. This will require a willingness by leaders throughout the university to occasionally make difficult decisions and take strong action without the traditional consensus-building process" (p. 41). Governance in the future should restore the balance of respect that the AAUP's Committee T Report recognized in 1920 but that many faculty advocates today overlook.

Second, given the increasing segmentation and variety in academe due to U.S. mass higher education, pluralism rather than standardization should become the norm in academic governance. Daytona Beach Community College with 10,000 students needs a different governance scheme than does Eckerd College with 1,500 students, and Iowa State University should exhibit a different form of governance from Grinnell College. Texas Women's University, the University of Notre Dame, and Massachusetts Institute of Technology will, and should, differ in their style of governance. Whether a school is small or huge, religiously sponsored or secular, rich or struggling, liberal arts or research-oriented, two-year or four-year, public or private will shape the pattern of faculty governance and administrative assertiveness. To argue, as numerous advocates for greater faculty powers do, as if all faculty were truth-seeking scholars, devoted teachers, and persons eager to assist in their university's administration, is to mischaracterize America's multifarious full-time, part-time, and adjunct postsecondary instructors. Furthermore, to believe that small, underendowed colleges should be governed pretty much as, say, Cornell University, Baylor University, and the University of Michigan, is folly.

Given the new kinds of institutions and new kinds of faculty, the period ahead should be one of experimentation and innovation in campus governance. This has begun bravely at a few institutions such as William and Mary

(Baldwin and Leslie 2001). Sure, the faculty should continue to be given the dominant voice in matters in which they are most expert, such as what is happening in their field of scholarship. Likewise, the president, deans, and vice presidents, as well as the trustees, should exercise major influence in those areas for which they are most responsible. The general principle persists. However, adherence to some sort of quaint, old standard or the desire for a new decree applicable for all institutions should be viewed with great suspicion and a touch of risibility.

Third, in the United States, government takes place at the federal, state, county, city or town, and even village or neighborhood levels. So it is in higher education. Government occurs within an academic department, a division, a school (of business, education, or arts and science), and the entire college or university. Hence I suggest that we think of the government of academic institutions as more than participation in large, all-college issues, and that faculty influence in decisions should be greatest at the local level but less controlling at the total university level, where student, trustee, alumni, legal, state, employer, and even media interests must be considered as well. That is, the kind and degree of governance should depend largely on the level at which it is practiced.

At the department level, professorial governance can and should be highly democratic, with little administrative interference unless the faculty in the department drift from the institution's policies or fall into disarray or decline. This is also the best level at which to engage the "other" faculty: part-timers, adjuncts, and graduate assistants. Shared governance often works best, especially at large universities, at the level of specialized school or college: agriculture, social work, medicine, communications, business, and the like. The unit is small enough, the academic purposes are more focused, and the deans are not responsible for such a wide spectrum of chores as presidents. At the all-college or whole university level, shared governance increasingly is a failure, although it can work quite effectively at smaller institutions if there is mutual understanding, mutual respect, and generosity of spirit. Yet large faculty senates are frequently quarrel pits, garbage cans for the disposal of personal grievances, and platforms for harangues. Many members are in reality lobbyists for their own disciplines, schools, or ideological causes. And the pace is often snail-like. William Tierney, this book's editor and former president of the academic senate at the University of Southern California, found that "the leisurely pace of decision-making by the Senate seems quaint, at best. The Senate meets once a month for two hours. We take the summer months off . . . The Senate needs a structure that is agile" (n.d., p. 13).

Berkeley scholar Martin Trow, who once headed his institution's faculty senate, goes further. He says flatly that faculty senates cannot lead. To him, "Members of academic senate committees are part-time amateurs, usually with minimum staff and dependent on the administration for information." As a result, "the advice of academic senates is often tardy or incompetent." Trow believes that academic senates can be most useful "for setting limits on the arbitrary power of deans, provosts, and presidents" (1990, p. 26–27).

Fourth, faculty participation in all-university governance should be largely through special task forces or Kleenex structures that help solve a major problem or provide advice on a significant issue and then dissolve. Many professors are superb analysts, first-rate thinkers, and exceptionally knowledgeable persons, so when their attention is captured for a special purpose and for a limited period, and they are given adequate and detailed information about the topic and reasons for a decision on the topic, their counsel and suggestions can be invaluable. Presidents and trustees are usually not well informed about particular academic matters or emerging intellectual trends; they should seek advice, criticisms, and proposals from the wiser faculty members (Sample 2002). Faculty at numerous campuses have offered excellent guidance about such matters as technology, performing arts, the athletic program, strategic priorities, and graduate programs, among others.

The fifth suggestion is that more heed be given by faculty and administrators to their sense of duty and to their obligations to each other and to their colleges or universities. Good governance requires more than a preoccupation with rights and advocacy of individual needs. We live in a time of rampant individualism (Taylor 1992; Putnam 2000), of an epidemic of contentions about rights and purported victimizations. If it is to be governed better, higher education must receive greater concern from its members for each institution's welfare.

Edward Shils once reported that Sidney Hook told him how John Dewey in his later years remembered that when the AAUP was born in 1916, a committee A and a committee B were created. Committee A was to deal with academic freedom and tenure, while the other committee was to deal with the obligations of being an academic. Committee A quickly became a preoccupation of the association, but committee B never met (Shils 1997, p. 153). Presidents too can forget their obligations and duties. In my home state of Maryland, for example, the new president of Towson State University immediately had a luxurious home built for his residence with $2 million of state monies and a $50,000 gold medal made for him to wear at his inauguration; this, when the state was cutting back on appropriations for higher education. The state's board of regents fired him shortly thereafter. Everyone in higher education needs to balance his or her intellectual interests and personal values with the requisites of a strong, high-quality, amiable, and financially solid organizational life at his or her college or university (Kennedy 1997; Etzioni 1996).

Academics have a special obligation to help govern their institutions in some principled but modern, innovative way. Not only have knowledge and the colleges and universities that preserve and foster knowledge become newly central in our postindustrial society, but academics can only prosper and produce in a college or university setting. The campus traditions and culture, resources, fellowship, wonderful talk and classroom exchanges, special equipment, a warehouse of books and network of electronics, and a semi-sacred and often lovely setting are indispensable to a life of learning and research. Professors are embedded agents.

Updating the Dogmas

Abraham Lincoln said in 1862: "The dogmas of the quiet past are inadequate to the stormy present. The occasion is piled high with difficulty, and we must rise to the occasion. As our case is new, so we must think anew. We must disenthrall ourselves" (Boritt 1996, p. 56).

Much the same could be said about the governance of U.S. contemporary colleges and universities. Mass higher education, with its more varied institutions and newly heterogeneous teaching faculty, the greater size of its institutions, its more competitive conditions, heavier financial needs, and the new sensibilities of its students, faculty, and administrators, has rendered the dogmas of our quieter academic past inadequate. We must disenthrall ourselves and think anew (Keller 1989). We can safeguard the tattered ideal of shared governance only by reinventing it for the new environment.

REFERENCES

American Association of University Professors (AAUP). 1920. Committee T report on the place and function of faculties in university government and administration. *AAUP Bulletin* 6 (March): 17–47.
———. 2001. Policy documents and reports. 9th ed. Washington, DC: American Association of University Professors.

Association of Governing Boards (AGB). 1996. Stronger leadership for tougher times. Report of the Commission on the Presidency. Washington, DC: Association of Governing Boards.

Baldwin, R., and D. Leslie. 2001. Rethinking the structure of shared governance. *Peer Review* 3 (Spring): 18–19.

Baumol, W., and S. A. B. Blackman. 1995. How to think about rising college costs. *Planning for Higher Education* 23 (Summer): 1–7.

Boritt, G. S. 1996. *Of the people, by the people, for the people: Quotations by Abraham Lincoln.* New York: Columbia University Press.

Chait, R. 2002. The "Academic Revolution" revisited. In *The future of the city of intellect,* ed. Steven Brint. Stanford: Stanford University Press.

Coleman, J. S. 1973. The university and society's new demands upon it. In *Content and context,* ed. C. Kaysen. New York: McGraw-Hill.

Corson, J. J. 1960. *Governance of colleges and universities.* New York: McGraw-Hill.

Duderstadt, J. 2001. Fire, ready, aim! In *Governance in higher education: The university in a state of flux,* ed. W. Hirsch and L. Weber. London: Economica.

Etzioni, A. 1996. *The new golden rule: Community and morality in a democratic society.* New York: Basic Books.

Fulton, O. 1998. The academic profession in comparative perspective in the era of mass higher education. In *Universities and their leadership,* ed. W. Bowen and H. Shapiro. Princeton: Princeton University Press.

Gappa, J., and D. Leslie. 1993. *The invisible faculty.* San Francisco: Jossey-Bass.

Herbst, J. 1982. *From crisis to crisis: American college government, 1636-1819.* Cambridge: Harvard University Press.

Hofstadter, R., and W. Metzger. 1955. *The development of academic freedom in the United States.* New York: Columbia University Press.

Hutcheson, P. 2000. *A professional professoriate: Unionization, bureaucratization, and the AAUP.* Nashville: Vanderbilt University Press.

Keller, G. 1983. *Academic strategy: The management revolution in American higher education.* Baltimore: Johns Hopkins University Press.

———. 1989. Shotgun marriage: The growing connection between academic management and faculty governance. In *Governing tomorrow's campus,* ed. J. Schuster and L. Miller. New York: ACE/Macmillan.

———. 1997. Examining what works in strategic planning. In *Planning and management for a changing environment,* ed. M. Peterson, D. Dill, and L. Mets. San Francisco: Jossey-Bass.

———. 1999–2000. The emerging third stage in higher education planning. *Planning for Higher Education* 28 (Winter): 1–7.

———. 2001. Governance: The remarkable ambiguity. In *In defense of American higher education,* ed. P. Altbach, P. Gumport, and D. Johnstone. Baltimore: Johns Hopkins University Press.

Kennedy, D. 1997. *Academic duty.* Cambridge: Harvard University Press.

Kerr, C. 1964. *The uses of the university.* Cambridge: Harvard University Press.

Kors, A., and H. Silvergate. 1998. *The shadow university: The betrayal of liberty on America's campuses.* New York: Free Press.

Light, D. 1974. The structure of the academic professions. *Sociology of Education* 47 (Winter): 2–28.

Metzger, W. 1993. The 1940 statement of principles on academic freedom and tenure. In *Freedom and tenure in the academy,* ed. W. VanAlstyne. Durham, NC: Duke University Press.

Mortimer, K., and T. R. McConnell. 1986. *Sharing authority effectively.* San Francisco: Jossey-Bass.

O'Neil, R. 1997. *Free speech in the college community.* Bloomington: Indiana University Press.

Poskanzer, S. 2002. *Higher education law: The faculty.* Baltimore: Johns Hopkins University Press.

Putnam, R. 2000. *Bowling alone: The collapse and revival of American community.* New York: Simon and Schuster.

Rosovsky, H., and I. Ameer. 1998. A neglected topic: Professional conduct of college and university teachers. In *Universities and their leadership,* ed. W. Bowen and H. Shapiro. Princeton: Princeton University Press.

Sample, S. 2002. *The contrarian's guide to leadership.* San Francisco: Jossey-Bass.

Scott, J. 1997. Death by inattention: The strange fate of faculty governance. *Academe* 83 (November-December): 28-33.

Shapiro, B., and H. Shapiro. 1994. Universities in higher education: Some problems and challenges in a changing world. October. Unpublished manuscript.

Shils, E. 1997. The academic ethic. In *The calling of education,* ed. S. Grosby. Chicago: University of Chicago Press.

Taylor, C. 1992. *The ethics of authenticity.* Cambridge: Harvard University Press.

Tierney, W. G. (n.d.). Reflections on academic governance. Los Angeles: Center for Higher Education Policy Analysis, University of Southern California.

Trow, M. 1990. The academic senate as a school for university leadership. *Liberal Education* 76 (January-February): 23-27.

Wilson, R. 2000. They may not wear Armani to class, but some professors are filthy rich. *The Chronicle of Higher Education,* March 3, pp. A16-18.

CHAPTER SEVEN

University Governance and Academic Freedom

Robert M. O'Neil

When Christina Axson-Flynn enrolled in the Actor Training Program at the University of Utah in the fall of 1998, she could hardly have anticipated the intense conflict between governance and academic freedom which her curricular choice would soon trigger. A devout Mormon, Axson-Flynn had warned faculty members during her audition that she would be uncomfortable "taking the Lord's name in vain" or uttering certain taboo words. On two occasions during her first semester, she substituted acceptable language for words she found offensive in the assigned scripts—once with her instructor's knowledge and reluctant approval, and the other time on her own initiative. During a discussion of plans for the ensuing semester, the gap between Axson-Flynn's standards and her instructors' expectations became starkly clear.

When the faculty warned that future scripts must be read verbatim, Axson-Flynn withdrew from the program. She soon filed a lawsuit in federal district court, charging that the conditions that the drama faculty had imposed upon her effectively abridged her federally protected constitutional rights. Specifically, she claimed that the Utah drama professors with whom she had tangled during the fall semester had abridged her religious liberty and her freedom of speech by insisting that, as a condition of completing the Actor Training Program, she must utter words that she deemed abhorrent by reason of her faith and beliefs. The district judge dismissed her suit, upholding the curricular mandates imposed by the theater faculty.[1]

The *Axson-Flynn* case juxtaposes, in a federal courtroom, the freedom of students to learn and the freedom of professors to teach. Simply put, it presents at one and the same time two questions that usually arise quite separately—

on the one hand, the issue of "whose academic freedom?" and on the other hand the issue of how (and where) that quandary is to be addressed and resolved. Curiously, there appears in this case to have been no resort to whatever campus channels might have availed either party, although one would normally expect that internal university processes would be given a chance to address such a dispute before it reached a federal courtroom. It may be that the very novelty of the case clouded the quest for internal relief or resolution. In any event, the prospect that a federal appeals court would be called upon to decide between a student's right to learn and a professor's right to prescribe how that student should learn is a frightening one indeed. Those who appraise systems of academic governance await the outcome with understandable anxiety.

This chapter focuses on several areas in which the relationship between university governance and academic freedom deserves closer scrutiny. I begin by probing several intriguing and unresolved issues surrounding the granting and the removal of faculty tenure, the relationship of which to academic freedom needs little elaboration here. I then turn to issues of academic freedom and the structure of university governance, including special attention to the inevitably complex relationship between academic freedom and collective bargaining. I then revisit the most perplexing issue posed in the *Axson-Flynn* case—Whose academic freedom?—where I also appraise the increasingly contentious debate between individual and institutional claims of academic freedom. I conclude with a brief analysis of the potential impact of the events of September 11, 2001, upon the governance/academic freedom nexus.

Because they are central to each of the sections that follow, I wish to elaborate on George Keller's initial discussion and offer a basic understanding of the principles of academic freedom that may be helpful at the outset. By far the most authoritative voice over the past three quarters of a century has been that of the American Association of University Professors (AAUP), a faculty group that declares positions and policies, investigates violations of academic freedom (which in extreme cases may lead to censure of the administration), and gathers data on issues important to faculty interests and welfare. The basic declaration of academic freedom is found in AAUP's 1940 statement, which has now been endorsed by most scholarly and learned societies, and by a large number of colleges and universities. That statement declares that "teachers are entitled to full academic freedom in research and in the publication of results, subject to the adequate performance of their other academic duties." Specifically, the statement declares that "teachers are entitled to freedom in the classroom in discussing their subject" but adds that "they should be careful not to introduce into their teaching controversial material which has no relation to their subject" (AAUP 2003).

Recognizing that university professors may also seek and merit protection outside the classroom and the laboratory, the statement adds that "when they speak or write as citizens, they should be free from institutional censorship or discipline, but their special position in the community imposes special obligations." Specifically among those obligations, "they should at all times be accurate, should exercise proper restraint, should show respect for the opinions of others, and should make every effort to indicate that they are not speaking for the institution." A closely related guarantee is that of due process—the insistence of AAUP (indeed of the academic community as a whole) that continuing appointments of nontenured faculty, and even more clearly of those who have been granted tenure, may be terminated only for the gravest of reasons (subsumed under the general heading of *cause*) and only through a process that ensures fairness and impartiality to an accused professor.

Curiously, AAUP has never defined just what its members believe should constitute "cause" for such terminations, preferring to leave the evolution of a kind of academic "common law" to the myriad reports resulting from campus investigations of alleged academic freedom infringements. That, in a nutshell, is the corpus of faculty rights and interests which academic tenure protects—making appropriate as a starting point in our examination the processes by which tenure is achieved and may be lost.

Tenure: How It Comes and How It Goes

The intriguing and vital relationship between tenure, academic freedom, and faculty governance has been curiously neglected.[2] In a study summarized in his new book, *The Questions of Tenure*, Harvard professor Richard Chait focuses on one significant facet of that relationship—the links between faculty status and governance. Chait reports that "the presence of a tenure system provides a reliable indicator of greater faculty voice in governance." It is far from clear, however, that greater faculty security was the cause or catalyst for more collegial governance; indeed, Chait cautions at the conclusion of his report, "it is far more likely . . . that tenure signaled rather than created these conditions." The converse is, however, equally noteworthy. The report of this important study observes that "the *absence* of tenure suggested a comparatively vulnerable college where faculty have relatively limited authority or interest in shared governance" (Chait 2002, p. 96). Beyond this intriguing correlation between status and structure, it may be worth probing several implications of university governance for the process by which tenure is conferred, and therefore by which academic freedom is enhanced, within the academic profession.[3] There are some fascinating case studies, and abundant raw material for further analysis.

In the late 1970s, the administration of the University of Wisconsin system faced a novel and troubling dilemma about the conferral of tenure. The chair of a relatively small department at one of the rural northern campuses was approaching the end of the probationary period, so a tenure decision had to be made soon. That fact alone revealed at least one lapse in the process, since a nontenured professor should not in good conscience be asked to head an academic unit within which decisions about granting (or denying) tenure to colleagues must be made under his or her aegis. The Wisconsin administrative code contained a provision that (like many mandates that govern the university system's affairs) had been drafted to protect faculty interests. Under the code, tenure could only be awarded on the basis of a positive recommendation by the faculty members of the relevant academic unit (department or professional school). The particular department in question was dysfunctional, and its already tenured members were reportedly quite hostile to its nontenured chair for reasons that seemed unrelated to his academic prowess and potential.

Herein lay the dilemma: If the tenure issue were entrusted to the senior faculty of the department, as the state's code seemed to require, a negative but untrustworthy judgment would certainly ensue. If, on the other hand, campus administrators outside the department were to initiate a favorable personnel action, as they undoubtedly would have done, and had the board of regents eventually granted tenure, such a seemingly benign intervention would not only violate state law but also would flout a legal provision that had as its central goal safeguarding the role of the faculty in what is arguably the most sacrosanct of professorial powers, the conferral of tenure upon immediate colleagues. The only other option that seemed even vaguely viable would have been to terminate the probationary appointment of a promising scholar and teacher, on the technically defensible but clearly unconscionable ground that a governance system that was designed to ensure faculty interests provided in this instance no process by which tenure could have been granted. So callous an explanation for ending a faculty appointment, despite a case in favor of granting tenure that would have prevailed under any other conditions, would have turned the system on its head. It also would have been a clear, albeit ironic, affront to an individual's academic freedom, seemingly compelled by a collective interest in collegial judgment.

A Solomonic solution eventually emerged. An ad hoc group of tenured faculty from cognate social science departments was charged with reviewing the case. They were asked to apply, to the best of their ability, the tenure standards that the candidate's immediate colleagues would have applied had they been able to judge the case impartially and objectively. The ad hoc committee recommended the granting of tenure, finding the case to be clearly meritorious. The campus chancellor, the system administration, and the Wisconsin board of regents accepted that recommendation, and the case came to an end—though not without vigorous protest from the bypassed departmental colleagues, who insisted that such an action had forced upon them a lifetime colleague whom they had clearly wished not to embrace. That claim mercifully never ended up in court; had such a suit been filed, any state or federal judge would surely have dismissed it on the ground that no individual grievance could be based upon a breach of the departmental-initiation provision of the administrative code. It was, in short, an illegality in the abstract—and one necessitated by the absence of any acceptable alternatives. It was also, let us concede, a case of favoring individual academic freedom interests over the collective interests of departmental faculty governance to which we normally would defer.

The central lesson of this bizarre case now merits closer scrutiny. Normally, we deem peer evaluation and careful assessment of a nontenured colleague's potential absolutely vital to the granting or denial of tenure. Nonetheless, with all deference to such judgments, we accept on occasion the negative outcome of a process in which positive departmental action is reversed on the basis of an all-campus tenure committee's less favorable assessment, and tenure is ultimately denied. The notion that someone other than the candidate's immediate peers should make such momentous judgments is inherently suspect within the academic community. Thus, when a front-page *New York Times* story in mid-March 2002 noted that Columbia University's embattled English department had effectively ceded senior hiring decisions—with a clear implication of concomitant tenure—to a panel of five scholars from other institutions, many readers were troubled, even outraged, by what seemed to some an abdication of the most basic of professorial prerogatives (Arenson 2002). Of course, the ultimate personnel decisions would still be made on Morningside Heights before anyone could receive Columbia tenure. But the initiative seemed to have shifted to outsiders, as a desperate and last-ditch measure designed to heal deep and persistent wounds among Columbia's senior English scholars.

As a matter of sound policy, the conferral of tenure should not depend solely upon a positive peer recommendation, as the well-intentioned Wisconsin code section demands. There are times, like those in the contentious Wisconsin case, when some acceptable alternative must be available. A personal experience from the same period may illustrate. Soon after I became vice-president of Indiana University for the Bloomington campus, I received two personnel recommendations from a small, though highly distinguished, academic department. The unit was at that time dominated by a powerful and eminent scholar who had largely shaped the nature of the discipline as well as the unit he headed at Indiana. It happened that two of the five professors in that department came up for tenure in the same year.

The chairman recommended tenure for one and termination for the other. For various reasons far too complex to recount here, I eventually reversed both recommendations. My judgment was confirmed by the university system's president and by the trustees, though only after vigorous protest from the chairman and one other tenured colleague. Only exceptional circumstances, such as a persuasive rejection of the department's actions in this case, first by the arts and sciences tenure committee and later by the all-campus advisory group, would ever warrant such an extraordinary reversal. Moreover, one does not lightly repeat such action; mercifully, the tenure process during my remaining years at Indiana was relatively calm, if not always routine, and no need for comparable intervention recurred.

A third and very different situation expands the inquiry. In the late 1960s, soon after the University of Buffalo joined the State University of New York, president Martin Meyerson faced a personnel crisis for which even his tumultuous months as acting chancellor at Berkeley had not fully prepared him. A mature scholar had been recruited six years earlier to a joint chair in two professional schools that had been seeking closer collaboration. His salary and teaching duties were evenly split between the two schools. He participated actively in the work of both faculties and published papers at the intersection of the two disciplines. All went well until about an hour before the end of the final day of the dual appointee's probationary period. President Meyerson now learned for the first time that neither school was quite willing to recommend tenure, although both faculties had repeatedly expressed their esteem for their shared colleague and a strong hope that he would remain on the faculty.

The president's question to his staff, as the witching hour approached, was, of course, the proper one: "Do I have legal authority to grant him tenure by the stroke of my pen?" A quick call to Albany produced a positive answer. Tenure was conferred at 4:55, and the professor was so informed as the campus bells sounded five. Regrettably, this saga did not quite end there. Neither of the two faculties was yet ready to embrace this valued colleague as a member of its tenured ranks. The next semester brought plaintive and persistent phone calls to the president's office, both from the now legally tenured but not entirely welcome professor and from the two professional school deans, each of whom wished passionately to retain the professor, albeit on someone else's tenure roster. Granting presidential tenure did solve one set of problems and surely was the wisest course for the institution as well as the individual, but it created in its wake other issues that persisted until the eventual retirement of this "professor without a faculty."

These all appear to be classic situations in which the exception proves the rule. To preserve faculty governance and judgment and to ensure the credibility of a process that is not always fully trusted within, much less outside the academic community, the paradigm should be favorable action by one's immediate peers as the sine qua non of a positive tenure action. There should, however, be some possibility for exceptions in rare but meritorious cases, such as the two that have just been discussed. What we lack and urgently need is a clearer consensus on the circumstances that warrant departure from the norm. Creating a "shadow department" to substitute its judgment for that of a real but dysfunctional unit is surely not the answer. Nor should we need to resort to ad hoc variations even for the best of cases.

Perhaps we could simply agree that where there are demonstrable reasons for not accepting a department's normally decisive negative judgment, and where a strongly favorable recommendation emerges from one or more other faculty groups, which are credible and are empowered to make such judgments (for example, an arts and sciences tenure committee or an all-campus body advisory to the provost), we may proceed to award tenure despite an adverse appraisal by the candidate's immediate peers. In so doing, we should be candid in recognizing that such a process may well create an involuntary collegial relationship—a price we should be willing to exact in the exceptional case in which protection of academic freedom may indeed trump abstract interests of faculty governance.

The governance issues seem somewhat clearer on the other side of the coin, the removal of tenure. Here the policies of the AAUP are unambiguous: Dismissal for cause of a tenured professor or termination of a probationary appointment before its end requires an adversary hearing that meets full standards of due process, and it should be preceded by informal inquiry from an elected faculty personnel committee. Peer judgment is expected, as well, before the termination of a tenured (or continuation of a nontenured) appointment for reasons other than cause, which may include a bona fide financial exigency or the elimination of a program or department for valid educational reasons. Whatever the catalyst for such drastic action, AAUP policies contemplate that final negative action must either result from the recommendation of an elected faculty body or at least be subject to scrutiny by such a body before it becomes final, in order to ensure fairness, consistency, and faculty participation in making such draconian judgments.[4] Here again, the relationship between academic freedom and faculty governance requires the involvement, at an appropriate and meaningful stage in the process, of peer judgment by those who should be best endowed to advise on a proposed adverse personnel action.

A personal experience may illustrate the soundness of this mandate. During two decades of senior administrative service, I initiated four tenure-termination proceedings. Three cases resulted in eventual dismissal by the governing board, and none was challenged in court. The relevant faculty personnel committee concurred in each of those actions—indeed, the committee was at least as anxious as the administration to terminate the appointment of one confessed plagiarist and of two tenured professors who had for years unconscionably avoided any but the most minimal of professorial tasks.

The fourth case was, however, starkly different. The department chair who had begun the dismissal process was at that time an elected member of the National AAUP Council and thus could hardly be thought insensitive to academic freedom concerns. The case he presented seemed to show a consistent and inexcusable dereliction of duty. Yet the faculty personnel committee, when asked to undertake a preliminary review of the case before formal charges were filed (as AAUP policy strongly recommends), advised against dismissal because of what seemed to its members to be vaguely extenuating circumstances. The administration decided nonetheless to proceed and lodged formal dismissal charges. Just before those charges were taken to the faculty personnel committee, we received a physician's report that the about-to-be-accused professor had an inoperable brain tumor. A profuse apology to the terminally ill colleague and his grieving family was the least that could be done by way of confessing error and trying to set matters aright. Clearly, the faculty committee (which had little sympathy for the aberrant behavior but feared a potential miscarriage of justice) was right. Anyone who doubts the soundness of AAUP policy in this realm of procedure should have experienced the trauma of this case, which still evokes haunting memories after three decades.

Whose Academic Freedom Is It—and Who Decides?

At one time, we in the faculty universe would have assumed a fairly simple answer to the question "whose academic freedom is it anyway?" We would have insisted, as the AAUP's 1940 statement clearly posits, that academic freedom exists to enable individual professors to teach, write, and pursue research without fear of reprisal because their views may offend government officials, trustees, alumni, students, or even their own colleagues. As University of Texas law professor and AAUP general counsel David Rabban noted in a recent article, "the two most important early Supreme Court decisions on academic freedom . . . identified it as an individual liberty of professors" (2001, p. 18; see also Rabban 1993). Later rulings have, however, complicated that equation substantially. The U.S. Supreme Court's 1978 *Regents of University of Calif. v. Bakke* decision validated the use of race in the admissions process, in part through recognition of an institution's academic freedom–based interest in determining "who may be admitted to study".[5] Another Supreme Court case several years later, involving claims of access to university facilities by student religious organizations, invoked "the academic freedom of public universities" as a reason for the abstention of federal courts, insisting that educational decisions about the content of expression "should be made by academicians, not by federal judges."[6]

Thus, for the first time, there were strong suggestions that colleges and universities, as well as the individuals who comprise their faculties, merit some protection under the broad heading of "academic freedom," at least against external threats of a comparable character. Such early judicial recognition of an institutional dimension of academic freedom did not, however, evoke faculty concern at the time because professorial interests benefited substantially, if indirectly, from such judicial deference to institutional claims of academic freedom. It was, in short, a win-win situation, with no suggestion that we were heading toward what would eventually look far more like a zero-sum game.

All that has now changed dramatically, as Rabban notes, by reason of recent court rulings. Two federal appeals courts have not only recognized a ten-

sion between the academic freedom claims of individuals and those of institutions but also have embraced the latter at the expense of the former. In 2001
the U.S. Court of Appeals for the Third Circuit ruled that a public university
may actually invoke its academic freedom interests in a grading dispute with an
individual professor, and that the institution's academic freedom may trump
the faculty member's plea that grading has always been an indispensable part
of the teaching process.[7] Instead of the professor and the president jointly asserting shared interests in academic freedom against hostile forces off campus,
which had been the prior model, we have now entered the zero-sum game. In
this new and fearsome environment, one set of academic freedom interests pre-
vails only at the expense of the other. If, in a court's view, the administration is
right and has final authority over grading decisions, the power which it holds
and asserts in this arena reflects a direct diminution of what had historically
been the professor's prerogative to assess the performance of his or her own students. This remarkable ruling reflected a decision two years earlier, involving
the same institution, in which the same court had said that the university may,
as a matter of academic freedom, determine (even contrary to professorial judgment) "what will be taught in the classroom."[8]

The most ominous of the recent judgments, though, is that of the fourth circuit appeals court, in a case involving the seemingly peripheral topic of computer-
use policies. The Virginia General Assembly in 1996 barred state employees from
using state-owned or state-leased computers to access sexually explicit material, save where the demands of a bona fide research project warranted per-
mission from an "agency head." Six Virginia public university professors challenged the law in federal court and prevailed at the trial level on a variety of free
speech claims. But the appeals court reversed, first through a three-judge panel
and later through the entire circuit sitting en banc.[9]

Although a lengthy discussion of academic freedom was hardly necessary to
the judgment, the majority felt this an appropriate occasion to convey its views
on that issue. To the extent the Constitution might protect academic freedom
more broadly than it embraced any citizen's First Amendment speech rights,
said the fourth circuit, "the right inheres in the University, not in individual
professors." However often the U.S. Supreme Court and other tribunals had up-
held professorial free speech claims, this was merely an accident of the fact that
"teachers were the first public employees to be afforded the now-universal protection against dismissal for the exercise of First Amendment rights" (Rabban
2001, p. 19). The abstract possibility that institutional policy might abridge in-

dividual faculty freedoms was dismissed in a footnote as "not presented here" because none of the six plaintiffs alleged that they had actually been denied Internet access because of the subject matter of their research. The circuit's chief judge, J. Harvie Wilkinson, a former University of Virginia law professor, although concurring about the validity of the computer-use law, took strenuous issue with his colleagues' novel and alarming views on academic freedom and in that departure was joined by several dissenting judges.

Rabban concludes his recent article on a hopeful and portentous note: "Although it is unlikely that the weight of judicial authority will follow the majority in the [computer-use] case and deny First Amendment protection to the academic freedom of individual professors, the tension between individual and institutional claims to academic freedom will almost certainly persist" (2001, p. 20). That prognosis is also highly germane to our current inquiry into the issue of "whose academic freedom?"

The short answer to that question has been, until quite recently, "it depends on who asserts it." The premise was that protection of academic freedom could not be a zero-sum game, in which recognition of an *institution's* academic freedom claim (as in the Bakke case with regard to race-based admissions) in no way diminished—indeed, invariably enhanced—the *individual* faculty member's claim. A professor serving on a medical school admissions committee shares in the exercise of the very academic freedom that the institution has successfully pressed to support its use of race in deciding "who may be admitted to study." Bakke's basic assumptions have never been rejected or even substantially qualified, at least by the U.S. Supreme Court, despite some less-than-faithful adherence by several lower federal courts. Now, however, the prospect is more ominous. The tendency of major challenges (currently against the University of Michigan [Schmidt 2001]) to race-based admissions programs could lead the Supreme Court to revisit the academic freedom rationale as well as the immediate issue of how far race and ethnicity may shape the selection of students for highly competitive programs. Several federal circuits have reached conflicting results, a situation which often invites Supreme Court intervention.

Should the Supreme Court agree to review any of the lower court rulings on the role of race—something it has thus far declined to do despite contrasting, if not directly conflicting, judgments—the academic community should be fully prepared to support not only the use of race in the admissions process as an essential ingredient of diversity but also the academic freedom rationale for the process by which faculties achieve and maintain diversity through determination of "who may be admitted to study." Given our natural and predictable preoccupation with the role of race and affirmative action, there is a grave risk that the "whose academic freedom" issue might be decided by default in ways that could profoundly impair future claims of professorial as well as institutional interest.

This appraisal of the respective claims of university and professor brings us to one other dimension of "whose academic freedom." It is the specific issue with which we began and to which we promised eventually to return. Recall the case of Christina Axson-Flynn, the University of Utah student who went to federal court seeking protection against an acting curriculum that would compel her to utter words she found religiously abhorrent. The faculty members who assigned the scripts that contained those words were vindicated in the trial court, where the district judge deferred substantially to professorial judgment about what should be learned and how, despite the unusual and unavoidable conflict created by the student's objection. The judge observed that, among other factors favoring deference, there was a close nexus between the prescribed curriculum and the theater faculty's capacity to ensure the competence of its graduates who were headed for the professional stage.[10] That ruling is being directly challenged in the tenth circuit appeals court, which will soon have to settle the question of "whose academic freedom" unless it can avoid deciding the merits of the case. One path of possible escape would be the student's voluntary withdrawal from the program; another would be the district court's failure to consider possible avenues of accommodation that might have forestalled the litigation.

Whether in this case or in some other, the issue of "whose academic freedom" as between student and teacher eventually must be addressed. There have been a few inconclusive antecedents, such as the unsuccessful suit a few years ago by an Ohio State veterinary student who sought an exemption, based on conscience, from having to perform surgery on live, healthy animals.[11] The court of appeals in that case deferred almost totally to the faculty's judgment, strongly hinting that a student who balked at such a procedure had simply chosen the wrong profession. When the moment of decision comes, the best argument in support of the district judge's ruling is not that the professor is always right—a claim that could hardly be made with a straight face even by a forty-year veteran of the classroom. Nor could it plausibly be argued that a university is a paramilitary setting where the professor's every word must be obeyed without question to maintain discipline, least of all in the performing arts.

The rationale is quite different—a conviction that (as the U.S. Supreme Court has insisted on several occasions) judges "should show great respect for the faculty's professional judgment" and should accord substantial deference on curricular matters, even where a judge as an original matter might differ.[12] Courts have deferred equally to other forms of expertise, which judges properly disclaim, and recognize in this way the province of those who are best qualified to make judgments. Thus the issue ought not be which of two people— the student or the professor—has the stronger claim on the merits. Rather, what we should ask is which *judgment* of the two deserves the higher level of deference when they are in direct conflict before a court. On that basis, the district court's dismissal of the student's claim seems indisputably sound, if unsettling.

If we step back a bit from the current litigation, there is a markedly different view of the Axson-Flynn case, one which stresses governance and wonders why the dispute is in court at all. The short answer (because the student hired a lawyer and filed a lawsuit) is hardly responsive. The deeper question, which has somehow gotten lost amid the pleadings and affidavits and rulings, is where and how such issues should best be resolved. If we take a broader view, even lawyers should recognize that a federal courtroom may be about the worst possible forum for the interests of all parties—the student, her professors, the university, the academic and professional theater. While neither side seems to have raised this issue anywhere in the litigation, one would hope that such ultimate disputes over "whose academic freedom" could be kept out of the courts, if only to forestall the possibility of judgments that may please no one and ill serve the collective interests of the academic community.

If we care deeply about the future relationship between academic freedom and university governance, we should realize that the case for better internal channels of dispute resolution is a compelling one. Even where the path to court is fairly straight, the legal rules are reasonably clear, and the possible outcomes are potentially acceptable to both sides, conscientious law teachers caution their students that litigation reflects a failure of the legal system, not its finest hour. Where there are no clear precedents, and where the range of possible outcomes seems as unappetizing as it does here, the lesson should be even clearer and more readily apparent. Suppose the parties in Axson-Flynn had been determined never to go to court, or suppose the district judge had insisted that they not take up any time on her docket until they had tried every conceivable alternative short of litigation?

At the very least, an objective arbiter might have discovered that the parties have exaggerated or artificially sharpened the dispute, either through misunderstanding or from the excessive rigidity that partisans often develop when they feel they have been attacked or challenged. Even more promisingly, it might have developed that the parties have simply failed to explore options that might avoid direct conflict. It may be significant, as both parties recognize, that other Mormon students in the University of Utah Actor Training Program did not object to the language that Axson-Flynn found unacceptable. Moreover, even she did not object to reciting all taboo four-letter words. Perhaps most notably, she was willing to assume the role of an unwed mother who has an abortion, thus portraying two behaviors that her church condemns as fervently as it does the blasphemy she refused to utter. Indeed, on the only two occasions when the student did flatly object, the faculty were willing to tolerate a substitution—one time by acquiescence after the fact and the other by grudging accommodation before the fact.

Finally, among the potential benefits of campus resolution, there is the heightened level of deference that courts will invariably pay to academic judgments that reflect a thorough internal process. Though, as we noted, judges properly defer to faculty determinations on curricular matters, process or not, there seems little doubt that a policy that has been tested and validated within the institution deserves an even greater measure of deference. Here, then, is the clear implication for governance and academic freedom: While the faculty of the University of Utah Actor Training Program may well prevail in the appeals court, as they did in the district court, their claims would rest on even stronger ground had there been an opportunity within the university to address and resolve a student's faith-based concern about the assigned curriculum. The challenge, of course, is to discover or define processes for that purpose which do not threaten academic freedom and professorial judgment to the same degree as would the intervention of a federal judge to whom an aggrieved student took her plea for curricular dispensation. The outcome of the Axson-Flynn case in the court of appeals may or may not aid in meeting that challenge.

Academic Freedom, Decision-Making Structure, and Governance

Another vital dimension of the academic freedom–governance relationship is the structure by which basic decisions and policies are formulated within the academic community. Before the 1970s this matter was far simpler; faculties were typically represented in their dealings with administrations and governing boards by faculty senates or similar entities, and many issues (such as salaries and benefits) were seen as nonnegotiable, even though institutional policies and judgments did not always evoke universal acceptance. Lately the entry of faculty unions, through collective bargaining, has changed the equation for a substantial portion of the academic profession. Much has been written of the pros, cons, and variations of faculty bargaining. What has been largely and curiously neglected—and clearly merits some attention here—is the degree to which faculty bargaining may alter settled assumptions and expectations derived from an earlier, simpler time before unions were part of the equation.

Conventional wisdom would suggest that a faculty whose interests are formally represented by an organization empowered to negotiate a contract with the administration and governing board would be at least as well, if not better, protected than would a nonunionized faculty under comparable conditions. When it comes to economic interests such as salaries and tangible benefits, there is considerable evidence of a positive correlation. The less tangible the faculty interest, however, the less clear that nexus becomes. By the time one gets to faculty governance and academic freedom, the correlation becomes more problematic.

This relationship was starkly posed in March 2002 by a faculty collective bargaining bill that passed the lower house of the Washington state legislature. Since faculty bargaining at public universities must be specifically authorized by state law, such enabling legislation was a necessary prerequisite to faculty organization. In other states where such laws have been enacted and bargaining has ensued, governance issues have seldom if ever been addressed. However, the Washington bill contained a late amendment with a novel twist: Faculty bargaining would be permitted only at those institutions where the faculty agreed to eliminate the existing faculty senate, effectively substituting one form of representation of faculty interests for another.

Although the statutory preamble recognizes that "joint decision-making between administration and faculty is the long accepted manner of governing [at Washington's public colleges and universities]," it posits that "collective bargaining can fill the same role." One of the bill's sponsors, Senator Jim Honeyford, acknowledged that Washington's public university faculties "currently have the faculty senate to represent them in negotiations" and that "both bargaining and the faculty senates have some different functions." But, in defense of the amendment, he added his conviction that forcing unionized faculties to choose between the two structures was warranted because "I do not believe that they need them both" (Fogg 2001, p. A12).

Reaction to the "either-or" amendment has been varied across the academic landscape. Some supporters of the bill viewed the amendment as a kind of poison pill intended to defeat the basic bargaining authorization. Others believed the proviso could be removed at a later stage or that the governor might even be persuaded to sign the bill but veto the amendment. Curiously, Washington state does have one campus at which there is both a union and a senate. Eastern Washington University has the only public sector faculty collective bargaining arrangement. The university's president, Stephen M. Jordan, reported that "we have a very cooperative process among the faculty senate, the union, and the administration" (Fogg 2001, p. A12). He expressed deep concern that, if the amended bargaining bill were to pass, and if it were applied to the one existing unionized public institution in the state, faculty-administration relationships could be jeopardized severely if his faculty were forced to choose between a union and a faculty senate.

The Washington proposal is as unsettling to faculty interests as it is novel. However one might grade the sponsoring lawmakers on their understanding of faculty governance and collegial relations, there seems little doubt that if any state wished to enact such a law—and thus to make faculty bargaining contingent on the abandonment of traditional governance structures—it would be free to do so, save for the question that would arise uniquely at Eastern Washington of the retroactive impact upon an established dual system of governance. (Of course, such a law could hardly forbid Washington professors from meeting informally to discuss governance issues and faculty interests. Even the Washington legislature's infamous Canwell Committee, which in 1948 presaged McCarthyism by forcing the dismissal of several tenured faculty at the University of Washington, would not have gone that far.) Merely forcing so draconian a choice between traditional governance and collective bargaining seems well within the power of state lawmakers. Whatever the final outcome in Olympia, the attention that one state has given to subjecting its professors to such a dilemma warrants a deeper inquiry into the potential implications for governance and academic freedom.

Suppose such a bill were to pass and become law, and a Washington state faculty were put to such a choice, eventually opting for collective bargaining, knowing that their senate would cease to exist. In theory, there would be no reason why a union could not demand and obtain many of the same formal functions as the preexisting senate had enjoyed. Yet there would be inevitable and important limitations. Most basically, representatives of a unionized faculty could no longer convene as a senate, at least in any official sense on the university campus, whatever faculty groups might be able to do by meeting informally and unofficially off campus. Moreover, the administration might properly refuse to discuss with the union a number of issues that in the past would have dominated a faculty senate's agenda, on the ground that such matters were not "terms and conditions of employment" under the bargaining law. Undoubtedly, the opportunities that a healthy faculty senate affords for discussion and resolution of such weighty matters (with or without administrative involvement) would now be missing from the governance equation. In this sense Washington state senator Honeyford seems seriously misguided in his belief that forcing a choice between structures is warranted because "they [do not] need both" (Fogg 2001, p. A12)

The remaining issue posed by the Washington saga is the one most clearly deserving of our attention: In what ways may the choice of governance structures, especially the role of collective bargaining, affect the condition and vitality of academic freedom on U.S. university campuses? Here it is useful to recall Chait's recent and revealing study of the highly positive correlation between faculty tenure (or at least tenure systems) and the health of faculty governance. While the study cautions that one condition probably did not cause or create the other—most likely they share a cause—the correlation is surely meaningful.

Take away the senate, as the Washington bill would do, and academic freedom and tenure would not expire overnight, especially if a strong union replaced the senate. Yet in subtle ways, the absence of a traditional, collegial forum for campus-wide discussion and shaping of policy over time would leave most institutions vulnerable in matters of academic freedom. To be sure, as Neil Hamilton, James Duderstadt, and Keller note, different reasons for faculty involvement in governance and different levels of faculty governance exist. Knowledge production does not have to be related in every way with academic freedom, but faculty involvement is useful. Departmental-level governance is also useful. But I maintain that the absence of a campus-wide forum for faculty deliberation is troubling. (Like any generalization, this one admits a few exceptions. The one major university that does not have, and never has had, an all-faculty senate, is Harvard. Somehow academic freedom and tenure remain quite secure in Cambridge despite the absence of a governance structure of the type that exists at virtually every other major institution. In that respect, as in many others, Harvard can afford to be different.)

Academic freedom and collective bargaining as a form of governance are of course not inescapable adversaries. Yet there are inevitable tensions between a union's essential quest for maximum tangible benefits, notably higher salaries and annual increments for a chronically underpaid profession, and less tangible faculty interests such as dismissal or termination procedures and other safeguards of academic freedom. Notably, several formal investigations of academic freedom violations, which eventually led to censure by the AAUP, condemned practices and procedures that had been expressly authorized by a collective bargaining agreement but were incompatible with AAUP policies.[13]

In two especially notable cases, the bargaining agreement had actually been negotiated by an AAUP chapter that was the faculty's recognized bargaining agent. The administrations in those cases understandably resisted a threatened censure by pleading that they could not fairly be faulted for having followed the provisions of an AAUP-negotiated contract. How, in short, could one be slapped by the left hand for doing precisely what the right hand told it to do? The AAUP answer was clear and consistent: Basic principles of academic freedom and due process, including the length of notification periods and severance protections, may no more be bargained away by an AAUP chapter than they could be removed or truncated by an administration or governing board, or for that matter bargained away by an American Federation of Teachers (AFT) or National Education Association (NEA) affiliate.[14]

One should resist the temptation to overgeneralize on the basis of a few examples. On many occasions, not only AAUP bargaining agents but also those affiliated with other faculty organizations have negotiated contracts containing model protections for academic freedom and faculty due process—whether by incorporating verbatim the language of policies found in the AAUP guide or at least by adapting the substance of those policies without the precise words. Indeed, unions have managed to bargain many an agreement that included more benign protection for intangible faculty interests in academic freedom and due process than the provisions that would have been found in a pre-bargaining faculty handbook. Even the occasional case of bargained-away faculty interests does, however, pose a cautionary note for those who probe the complex relationship between faculty governance and academic freedom.

One other issue of structure bears centrally on the nexus between academic freedom and university governance—the locus of decision making about *legal matters.* The role of the university attorney or general counsel has been curiously neglected, save possibly within the National Association of College and University Attorneys (NACUA), whose members obviously care deeply about where, how, and by whom legal questions are decided which bear directly upon academic freedom and faculty rights. A poignant experience from many years ago may provide a useful point of departure. In the mid-1960s, disclaimer-type loyalty oaths, which were still on the books in many states, plagued conscientious faculty members and widely threatened academic freedom. Colorado's was one of the worst; it was legally indistinguishable from a Washington state oath that the U.S. Supreme Court had struck down on due process grounds several years earlier. The national AAUP was eager to file the test case that would declare the obvious and terminate Colorado's oath. While we were seeking possible faculty plaintiffs—a mission that posed some hazards given the vagaries of Rocky Mountain politics—I received a call one day from John Holloway, then University of Colorado general counsel. There should be no need, he insisted, to put individual professors at risk; rather, he would file on behalf of the board of regents a suit that would challenge the constitutionality of the oath. We eagerly accepted this exceptionally generous and sensitive offer.

Such a suit was soon filed in state court, although it was quickly dismissed because of a Colorado procedural rule that prevents state agencies from going to court to contest the validity of laws they are charged to enforce. Mr. Holloway assured us he would appeal and did so at once. Before the appeal could be heard, however, a new majority replaced the liberal bloc on the board of regents. One of their first official acts was to order the general counsel to withdraw the appeal in the oath case. The disclaimer requirement was eventually removed from Colorado law but only after a series of court challenges in other states.

John Holloway's remarkable offer to the AAUP provides eloquent proof that the university attorney may sometimes be the best friend that the cause of academic freedom could claim. His role was hardly unique among the annals of university law, for those who represent institutions of higher learning are usually able attorneys who could find far more lucrative practice with wealthier (and often less demanding) clients. Yet the converse is also occasionally demonstrable; the general counsel can as easily be part of the problem when it comes to faculty interests.

There are two situations, at opposite ends of the spectrum, in which the role of the general counsel is so clear that few would disagree. On one hand, when a faculty member sues the institution, the attorney's primary allegiance immediately makes the professorial plaintiff (even if a close personal friend or neighbor) a legal adversary. Yet even in that situation, the college lawyer may be able to play a modestly helpful role, for example, in recommending a responsible and experienced lawyer before the case gets to court—a step that may benefit the university as well as the plaintiff, without the slightest hint of collusion. If settlement prospects emerge, a supportive university attorney may be able to play a constructive role despite the adversity of the relationship. However, once any faculty member has filed formal action against the institution, whether in court or in some other legal forum, there is little the general counsel can do other than represent the institution, its administration, and its governing board as vigorously as possible.

There are also relatively easy cases at the other end of the scale. If a faculty member is sued or otherwise placed in legal jeopardy because of the conscientious execution of an official university assignment, the general counsel will invariably either directly defend such a person or will secure (and cover the cost of) effective representation if for some reason outside counsel seems preferable. Thus in the Axson-Flynn case, the University of Utah immediately secured counsel from the state attorney general's office for the Actor Training Program faculty members who were sued solely because they had insisted that one of their students carry out a standard assignment. Such a solution would obtain in most institutions; it would be unconscionable not to provide a legal defense for faculty members who were only doing what the university had asked them to do in their professorial (or administrative) roles.

The hard cases, on which there is far less clarity or consensus, fall between these two extremes. They typically involve a faculty member who encounters legal problems because of a controversial research project or a contentious publication, which may be authorized and may have been conduced or written in university facilities but which lacks the certainty of the "carrying out university assignment" situations. Increasingly, responsible institutions do provide legal representation in such cases and thus place the institution on record as a defender and protector of academic freedom. Such was the role several years ago of Cornell University general counsel James Mingle, who came to the aid of beleaguered labor relations professor Kate Bronfenbrenner when she was challenged by a nursing home chain on the basis of expert testimony she gave in an administrative proceeding, to the dismay of the powerful corporate interests who sought reprisal against her (Dickey 1998). That was also the role earlier in

2002, when Johns Hopkins University general counsel Estelle Fishbein vigorously defended several of her medical faculty when tobacco companies issued subpoenas seeking reams of research data from cigarette smoking studies that went back decades.

In contrast, as though to remind us that not all university lawyers are Holloways, Mingles, or Fishbeins, a decade or so ago the Georgia attorney general's office not only did not help but actually took a position adverse to Medical College of Georgia researcher Paul Fischer when his smoking-related research materials were sought by tobacco companies under the state's freedom of information law (Lerner 1998). The university lawyer's role there is analogous to the brigade that goes onto the field after the battle to shoot the wounded—clearly a part of the problem rather than, as in the cases we noted earlier, part of the solution.

There are few firm guidelines on the role that a university general counsel should take in these less obvious situations (of which controversial research is the best but hardly the only example). Part of the difficulty is that the university attorney serves multiple clients, with often subtly variant (if not conflicting) interests and needs. When the lawyer is also a member of the state attorney general's staff, the potential for dissonant directions is compounded.[15] What is sorely needed is further discussion of the complex role of the university attorney and general counsel, with the benefit of the vast experience of those who (like Holloway, Fishbein, and Mingle) enter the battlefield to treat the wounded and protect the healthy. They set an example as defenders and protectors of academic freedom which we would hope most university lawyers would emulate, even if in the real world we realize that not all will do so.

The role of governance in the process also deserves closer scrutiny. While the complexity of the state attorney general's staff member on campus may be obvious, there are other issues with structural dimensions. Within and outside the university legal office, for example, there is vigorous debate whether the chief campus counsel should stick exclusively to providing legal advice or should also serve (if time and proximity permit) as a member of the president's cabinet or group of senior advisers.

There are good arguments on both sides of this issue. Yet the case for having the lawyer present for discussion of what might appear to be nonlegal issues seems compelling, if only because there are few major campus policy issues these days that have no legal implications. Moreover, the general counsel is likely to have one of the longest memories around, as well as a range of contacts on campus and in the community which most provosts and other academic administrators would envy. Even so, we should listen closely to those who argue that the most effective advice and representation may come from a general counsel who is a specialist and confines attention to strictly legal matters; such a person seldom risks blurring the lines by becoming deeply immersed in policy decisions, the legality of which may eventually need to be assessed with an objectivity difficult for one to preserve as a full-fledged member of the administrative team.

Academic Freedom and Governance after September 11

When on the afternoon of September 11, 2001, Professor Richard Berthold joked to his freshman history class at the University of New Mexico, "anyone who can bomb the Pentagon gets my vote," we knew things would be different after the horrendous attacks of that morning. As soon as news of his remark got beyond the campus, New Mexico legislators and citizens began demanding that Berthold be disciplined, suspended, or even dismissed. The administration reacted quickly and firmly, suspending Berthold with pay and launching an investigation that would take most of the fall semester. Berthold himself apologized profusely, admitting he had been "a jerk." Three months later, as the semester came to a close, the administration announced that Berthold was being officially reprimanded and would be teaching no freshman classes for the foreseeable future. New Mexico's provost, Brian Foster, explained the reprimand by noting that "Professor Berthold failed to act responsibly toward his students." Berthold himself, apparently relieved that the sanction was not harsher, saw the reprimand as "an appropriate response to the callousness and stupidity I demonstrated on September 11" (Wilson and Smallwood 2002, p. A12). In the end, everyone seemed reasonably satisfied. Nothing was heard to the contrary, either from the legislators who had once demanded Berthold's ouster or from any faculty who might have come to his defense had they deemed the sanction to be excessive or the process deficient.

Much the same could be said of other incidents that might have severely tested the system in terms of academic freedom and of governance. At a teach-in held at City College of New York soon after the attacks, several faculty members sharply criticized U.S. economic and foreign policy. The chancellor verbally took them to task and at the urging of several CUNY trustees placed the issue on the agenda for the board's next meeting (Wilson 2001, p. A11). One of those trustees called statements at the teach-in "outrageous" and suggested that any aggrieved professors "have an invitation to take a hike," though he was careful to add his understanding that even the most outspoken of the teachers at the teach-in could not be summarily or peremptorily dismissed.

Meanwhile, through a seemingly providential coincidence, Benno C. Schmidt, formerly president of Yale University and, more importantly, a lifelong First Amendment scholar, just happened to be vice-chairman of the CUNY board. The qualities that such an individual brings to the board table are indeed rare and underscore the concerns outlined by David Collis, Duderstadt, and Keller. In that capacity, Schmidt seized the moment to educate his fellow trustees on the fine points of free speech and academic freedom. In a truly inspired essay, he acknowledged the anger and despair that most New Yorkers felt in those early weeks but stressed the transcendent values of free expression, even to the extent of protecting hateful messages in stressful times (Nidry 2001). Schmidt's piece was so persuasive that by the time the trustees convened, the item had been completely removed from the board agenda and nothing further was heard. Interestingly, there were no further teach-ins at any CUNY campus.

While much more may yet happen in the years ahead, it seems appropriate to conclude on a rather optimistic note. The initial post–September 11 events attest to a remarkable resiliency of the governance system as a whole. They also suggest how different conditions are today from the McCarthy era, when the system (as well as the people charged with leading it) largely failed in its presumptive duty to protect and defend academic freedom. When AAUP's Committee A on Academic Freedom and Tenure convened in early November, it issued a brief but remarkably sanguine statement about the way in which all of U.S. higher education had responded to events that surely could have wrought far worse reactions on both sides.[16] It is far from clear why all sectors of the academic community—trustees, administrators, faculty, and students—have proved to be relatively flexible and understanding. Suffice it to say that I disagree somewhat with George Keller's assessment of governance. The current state of affairs strongly suggests that our governance systems are remarkably resilient and that the status of academic freedom in this country is healthier than most of us would have imagined had we assessed that relationship on the afternoon or evening of September 10, 2001.[17]

NOTES

1. *Axson-Flynn v. Johnson,* 151 F. Supp. 2d 1326 (D. Utah 2001).

2. There is, to be sure, a 1993 Statement of the American Association of University Professors which specifically addresses "The Relationship of Faculty Governance to Academic Freedom" and identifies important links, concluding that "sound governance practice and the exercise of academic freedom are closely linked," though conceding that "a good governance system is no guarantee that academic freedom will flourish." For a more recent analysis of these issues, see Larry G. Gerber, " 'Inextricably Linked'— Shared Governance and Academic Freedom," *Academe,* May-June, 2001, pp. 22–24.

3. There should be little need here to elaborate the close links between academic freedom and tenure. See Ralph S. Brown and Jordan E. Kurland, "Academic Tenure and Academic Freedom," in *Freedom and Tenure in the Academy,* ed. William W. Van Alstyne (Durham: Duke University Press, 1993), pp. 325–55, for a definitive assessment.

4. The relevant policies are found in "Recommended Institutional Regulations on Academic Freedom and Tenure 4 and 5," in AAUP *Policy Documents and Reports,* 9th ed. (Washington, D.C.: AAUP, 2001), pp. 23–27.

5. *Regents of University of Calif. v. Bakke,* 438 U.S. 265 (1978).

6. *Widmar v. Vincent,* 454 U.S. 263 (1981).

7. *Brown v. Armenti,* 247 F.3d 69 (3d Cir. 2001).

8. *Edwards v. California University of Pennsylvania,* 156 F.3d 488 (3d Cir. 1998), cert. denied, 525 U.S. 1143 (1999).

9. *Urofsky v. Gilmore,* 216 F.3d 401 (4th Cir.), cert. denied, 531 U.S. 1070 (2001).

10. *Axson-Flynn v. Johnson,* 151 F. Supp. 2d 1326 (D. Utah 2001).

11. *Kissinger v. Board of Trustees of the Ohio State University College of Veterinary Med.,* 5 F. 3d 177 (6th Cir. 1993).

12. See, e.g., *Regents of Univ. of Mich. v. Ewing,* 474 U.S. 214, 225 (1985). The high court observed that federal judges are unsuited "to evaluate the substance of the multitude of academic decisions that are made daily by faculty members of public educational institutions," and that courts "should show great respect for the faculty's professional judgment."

13. For example, the State University of New York, was placed on censure in 1978 and is still on the list. The most recent AAUP report on "Developments Relating to Censure by the Association" notes that while the adverse personnel actions that triggered the investigation were "apparently consistent with the provisions on retrenchment in a collective bargaining agreement," Committee A had stressed in its report, which led to censure, that "an action cannot be viewed as sound academic practice merely because it may be contractually permissible" (*Academe,* May-June, 2001, p. 45).

14. The two cases were the Polytechnic Institute of New York (cited for excessive probation in 1974, reported in the Winter 1974 *AAUP Bulletin*) and Temple University (cited for inadequate termination or dismissal procedures in 1985, reported in the May-June 1985 issue of *Academe*).

15. For a much fuller discussion of these and related problems and dilemmas that face the university attorney, see Robert M. O'Neil, "The Lawyer and the Client in the Campus Setting: Who Is the Client, What Does the Client Expect, and How May the Attorney Respond?" *Journal of College & University Law* 19 (1993): 333–41. See for a more recent reprise on these issues, "The University Counsel—A Roundtable Discussion," *Academe,* November-December 2001, pp. 26–31.

16. Statement by the Committee on Academic Freedom and Tenure on Academic Freedom in the Wake of September 11, 2001. Retrieved from www.aaup.org/statements /SpchState/9-11stmt.htm

17. There has not been perfect accord on this front. For a much less benign view of what happened on U.S. campuses in the six weeks after September 11, see Stanley Kurtz, "Free Speech and the Orthodoxy of Dissent," *Chronicle of Higher Education,* October 26, 2001.

REFERENCES

American Association of University Professors (AAUP). 2003. *1940 statement of principles on academic freedom and tenure.* Retrieved September 17 from www.aaup.org /statements.

Arenson, K. W. 2002. Columbia soothes the dogs of war in its English department. *New York Times,* March 17, p. 1.

Chait, R. P. 2002. *The questions of tenure.* Cambridge, MA: Harvard University Press.

Dickey, J. L. 1998. Lawsuit impacts academic freedom. *Minnesota Daily,* June 3.

Fogg, P. 2001. Bill in Washington state would allow professors to bargain collectively, if . . . *The Chronicle of Higher Education,* March 29, p. A12.

Lerner, M. 1998. Universities play key role in how requests were handled. *Star Tribune* (Minneapolis), May 17, p. 20A.

Nidry, J. P. 2001. CUNY trustees: Let free speech flourish. *Newsday,* October 19, p. A50.

Rabban, D. M. 1993. A functional analysis of "individual" and "institutional" academic freedom under the first amendment. In *Freedom and tenure in the academy,* ed. W. W. Van Alstyne. Durham: Duke University Press.

———. 2001. Academic freedom, individual or institutional? *Academe* 87, no. 6: 16–20.

Schmidt, P. 2001. Full appeals court will consider U. of Michigan affirmative-action case. *The Chronicle of Higher Education,* November 2, p. 32.

Wilson, R. 2001. CUNY leaders question faculty comments on terror attacks. *The Chronicle of Higher Education,* October 19, p. A11.

Wilson, R., and S. Smallwood. 2002. One professor cleared, another disciplined over September 11 remarks. *The Chronicle of Higher Education,* January 11, p. 12.

CHAPTER EIGHT

Improving Academic Governance

Utilizing a Cultural Framework to Improve
Organizational Performance

William G. Tierney

Shared governance is to higher education what mom and apple pie are to American culture. Many view those who speak against shared governance as academic heretics who have disavowed one of higher education's central totems. As I noted in the introduction, in a survey to 3,500 provosts, department chairs, and faculty leaders, for example, close to 80 percent expressed the belief that "shared governance is an important part of my institution" (Tierney and Minor 2003). Yet, like the U.S. population's definition of democracy, there are multiple and conflicting interpretations of shared governance, not simply from campus to campus but also within institutions. One individual equates shared governance with the faculty senate, and another opines that shared governance is when the president consults with a handful of selected faculty before making a decision. Only when a board is overly intrusive do individuals tend to comment on their role even though, as James Duderstadt has observed, their decisions are critical.

A small minority of individuals question the worth of shared governance, but for the foreseeable future, governance of traditional colleges and universities is likely to involve administrators, boards, and faculty. However much one individual might like to wave a magic wand and dispense with a decision-making structure that many see as lethargic or overly consultative, most survey respondents realize that academe's current governance structures not only are not going away but serve useful purposes. Indeed, the tension with governance on most campuses comes not so much from attacks that try to destroy structures as from the lack of a common language about the role of different constituencies in making decisions.

Such misunderstandings are important in any period but are especially so when participants in an organization find themselves in a turbulent environment of the kind that Simon Marginson and David Collis have outlined. Given the various arguments that the authors have put forward in this book, I suggest that an appropriate stance for those of us involved in the governance of postsecondary education is to recognize that colleges and universities are organizational cultures composed of structures and processes that continually change and adapt (Tierney 1998, 1999). An organization's culture has a considerable effect upon academic quality. The challenge is to consider ways to enhance quality in a landscape that has changed, and the goal is not to do away with shared governance or to insist that yesterday's structures must be rigidly adhered to in today's environment. Instead, the question revolves around creating a sense of shared governance that enables the organization to compete successfully in the conditions of the twenty-first century, while holding onto central beliefs such as those about academic freedom outlined by Robert O'Neil in chapter 7.

Just as it is foolhardy to assert that the structures for decision making are irrelevant to the quality of decisions that are reached, it is equally flawed to assume that there is one best system that will ensure good decision making. Because governance structures are cultural configurations, the way to improve governance is through an interpretation of the organization as a dynamic culture. The interaction of individuals and structures can be oriented toward improvement and high performance when an institution's leaders utilize cultural strategies aimed at organizational redesign rather than structural arguments over one or another decision-making apparatus.

I utilize a survey of 3,500 individuals and phone interviews with seventy administrative leaders and faculty senate presidents in order to offer four mental models of shared governance.[1] The focus of the survey and the interviews pertained to the role faculty might play in governance. Once I have sketched these models, I consider how one might govern more effectively in today's cultural milieu. I suggest that if we think of the organization as a culture that is interpretive and dynamic, the manner in which we construct and participate in the processes and structures of governance will be different for the faculty and for other constituencies such as boards and administrators who participate in the decision-making process.

Interpretations of Shared Governance

A Legislative Model. One interpretation of shared governance assumes formalized structures of decision making. "If faculty do not have a structure for debate and consideration of the full range of academic issues, then I would not say a healthy system of shared governance exists," noted one individual. A second added, "Simply consulting with one or another individual or group is not what I would call shared governance." A third person said, "Successful shared governance means that the faculty are involved, that we are not put off to the side while the administration decides things." A fourth concurred: "The opposite of shared governance is what I think of as summertime decision making, in which decisions get made while the faculty are away from campus."

A legislative interpretation frequently uses the faculty senate as a synonym for shared governance. Curiously, as Neil Hamilton observed, the respondents overlooked faculty involvement at the system level. They used the individual college or university as the unit of analysis. From this perspective, without a deliberative body at the unit level, there can be no shared sense of governance. "Somehow they have to gauge the faculty's viewpoint on an issue. How can that be done without a formalized mechanism?" asked one legislative supporter. A legislative framework often is viewed as a hierarchical and flat decision-making structure. The structure is viewed as flat because power is diffuse and decentralized. The structure presumably functions through a hierarchical chain of command in which a committee makes a recommendation to a senate, which gives it to the provost for further input and deliberation.

There were many concerns about the legislative aspects of shared governance. "If governance is a funnel where everything has to go through a senate to get decided then nothing would get done," summarized one critic. Another individual observed, "The U.S. Senate is a deliberative body that allows unlimited time for discussion; that works well in the enactment of legislation, but not for organizational decision making." A third person lamented, "Highly formalized structures may be where we are headed, but if that's the future, then it's bleak. We'll never be able to compete." Such comments echo the concerns raised by George Keller and seconded by Duderstadt about the need for greater presidential power and prerogative.

A Symbolic Model. If a legislative view assumes a fundamentalist stance toward shared governance, than a symbolic view adopts an interpretive posture.

"Shared governance is not in the formal rules, really, but in their interpretation," offered one individual. A similar comment utilized religious overtones: "Governance is the formal rules, but that's like the bible. How the institution articulates and elaborates the rules is what shared governance actually is." Two other individuals extended this point of view, with one saying, "The faculty senate is a necessary theater—a boring play. Occasional votes in something like the senate is not governance. Governance is the symbols we utilize to show we're all in this together." The other summarized: "Faculty interpret, criticize, analyze everything. If we want to understand shared governance and if it's working, then we need to look on the symbolic means by which we get things done." The assumption is that structures are empty and lifeless vessels without actors providing meaning and interpretation.

A symbolic perspective on governance is less concerned with the structural aspects of decision making and more intrigued by its cultural nuances. Whereas one person will look to the faculty handbook for the rules of engagement, another person will try to make sense about how those rules are interpreted by different actors in the organization. A legislative proponent will look at the end of the academic year for the issues that were voted on and how they got decided. An interpretivist will be more interested in the multiple processes called upon to consider issues and how they got decided.

As one might expect, those who subscribe to a legislative view are critical of a symbolic perspective: "Shared governance has to be more than chattering. It's votes, decisions, about important things." Another added, "Simply being invited to a meeting or having a senate means nothing." A third summarized, "Collective bargaining is structural. The faculty have a clear say in specific issues. There are clear lines of authority. That's what we should have. Governance shouldn't depend on nuance."

A Consultative Model. One confusing aspect of individuals' interpretations of shared governance is that the mental models they use to define governance are not parallel categories. A consultative viewpoint, for example, does not pertain to formalized structures of approval or the interpretation of what occurs within those structures. As the term suggests, faculty are consulted on issues. Such consultation is not diametrically opposed to some interpretations of the legislative model if an individual views senates as providing advice rather than formalized decisions. Although those individuals who subscribe to a symbolic model may be interested in the processes of consultation, those who speak from a consultative perspective are more interested in the range of issues discussed and constituencies involved.

"Faculty generally understand how the process works," offered one individual. "They want to have their day in court, so to speak, to voice their opinion, but once they have been heard, then they accept that it's in the administration's hands on what to do." "Shared governance means consultation," one person succinctly said, and another added, "If governance is successful then there are very few surprises. Faculty will have been advised of what's being considered and their opinions will have been sought." Someone else remarked, "Critics always criticize the speed of change, but some issues should be slow because you have to consult. Reforms won't work without faculty having a lot of input."

Criticisms of the consultative model are twofold. On the one hand, "Consultation makes me think of parents consulting the kids about where to take the summer vacation. Asking someone's opinion is nice, but it's clear who decides. That's phony governance." On the other hand, "Consultation usually means a level of decision making. When you speak about this you've got to look at who gets consulted on what. Usually it's a charade. It can work, but power is hidden. They [faculty] think they have power, but they don't."

A Communicative Model. Those who subscribe to a communicative model of shared governance have a different approach than their symbolic colleagues. Whereas symbolic proponents look for how processes are discussed and by whom, those who employ the communicative model concern themselves with the degree to which identity-defining ideas are understood and agreed upon. Agreement is not so much a matter of formalized voting mechanisms as it is a matter of communication. Thus, a communicative model of shared governance is not so concerned with the structures in which communication occurs or that simply one or another group has been consulted in a formal or informal manner. Instead, the success of shared governance from a communicative standpoint refers to the degree to which there is broad agreement on the strategic direction of the institution.

"What's it mean to have a university anymore?" asked one individual. "The business school receives money from a company, the university doesn't. Scientists work in labs funded outside the university and are more interested in their labs than what's happening in the English department. The English department has no clue about what the scientists are doing. Shared governance is when there is some degree of shared understanding." "There is a trend toward disengagement," commented another observer. "Faculty are disengaged at the university level, but are very engaged in their own work. But we can't succeed like that. Shared governance needs to make people see how we're all in this together." These individuals pointed out something more than simply the well-understood observation that faculty are wedded to their disciplines. The proponents of the communicative model paint a picture in which a hollow core exists due to the changed circumstances of the early twenty-first century. The success of shared governance depends not upon well-built structures, an understanding of symbolic processes, or a fulsome consultation process. Shared governance gets equated with the ability to provide organizational meaning and identity such that the organizational sum is greater than the individual parts.

"The loss of institutional autonomy makes everything that much harder," a respondent explained. "The complexity and pace of decision making can make a shambles of shared governance if we don't concentrate on broad understandings of what we're doing, where we're heading." "To say that we just need to speak with one another more is hogwash," countered one academic. "I support democracy. Democracy means that people are accountable, that different groups voice their opinions, and they are in some way counted and administrators are held accountable." Added a third: "A president has to be able to communicate, but that's not shared governance." "I wish we could do away with the whole phrase *shared governance*," another concluded. "It implies processes. I'm not concerned about process; I'm worried about getting results, in getting the job done."

The Problem of Mixed Models of Shared Governance

What are we to make of the various interpretations of shared governance? How might those in leadership positions deal with competing definitions on their campuses? Do such differences matter, or are they merely the vagaries of academic life and relatively unimportant? From the results of the survey, which went to 763 four-year institutions, we know that 83 percent of the respondents believe that shared governance is important—as do the authors in this book—despite having competing conceptions of the term (Tierney and Minor 2003). The belief that shared governance is important is equivalent across institutional type and across the various positions surveyed—academic vice presidents, senate/faculty leaders, and department chairs. The size of an institution or whether or not it has collective bargaining does not influence the importance individuals place on shared governance. Accordingly, from a practical perspective there seems to be very little purpose in trying to convince four-fifths of one's institution that shared governance is irrelevant—especially in times of change.

If shared governance matters, but no one holds the same interpretation of the term, then what is one to do? Finding an answer is important because competing conceptions of what individuals mean by shared governance influences the ability to make decisions. When influential and/or vocal members of the faculty subscribe to a legislative model and others work from a symbolic perspective, discussions revolve around structural matters rather than substantive ones. If faculty believe that they need to be consulted on all matters large and small, whereas an administrator assumes that only major strategic issues need to be brought to them, cries of lack of consultation will be heard. Such complaints frequently have two outcomes. First, the implementation of a decision stalls. Second, there is less willingness to get involved in additional plans and projects.

Often, the result of competing conceptions of governance turns on discussions about how to overcome or resolve differences of opinion. If faculty rigidly adhere to a legislative model that is time-consuming and a roadblock to reform, one might consider ways to get around the faculty. If consultative processes are of the utmost importance, individuals will work to ensure that everyone is represented at every meeting. If the articulation of the handbook is how symbolic proponents see the organizational world, they will try to gain common agreements on specific words and phrases.

What administrator has not wondered if a certain issue might be resolved more expeditiously if the faculty were not involved with the particulars of the idea? Which academic leaders have not sat in meeting after meeting in which the focus is on throwing out names for consideration to ensure that the "right" individuals get put on a committee? Such questions do not imply cynicism on the part of one or another group, or that academic life is entirely a political undertaking in which people, ideas, and processes need to be manipulated to personal advantage. When different perceptions of the organizational world exist, one expects to find individuals trying to figure out how to move an idea forward regardless of the roadblocks they have encountered.

Another response is to try to convince one's peers that their models are flawed. Instead of ignoring one's colleagues, the effort turns on argumentation. Again, what occurs is a structural response in which individuals try to win over others. If there are competing conceptions of governance, it seems logical to assume that one model is better than another. The arguments, however, move away from the particular problem under study and move to discussions about the nature of decision making. Thus, one hears about the need for greater speed in decision making to convince one's critics that the legislative model is no longer appropriate. Or one reads arguments about how colleges and universities are being run like widget factories and that intellectual work cannot function in such an atmosphere; greater deliberation is essential. Discussions focus on whether today is like yesterday and if the world will be more complex tomorrow. The assumption is that those who hold a contrary model will be convinced about a specific interpretation of the past or future, and then one model of shared governance will be employed.

As I noted at the outset to this chapter, although such responses are entirely understandable, they are flawed. To be sure, at times one ought to focus on reforming a shopworn structure. At other times, someone's interpretation of the past or future is so skewed that a discussion is warranted. However, from a cultural perspective, trying to dissuade individuals from their perceptions about organizational life is likely to fail and consume great amounts of time. Individuals possess deeply held beliefs about the way the world works which inform their models of shared governance. Although I have seen examples in which someone is persuaded by an alternative proposal, most often what happens is that a standoff occurs, or rather, faculty disengage from the process. "I'm worried that we're at a time where we really need faculty involvement," said one survey respondent, "and they're moving away." "Faculty are called upon to do more things," explained another, "so when they see that their opinions aren't included, they wonder why they should waste their time."

The point is surely not that one develops a model of governance in graduate school and that it never changes throughout one's career. As the sociocultural contexts in which academics and institutions are embedded change, perceptions and beliefs change as well. The challenge ought not to be to dissuade individuals from their structural perceptions of the world or try to work around them; rather than ameliorate structural differences, the goal in organizational life is to work creatively with multiple models from a cultural perspective.

Shared Governance from a Cultural Perspective

If one subscribes to structural notions of the organization, the commonsensical way to improve governance is to reform those structures. A cultural perspective stands such thinking on its head. The challenge is to focus on the culturally held beliefs of the organization's constituents about structures rather than to tinker with structures. The concept of equifinality is useful here. Individuals have different models of the organizational world, but if their basic assessments of desired end results are common, goals can be achieved.

The underlying tenet of a cultural perspective is that one needs to constantly interpret the environment and the organization to internal and external constituencies. Organizations and their environments are neither predetermined nor irrelevant (Tierney, in press). How might one orchestrate action from a cultural perspective that improves governance and enhances organizational performance? Based on previous work pertaining to organizational culture and high performance (Tierney 1999, 1998; Clark 1998), four ideas are prominent.

Demonstrate Trust. One common theme through many of the interviews was the need for trust. As one person succinctly stated, "Trust trumps structure every time." Without trust, legislative structures, symbolic processes, and formal and informal means of consultation and communication are irrelevant. To the interviewees, trust meant that when someone made a point, others would listen and be respectful; in return, when an individual promised that a particular route to a decision would be followed, the individual followed it. A faculty member pointed out, for example, that an academic senate is not necessary—and would be impractical—for all academic decisions, but without a reasonably trustful relationship between the faculty and the administration, individuals tended to revert to structural needs. A former university president concurred: "[Without trust] the faculty will slow you down. I had to be able to speak frankly to people, but to do that I also had to trust people."

How does one demonstrate trust? My purpose here is not to embark on an epistemological exegesis about trust, but the core idea turns on the assumption that faculty, administrators, and trustees need to trust one another to believe that each is trustworthy (Tierney and Minor 2003). Trust is something nurtured and earned; it rarely comes by way of title or office. By the end of his tenure, individuals tended not to trust what Bill Clinton had to say in large part because he parsed his language with legalisms; one was never certain if he meant what he said and if he would do what he seemed to say. Catholic parents trusted priests with their children because these men were priests. Trust came with the role, but trust in that role has long since been eroded because of what some priests did.

Russell Hardin speaks of encapsulated trust: "I trust you because I think it is in your interest to take my interests in the relevant matter seriously" (2002, p. 1). Trust as encapsulated interest has to be learned over time. Such an assumption is particularly germane to academic life. It is in the interests of boards, administrators, and faculty to take one another's concerns seriously, but trust does not occur instantaneously. In the academy, no one enters office endowed with a halo of trust. Indeed, academic life is circumscribed by argumentation and proof. If someone were to simply say, "trust me," the likely response is to be "prove you are worthy." Making a case for a new initiative is different from having a foundation in which trust exists across the campus. A culture of trust is founded on three premises.

First, individuals are able to meet one another in dialogues in which they believe that all are involved for the common good. In essence, the underlying assumption is that men and women of good will may have differing opinions about a particular topic, but such differences do not negate the importance each brings to promote the common good. The differences of opinion, for example, outlined in the preceding chapters presumably can be worked out within an organization in which individuals trust one another. Strong presidential authority may be needed and enacted in one institution and greater faculty voice utilized in another. The point, then, is to move away from a one-size-fits-all mentality and instead to have colleges and universities in which a culture of trust permeates organizational life.

Second, since all campuses exist as a loosely coupled system in which there is usually no consensus about the route to decision making, those who are involved in making a decision outline how the decision will be made, and they stick to that plan. The quickest way to lose trust is for an ad-hocracy to exist in which decisions are made without any reference to how they are to be decided, or worse, decisions are made, but an alternative path is taken.

Third, in a culture that values language, individuals are precise with their words. An individual invites criticism by saying, "I value your opinion," for example, and then making no provisions for others to offer their opinions. If an administrator presses a group of faculty to make a decision before the end of the school year because "we'll really lose out if we don't decide," that individual is open to criticism and cynicism when the faculty find out that once they made their decision, it sat on the president's desk for three months. The decision was not time dependent after all. The creation of trust will not resolve all problems, but without it, governance becomes much more difficult.

Develop a Common Language. A second way to enhance governance from a cultural perspective is to ensure that the organization's participants are speaking the same language. While one may be well advised to avoid trying to resolve different approaches to governance, a common language can be developed that unites rather than divides individuals. Many individuals recoil, for example, over the substitution of the word *customer* for *student* because the words connote different ways to treat an individual. In a similar vein, a group that prides itself on precision and specificity ought not to use words such as *collegial* or *community* without elaborating on their meanings.

Attempts to develop common understandings will be rooted in dialogues that take into account the history and future of the institution. Curiously, such dialogues have finite endpoints and yet are ongoing. The development of a strategic plan is one effort in which its creation is an end in itself. Multiple individuals are involved in discussing the future of the institution. However, simply producing a written document is insufficient if the basic tenets of the plan are not continually articulated, discussed, and refined. Common understandings about where the organization is headed enable governance to be shared because the future of the university is jointly owned. When individuals assume that governance is only about meetings and processes, they mistake structures for the dynamics that account for the organization. The clearer the vision, the more likely that a common language can be developed.

The need for a common campus language should not presuppose that an academic community exists by way of consensus. As I observed in the introduction, academic organizations in the twenty-first century ought to be centers of creative conflict. Confrontations about the future can be healthy if they exist in an arena in which trust has been nurtured and a common language exists. Conversely, if everyone agrees on the future of the institution, but there are no claims to greatness, ought not the governance process be judged a failure? Governance is a process, not an end. Governance needs to facilitate good decisions that enable academic quality. Thus, the creation of a common language is aimed as much toward developing a climate for high performance as it is for ensuring that the processes of governance enable good decisions to occur.

Walk the Talk. The third way to improve governance and enhance performance is to keep one's words in sync with one's actions. Words are understood through actions. Faculty understand that research is important through a variety of organizational actions. They are provided with sabbaticals to refresh their research skills. At most four-year institutions their salaries are higher if they do research. Promotion and tenure committees frequently ask for outside letters of reference that focus on the quality of the candidate's research skills; these letters play a prominent role in the tenure decision. Is it any wonder that early career faculty believe that research is important?

My point here is not to debate the wisdom of giving such prominence to the research aspects of the professorate. Instead, the examples highlight how a shared understanding of governance can be developed through the actions one takes. Why ought one to assume that a senate president has the skills or knowledge to be effective without any training or background? I am not suggesting that a campus needs a professional senate president, but if sabbaticals, workshops, seminars, attendance at conferences, and a multitude of other activities are aimed at improving an individual's research or teaching capabilities, it behooves an institution's leaders to think about what similar kinds of activities might improve the leadership capabilities of the faculty.

Similarly, if a president never misses a meeting of the board of trustees, a signal is sent about its importance. What signal is sent if a president never meets with the faculty, or the academic dean consistently arrives late to meetings and is unprepared with various committees? One need not be a semiotician to decode the meanings of college campuses. From a cultural standpoint shared governance has multiple interpretations because very little is attempted by way of symbolic and communicative action to foster mutual responsibility. If one wants to enable quick action and maintain shared governance, an institution's leaders need to focus on the cultural phenomena of the organization and consider how the institution's actions support, distort, or ignore common understandings. The point is not to show up at meetings simply for appearances or to act "as if" governance is important. Governance matters because issues critical to institutional improvement get discussed—be it by a senate, a committee, or a department, in a meeting, or by any number of formal and informal means. The challenge, then, is not to debate whether the size of a group is too big or too small, or whether one or another group needs to be consulted, but rather to infuse each of these interactions with meaning and import.

Concentrate on Developing and Maintaining a Core Identity. The final way to improve governance and enhance performance pertains to defining the mission of the institution. The challenges that Marginson and Collis outlined in chapters 1 and 2 emphasize the importance of defining one's niche. In this light,

I echo comments made by the other authors who talk about the need for a clear sense of organizational identity. An organization's participants need to understand the core values of the organization. When one "walks the talk" or communicates values and ideas, the central purpose is to define what the organization does as well as what it does not do. As Burton Clark has observed, "Strong cultures are rooted in strong practices. As ideas and practices interact, the cultural or symbolic side of the university becomes particularly important in cultivating institutional identity and a distinctive reputation" (1998, p. 7). An understanding of the organization's mission infuses governance processes and structures with a sense of purpose.

The creation and maintenance of a core identity is neither something that occurs only at the college's convocation and commencement nor something on which only the president is able to elaborate. Identity is a group action that occurs again and again over time by way of actions, decisions, processes, and structures. The governance of the institution in large part needs to be nurtured in such a way that thoughtful discussions about the organization's identity are able to occur in multiple venues and among multiple constituencies.

Conclusion

When epic changes confront individuals, a variety of responses are possible. Some will try to ignore these warnings, others will not believe that anything significant is happening and remain wedded to the status quo, others will misinterpret what is taking place, and still others will accept what they see as an inevitable tidal wave and jump overboard or pledge to go down with the ship.

How a college or university responds depends in large part on its governance and decision-making structures, which in turn depend on the issues just raised. One need not be a management guru to acknowledge that different structures produce different kinds of outcomes. Individuals make a difference, but the degree to which they matter is in concert with the structures in which they reside. Paradoxically, the way to improve governance is usually not through an intensive restructuring of the organization but through paying attention to the culture of the organization.

I have argued here that the structures and processes for governance exist within an organization's culture. Rather than try to reconcile different conceptions of what shared governance is, the challenge for institutional leaders is to orchestrate these equifinal definitions toward unified outcomes. Quality comes about not because higher education has finally designed the one best governance system but because an organization's participants are able to effectively interpret the culture of the organization.

NOTE

1. This was a national survey of four-year baccalaureate, master's, and doctoral institutions, as defined by the 2000 Carnegie Classification of Higher Education Institutions. A total of 763 institutions were randomly selected from these three sectors, sampling approximately 50 percent of all schools in each sector. For example, of the 611 existing master's colleges in the United States, 302 were sampled, a rate of 49 percent. We also sought information from diverse campus constituents knowledgeable about governance and decision-making processes at their institutions. We invited responses from 763 Academic Vice-Presidents (AVPs), 763 Senate leaders, and 2,289 faculty. In total, 3,761 persons received the survey.

Of those receiving the survey, 2,010 provided responses—an overall response rate of 53 percent. The faculty Senate leaders showed a response rate of 53 percent; the faculty responded at a rate of 53 percent, and AVPs provided responses at 54 percent. We also calculated an institutional response rate. The number with multiple respondents was high; the total institutional response rate was 77 percent.

For further information on this survey, see Tierney and Minor (2003).

REFERENCES

Clark, B. 1998. *Creating entrepreneurial universities: Organizational pathways of transformation.* Oxford: Pergamon.
Hardin, R. 2002. *Trust and trustworthiness.* New York: Russell Sage Foundation.
Tierney, W. G., ed. 1998. *The responsive university.* Baltimore, MD: Johns Hopkins University Press.
———. 1999. *Building the responsive campus: Creating high performance colleges and universities.* Thousand Oaks, CA: Sage.
———. In press. A cultural analysis of shared governance: The challenges ahead. In *Higher education: Handbook of theory and research,* ed. W. G. Tierney. New York: Agathon.
Tierney, W. G., and J. T. Minor. 2003. *Challenges for governance: A national report.* Los Angeles, CA: Center for Higher Education Policy Analysis.

Contributors

Mary Burgan is the General Secretary of the American Association of University Professors.

David J. Collis is a senior lecturer at Harvard Business School.

James J. Duderstadt is president emeritus, professor, and Director of the Millennium Project at the University of Michigan.

Neil W. Hamilton is Associate Dean of Academic Affairs and Professor of Law at the University of Saint Thomas.

George Keller is a higher education consultant in Baltimore, Maryland.

Terrence J. MacTaggart is a research professor in the University of Maine system.

Simon Marginson is Director of the Monash Centre for Research in International Education and Professor of Education at Monash University.

Robert M. O'Neil is Director of the Thomas Jefferson Center for the Protection of Free Expression and Professor of Law at the University of Virginia.

William G. Tierney is the Director of the Center for Higher Education Policy Analysis and Wilbur-Kieffer Professor of Higher Education at the University of Southern California.

Index

151–52, 164–66; *vs.* culture, 209–10; of governance, 66, 77–103, 133, 202, 203; and paradox of scope, 66–68; and restructuring, 113, 114–17, 122, 127–28, 129, 146–48; of shared governance, 205, 208, 209, 214; and tenure, xiii
students: and academic freedom, 177, 188–89; and academic presidency, 137; and accreditation, 29; admissions of, xxvi, 187–88; associations of, 121; changes in, 46; enrollment changes in, 162; financial aid for, 165; foreign, 7, 8–10; and globalization, 1, 3, 19, 20; internationalization of, 47; and paradox of scope, 33, 34, 37, 38, 40, 46–47, 63; and periphery, 45; and traditional governance, 162, 170, 171; uprisings by, 165
Sullivan, Don, 120
sunshine laws, 165
Supreme Court (U.S.): and academic freedom, 186, 187, 189, 195; and unionization, 163; Yeshiva decision (1980), x–xi, 163
Switzerland, 25
symbolic model, 208, 210, 214
system-wide governance, 77–103, 126, 129, 133; *vs.* local, 108, 113, 118, 120, 122–23; models of, 79

teaching: and academic freedom, 179; and academic presidency, 142; and change, 151; and globalization, 2; and provider institutions, 11; and system-wide governance, 95, 97, 98, 99
technical colleges, 48–49, 112
technology: geo-location, 14; information (IT), 6; and paradox of scope, 33, 40, 41, 68; and traditional governance, 158, 164, 173
telic reform, xviii–xx
Temple University, 200n14
Tennessee, 80
tenure, xiii, xxi, 164, 179–85; and academic freedom, 159, 178, 185; and academic presidency, 138; and change, 148, 154; Columbia University case, 181; and faculty input, xxvi; Indiana University case, 182; process of, 180; removal of, 184–85; and shared governance, 160, 213; and system-wide governance, 96; and termination, 179; and traditional governance, 173; University of Buffalo case, 182–83; Wisconsin code of, 180–82

Texas, 113, 132
Thrasher, John, 119
Tierney, William G., xv–xxxi, 172, 202–15
Towson University, 117, 173–74
tradition, 143; and academic presidency, 139; *vs.* change, 146, 149, 167–70; in governance, 158–76
traditional core of university: contracting, 58; decline of, 41, 46, 49, 50, 54, 57; and internationalism, 158; percent of expenditures on, 52–53; *vs.* periphery, 43, 45–50, 52–57, 61; rate of growth of, 71n10, 71n14
Trow, Martin, 173
trustees. *See* governing boards
Turkey, 25
Tyco, 61

UNESCO, 20
unions, faculty, viii, x, xi, xiv, 55, 113, 121, 123; and academic freedom, 191, 192, 193; and academic presidency, 139; American Federation of Teachers (AFT), 194; *vs.* faculty senate, 191–93, 194; in Florida, 120; and shared governance, 205; and Supreme Court, 163; and system-wide governance, 85–91, 93, 94; and traditional governance, 163, 164, 169
United Kingdom (UK), 5, 7, 10, 12, 16, 17, 21, 25; Cadbury Committee in, 35, 61, 62, 64; and paradox of scope, 33, 62
United States (U.S.): and accreditation, 17, 29; and global governance, 16, 21, 25; and globalization, 3; and paradox of scope, 33; and system-wide governance, 95. *See also* government, federal; governments, state; Supreme Court
Universitas 21, 16
Utah, University of, 177, 190, 196

values, academic, 151, 152, 153–54, 214
Van Damme, M., 17, 18–19, 32
Veit, Richard, 91–92
Vermont, 80

Washington Accord (1997), 18
Weber, Luc, 146
Welch, Jack, 38
Western Governors University, 13